The *Best* of
COUNTRY COOKING
2000

Editor: Jean Steiner
Art Director: Claudia Wardius
Food Editor: Janaan Cunningham
Assistant Editor: Julie Schnittka
Food Photography Artist: Stephanie Marchese
Food Photography: Scott Anderson
Photo Studio Manager: Anne Schimmel
Publisher: Roy Reiman

©2000 Reiman Publications, LLC
5400 S. 60th St., Greendale WI 53129
International Standard Book Number: 0-89821-288-X
International Standard Serial Number: 1097-8321
Printed in U.S.A.

For additional copies of this book or information on other books, write *Taste of Home* Books,
P.O. Box 990, Greendale WI 53129, call toll-free 1-800/558-1013 to order with a credit card
or visit our Web site at **www.reimanpub.com**.

PICTURED ON COVER. From the top: Asparagus Yeast Rolls (p. 102), Prize-Winning
Jelly Roll (p. 105), Grilled Three-Pepper Salad (p. 77) and Sesame Steaks (p. 17).

PICTURED ABOVE. Pork Parmesan, Family Favorite Salad and Shortcake Supreme
(all recipes on p. 137).

Down-Home Cooking from The Best Cooks in the Country

ANOTHER YEAR of the best cooking in the country has been compiled into *The Best of Country Cooking 2000*—the third in our cookbook series of family-pleasing recipes from home cooks across North America.

This giant collection's 382 down-home recipes—one for every day of the year and then some—include the very best ones from recent issues of *Country Woman*, *Country*, *Country EXTRA*, *Reminisce* and *Reminisce EXTRA* magazines plus other proven favorites. All are hearty, wholesome and family-pleasing—guaranteed.

You see, these recipes weren't "developed" in some high-tech industrial "kitchen". Instead, they're from the personal recipe files of hundreds of home cooks across North America. Each has been sampled and approved by the toughest critic around—a hungry family just like yours!

But that's not all. Before being selected, *every* recipe in this book was thoroughly tested—many of them twice—by us as well. So you can be doubly confident it's a "keeper" that doesn't require a tryout first.

So go ahead *today* and take your pick of this beautiful book's 65 Main Dishes—Southern Sunday Chicken (a weekly dish on Maurine Seavers' Oliver Springs, Tennessee table), Old-Fashioned Pot Roast (Crystal, Minnesota cook Georgia Edgington's most-requested recipe) and 63 others.

There's also a Satisfying Soups chapter brimming with kettle creations like Southwestern Turkey Dumpling Soup from Lisa Williams of Steamboat Springs, Colorado. And turn to Breads & Rolls for a basket full of oven-fresh goodies such as Almond Streusel Rolls (rated a perfect "10" by Perlene Hoekema's family in Lynden, Washington).

Spring and Fall Pie—in the Pies & Desserts chapter—is requested year-round in the Rapid City, South Dakota home of Laura Collins. And Strawberry Ice Cream from Leone Mayne of Frostproof, Florida is a cool and creamy finish for any meal.

As you page through *The Best of Country Cooking 2000*, watch for the special symbol at right. It signifies a "best of the best" recipe—a winner of a coast-to-coast cooking contest one of our magazines sponsored.

That's just a *small* sample of what's inside this tried-and-true taste treasury that in addition contains a mouth-watering medley of hearty salads, show-stealing side dishes and lip-smacking snacks besides.

You'll enjoy some extra-special features, too, most other cookbooks overlook:

Thirty-Minute Meals—Six complete meals (19 recipes in all) that go from start to finish in *half an hour or less!*

Memorable Meals—Six complete meals featuring family favorites from home cooks.

Cooking for Two—A separate chapter with 48 recipes all properly proportioned to serve two people.

Want more? *The Best of Country Cooking 2000* offers individual sections on cooking quick-and-easy fare that you can whip up for your hungry family with little effort.

Finally, throughout this colorful compendium are lots of ingenious kitchen tips from everyday cooks plus dozens of "restricted diet" recipes marked with this check ✓ that use less fat, sugar or salt.

See why we call this book "The Best"? Now, wait 'til you and your family *taste* why!

CONTENTS

IN THE MOOD *for a snack? This chapter is full of lip-smacking snacks and thirst-quenching beverages sure to satisfy any craving.*

HITS THE SPOT. Clockwise from top left: Party Punch (p. 7), Pineapple Boat with Fluffy Fruit Dip (p. 7), Asparagus Snack Squares (p. 7) and Pepper Avocado Salsa (p. 8).

Snacks & Beverages

PARTY PUNCH

Verna Doerksen, MacGregor, Manitoba

(Pictured at left)

Filled with four kinds of fruit juice, this lively beverage will brighten any setting. I usually make two to three batches for family gatherings, and there's never any left.

2 cups sugar
2-1/2 cups boiling water
1 bottle (48 ounces) grapefruit juice
1 can (46 ounces) orange juice
1 can (46 ounces) pineapple juice
1 cup lemon juice
2 liters lemon-lime soda, chilled

In a large bowl, dissolve sugar in water. Add juices. Refrigerate for 2 hours or until chilled. Just before serving, stir in soda. **Yield:** 7-1/2 quarts.

ASPARAGUS SNACK SQUARES

Judy Wagner, Chicago, Illinois

(Pictured at left)

We have asparagus almost every day during the short Midwest growing season. This pizza-like dish is a great appetizer. For variety, you can saute half a pound of sliced fresh mushrooms with the onion and garlic.

1 cup chopped Vidalia *or* sweet onion
2 garlic cloves, minced
3 tablespoons butter *or* margarine
1 pound fresh asparagus, trimmed
1/4 teaspoon pepper
2 tubes (8 ounces *each*) refrigerated crescent rolls
1 cup (4 ounces) shredded mozzarella cheese
1 cup (4 ounces) shredded Swiss cheese

In a skillet over medium heat, saute onion and garlic in butter until tender. Cut asparagus into 1-in. pieces; set the tips aside. Add remaining asparagus to skillet; saute until crisp-tender, about 4-6 minutes. Add asparagus tips and pepper; saute 1-2 minutes longer or until asparagus is tender. Press dough into an ungreased 15-in. x 10-in. x 1-in. baking pan; seal seams and perforations. Bake at 375° for 6-8 minutes or until lightly browned. Top with asparagus mixture; sprinkle with cheeses. Bake 6-8 minutes longer or until cheese is melted. Cut into squares. **Yield:** 3 dozen.

PINEAPPLE BOAT WITH FLUFFY FRUIT DIP

Katie Adams, Red Oak, Texas

(Pictured at left)

At the root of this appetizer is a boatload of sweet, citrusy flavor. Everyone finds the carved pineapple appealing and is eager to dig into the delicious dip inside with fresh-cut chunks of fruit.

1/2 cup sugar
1 egg, beaten
2 tablespoons orange juice
2 tablespoons grated orange peel
2 teaspoons lemon juice
2 teaspoons grated lemon peel
1 package (3 ounces) cream cheese, softened
1 carton (12 ounces) frozen whipped topping, thawed
1 large ripe pineapple
Additional orange and lemon peel, optional
Assorted fresh fruit

In a saucepan, combine the first six ingredients; cook and stir over low heat until mixture reaches 160°. Remove from the heat. In a mixing bowl, beat cream cheese. Gradually add egg mixture, beating until smooth. Cool to room temperature. Fold in whipped topping. Refrigerate until ready to serve. Stand pineapple upright and vertically cut about a third from one side, leaving the top attached. Remove fruit and discard outer peel from the smaller section. Remove fruit from the larger section, leaving a 1/2-in. shell. Cut fruit into chunks. Fill shell with dip. Sprinkle with orange and lemon peel if desired. Serve with pineapple chunks and other fruit. **Yield:** 6 cups dip.

PEPPER AVOCADO SALSA

Theresa Mullens, Gill, Massachusetts

(Pictured on page 6)

Much of our summer menu is done on the grill, and peppers and avocados are family favorites. I created this recipe to spice up our barbecued entrees.

    2 medium tomatoes, diced
1/4 cup *each* diced green, sweet red and
       yellow pepper
1/4 cup diced red onion
    2 tablespoons olive *or* vegetable oil
    2 tablespoons lime juice
    1 tablespoon cider *or* white wine vinegar
    1 garlic clove, minced
    1 tablespoon minced fresh basil *or* 1
       teaspoon dried basil
    1 tablespoon minced fresh dill *or* 1
       teaspoon dill weed
    1 teaspoon sugar
3/4 teaspoon minced fresh thyme *or* 1/4
       teaspoon dried thyme
Dash hot pepper sauce
    1 large ripe avocado
Tortilla chips

In a bowl, combine the first 12 ingredients. Cover and refrigerate. Just before serving, peel and chop the avocado; stir into the salsa. Serve with tortilla chips or as an accompaniment to meat, poultry or fish. **Yield:** 3-1/2 cups.

CREAMY RED PEPPER DIP

Linda Murray, Allenstown, New Hampshire

This flavorful dip looks so pretty served in sweet yellow pepper halves. It's great with fresh veggies.

✓ Uses less fat, sugar or salt. Includes Nutritional Analysis and Diabetic Exchanges.

    1 garlic clove, peeled
    1 package (8 ounces) fat-free cream
       cheese, cubed
1/2 cup canned roasted red peppers, drained
    2 green onions, cut into 2-inch pieces
    2 tablespoons lemon juice
1/2 teaspoon ground cumin
    1 medium sweet yellow pepper, halved
Assorted raw vegetables

In a food processor or blender, process garlic until minced. Add cream cheese, red peppers, onions, lemon juice and cumin. Cover and process until smooth. Spoon into pepper halves; serve with raw vegetables. **Yield:** about 1-1/2 cups.
Nutritional Analysis: One 2-tablespoon serving equals 26 calories, 138 mg sodium, 2 mg cholesterol, 3 gm carbohydrate, 3 gm protein, trace fat. **Diabetic Exchange:** 1 vegetable.

CHEESY ARTICHOKE DIP

Ramona Larson, Andover, Minnesota

(Pictured below right)

I first tasted this warm, well-flavored dip at our daughter's house—and immediately asked for the recipe. Since then, I've served it myself at family gatherings.

    1 can (14 ounces) artichoke hearts,
       drained and chopped
    1 cup mayonnaise
    1 cup (4 ounces) shredded mozzarella
       cheese
    1 cup grated Parmesan cheese, *divided*
    1 tablespoon chopped onion
    1 tablespoon minced fresh parsley
1/4 teaspoon garlic salt
    2 to 3 fresh artichokes, optional
Assorted crackers

In a bowl, combine artichoke hearts, mayonnaise, mozzarella cheese, 1/2 cup of Parmesan cheese, onion, parsley and garlic salt. Spoon into an ungreased 1-qt. baking dish. Top with remaining Parmesan cheese. Bake, uncovered, at 350° for 20 minutes. If desired, use fresh artichokes as serving "bowls". Remove the center leaves, leaving a hollow shell; spoon dip into shell. Serve warm with crackers. **Yield:** 16 servings.

SPICED TEA

Mrs. J.D. McCollum, Memphis, Tennessee

(Pictured at right)

Ripe with citrusy tang, this easy-to-fix hot tea can be whipped up for almost any size group. It fills the house with its spicy aroma as it simmers.

    3 quarts water
    5 individual tea bags
    1 cup sugar
    1 cup boiling water
    3 to 4 cinnamon sticks (3 to 4 inches)
    1 tablespoon whole cloves
3/4 cup lemonade concentrate
    1 can (6 ounces) frozen orange juice
       concentrate
    2 cans (6 ounces *each*) pineapple juice
Additional cinnamon sticks, optional

In a large kettle or Dutch oven, bring water to a simmer; turn off heat. Add tea bags; cover and steep for 3-5 minutes. Remove and discard bags. In a large bowl, dissolve sugar in boiling water. Add cinnamon sticks and cloves; cover and steep for 15 minutes. Add concentrates and pineapple juice; mix well. Strain and discard spices. Stir into tea; heat through. Serve with cinnamon sticks for stirrers if desired. **Yield:** 3-1/2 quarts.

SPECIAL SAVORY LOAVES

Alanna Petrone, Terryville, Connecticut

(Pictured below)

This hearty, well-seasoned bread will be welcome at any gathering. The recipe is one my husband and I developed and served at a family picnic, where everyone loved it!

    2 packages (1/4 ounce *each*) active dry
      yeast
1-1/3 cups warm water (110° to 115°)
    1 can (10-3/4 ounces) condensed tomato
      soup, undiluted
    1/4 cup olive *or* vegetable oil
    1/2 teaspoon salt
6-1/4 to 6-3/4 cups all-purpose flour
FILLING:
    1 cup minced fresh basil
    1/2 cup minced fresh parsley
    1/4 cup minced garlic
    1/2 cup olive *or* vegetable oil
    2 large tomatoes, thinly sliced
    1/2 cup grated Romano cheese
TOPPING:
    1 egg white, lightly beaten
    2 tablespoons sesame seeds
    1 tablespoon cracked black pepper
    1/2 teaspoon garlic salt
    1/2 teaspoon crushed red pepper flakes

In a mixing bowl, dissolve yeast in water. Add soup, oil, salt and 3 cups flour; beat until smooth. Add enough remaining flour to form a soft dough. Turn onto a floured surface; knead until smooth and elastic, about 10 minutes. Place in a greased bowl, turning once to grease top. Cover and let rise in a warm place until doubled, about 1 hour. Meanwhile, combine basil, parsley, garlic and oil in a bowl; let stand for 30 minutes. Punch dough down; divide in half. Roll each portion into a 16-in. x 12-in. rectangle. Spread basil mixture to within 1 in. of edges. Cover with tomatoes and sprinkle with cheese. Roll dough, beginning at long end; seal edges. Place on greased baking sheets; brush tops with egg white. Combine remaining topping ingredients; sprinkle over loaves. Cut four 1/2-in. slits on top of each loaf. Cover and let rise until doubled, about 30-45 minutes. Bake at 350° for 40-45 minutes or until golden brown. Serve warm. **Yield:** 2 loaves (32 slices).

GUESTS will warm up to Spiced Tea, Cheesy Artichoke Dip and Special Savory Loaves (shown below, clockwise from top left).

NOODLE NIBBLES

Lee Denney, Cushing, Oklahoma

For a tasty alternative to potato chips, try this crunchy snack created from pasta. The spices and cheese that coat the fried noodles give them a terrific flavor.

>   **2 cups uncooked bow tie pasta**
> **Oil for deep-fat frying**
>   **1/2 cup grated Parmesan cheese**
>   **1 teaspoon dried oregano**
>   **1 teaspoon dried parsley flakes**
>   **1/2 teaspoon garlic salt**
>   **1/4 teaspoon onion powder**

Cook pasta according to package directions; drain. Pat dry with paper towels. Heat oil to 375° in an electric skillet or deep-fat fryer. Fry bow ties, a few at a time, for 1-1/2 minutes or until golden brown. Drain on paper towels. Combine remaining ingredients in a resealable plastic bag; add warm bow ties and shake to coat. Serve warm or cold. **Yield:** 3 cups.

STRAWBERRY SALSA

Angela Packham, Oakville, Manitoba

(Pictured above)

Guests often try to guess the secret ingredient in this tasty condiment. None think of strawberries...but many ask for the recipe.

> **2-1/2 cups finely chopped fresh strawberries**
>   **1 cup chopped green pepper**
>   **2 tablespoons chopped green onions**
>   **2 tablespoons minced fresh parsley**
>   **1/3 cup Catalina salad dressing**
> **Dash hot pepper sauce**
> **Pepper to taste**
> **Tortilla chips**

In a bowl, combine the strawberries, green pepper, onions and parsley. Stir in the salad dressing, hot pepper sauce and pepper. Cover and refrigerate for 2 hours. Serve with tortilla chips. **Yield:** 3 cups.

HOT CRANBERRY PUNCH

June Formanek, Belle Plaine, Iowa

With its spicy ingredients, this thirst-quencher packs a hearty harvest punch. The beverage is a cinch to brew for a crowd.

>   **1 bottle (64 ounces) cranberry juice**
>   **4 cups water**
> **3-1/2 cups pineapple juice**
>   **1/4 cup packed brown sugar**
>   **1/2 teaspoon red food coloring, optional**
>   **2 cinnamon sticks (3-1/2 inches), broken**
>   **1 tablespoon whole cloves**
>   **1 tablespoon whole allspice**

In a 24-cup percolator, combine cranberry juice, water, pineapple juice, brown sugar and food coloring if desired. Place the cinnamon sticks, cloves and allspice in percolator basket; cover and begin perking. When cycle is complete, discard contents of basket. Serve the punch warm. **Yield:** 18-22 servings (about 1 gallon).

DAFFODILLIES

Earleen Lillegard, Prescott, Arizona

Whether I take these savory flowers to a church gathering or make them for my grandchildren, they're always a hit. I've been making them for over 25 years.

>   **1 tube (12 ounces) refrigerated buttermilk biscuits**
>   **1 package (8 ounces) cream cheese, softened**
>   **2 tablespoons butter (no substitutes), softened**
>   **1 teaspoon dill weed**
>   **1 teaspoon prepared mustard**
> **Dash salt**
> **Dash white pepper**

Separate each biscuit into three equal layers. Place 1 in. apart on greased baking sheets. With a kitchen shears or sharp knife, cut eight slits a third of the way toward center to form petals.

Cowpoke Cuisine...in Your Kitchen

IT'S BEEN a mainstay with cowboys for many years. But beef jerky is also at home *off* the range, confirms Carol Brekke from near Duluth, Minnesota.

"Husband Tom and I have tried a lot of recipes for beef jerky over the years, adapting the seasonings each time," Carol, a mother of three, relates. "Everyone who tries it agrees the flavor of this version is the best.

"Chewy and savory, jerky's a satisfying and substantial snack. Plus, it travels well whether you're going fishing or camping. Or send it along as a treat in kids' school backpacks."

At right, Carol shares her recipe—so you can rustle up some for feeding the "cowboys" on your spread as well!

HOMEMADE BEEF JERKY

- 1-1/2 pounds boneless chuck roast
- 1/2 cup soy sauce
- 1/2 cup Worcestershire sauce
- 1/2 cup packed brown sugar
- 1 tablespoon onion powder
- 1 tablespoon liquid smoke, optional
- 1/2 teaspoon garlic powder
- 1/2 teaspoon pepper
- 1/2 teaspoon salt-free extra-spicy seasoning*

Partially freeze roast for 2 hours. Slice across the grain, removing excess fat. Cut into 3/16- to 1/4-in.-thick strips. Combine remaining ingredients in a shallow glass container or heavy-duty resealable bag; add beef. Cover tightly and refrigerate for 6-8 hours or overnight. Place meat in a single layer on a foil-lined baking sheet (slices can be placed close together). Bake at 140° to 160° (or the lowest temperature on your oven) for 8-10 hours, occasionally blotting beef with paper towels. Test jerky for dryness (or doneness) by cooling a piece. When cool, it should crack when bent but not break and there should be no moist spots. Cool; cut the jerky into 2- to 4-in. pieces with scissors. Store in an airtight container at room temperature for up to 2 weeks, refrigerate for up to 3 weeks or freeze for up to 2 months. **Yield:** 5 ounces. ***Editor's Note:** This recipe was tested with Mrs. Dash extra-spicy seasoning. It can be found in the spice section of most grocery stores.

Make a deep thumbprint in the center of each. In a mixing bowl, combine remaining ingredients; mix well. Place heaping teaspoonfuls in the center of each biscuit. Bake at 375° for 8-10 minutes or until golden brown. Serve warm or at room temperature. **Yield:** 2-1/2 dozen.

JALAPENO CHEESE DIP

Grace Reno, Wrightwood, California

Here's a great dip that cooks in the microwave in a matter of minutes. It's perfect to serve to unexpected company.

- 1 package (16 ounces) process American cheese, cubed
- 1 can (5 ounces) evaporated milk
- 1/2 cup canned diced jalapeno peppers, drained

In a large microwave-safe bowl, combine cheese and milk. Cover and cook on high for 2 minutes; stir. Cook 1-2 minutes longer or until cheese is melted; stir until smooth. Stir in jalapenos. Serve warm. **Yield:** about 2-1/3 cups. **Editor's Note:** This recipe was tested in an 850-watt microwave.

CREAMY ORANGE DRINK

Julie Curfman, Chehalis, Washington

I whip up this creamy, refreshing orange drink for my family all the time. They can't get enough of the citrusy orange flavor.

- 6 cups orange juice, *divided*
- 1/2 teaspoon vanilla extract
- 1 package (3.4 ounces) instant vanilla pudding mix
- 1 envelope whipped topping mix

In a mixing bowl, combine 3 cups of orange juice, vanilla, and the pudding and whipped topping mixes; beat until smooth. Stir in remaining orange juice. **Yield:** about 6 cups.

erate until ready to serve. Serve with tortilla chips. **Yield:** 16-20 servings.

※※※※※※※※※※※

TACO DIP PLATTER

Marieann Johansen, Desert Hot Springs, California

(Pictured above)

To make this zesty appetizer, you simply layer beans, salsa, cheeses and other taco-like ingredients onto a platter. I call it a "walking dip", because you can scoop some on a plate with a few tortilla chips, then take it with you as you stroll around and talk with guests.

　　1 can (15 ounces) refried beans
　　1 cup chunky salsa
　　1 cup guacamole
　　2 cups (16 ounces) sour cream
　　1 can (4 ounces) chopped green chilies
　　1 can (2-1/4 ounces) sliced ripe olives,
　　　　drained
　　1/2 cup finely shredded cheddar cheese
　　1/2 cup finely shredded Monterey Jack
　　　　cheese
Tortilla chips

Spread beans on a 12-in. serving plate. Layer salsa, guacamole and sour cream over beans, leaving 1 in. uncovered around edge of each layer. Sprinkle with chilies, olives and cheeses. Refrig-

※※※※※※※※※※※

STRAWBERRY FROSTIES

Shawnee Branek, Long Island, Kansas

This recipe makes a wonderful summertime sipper, but I find it so refreshing, I make it year-round.

　　2 cups frozen unsweetened strawberries
　1-3/4 cups whipped topping
　1-1/2 cups water
　1-1/2 cups crushed ice
　　1/4 cup sugar

Place all ingredients in a blender. Cover and process until smooth. Pour into glasses; serve immediately. **Yield:** 6 cups.

※※※※※※※※※※※

ALL-OCCASION PUNCH

Carol Van Sickle, Versailles, Kentucky

Here's a beverage that'll bring folks back for more! I prepare this punch for all sorts of get-togethers and often serve it with an ice ring made from cherry soda pop.

Snacks & Beverages

2 quarts cold water
2-1/4 cups lemonade concentrate
2 quarts ginger ale, chilled
1 quart Cherry 7-Up, chilled
Ice ring, optional

In a punch bowl, combine water and lemonade. Stir in ginger ale and 7-Up. Top with an ice ring if desired. Serve immediately. **Yield:** 5-1/2 quarts.

STUFFED SNOW PEA SNACKS

Helen Cornet, Carmel, Indiana

What happens when you combine a creamy seafood concoction with a plain old bunch of vegetables? Magic—in the form of these engagingly different snacks!

1 package (8 ounces) cream cheese, softened
1 tablespoon mayonnaise
1 teaspoon Worcestershire sauce
1 can (6 ounces) crabmeat, drained and cartilage removed
6 bacon strips, cooked and crumbled
1/2 cup chopped onion
1 hard-cooked egg, chopped
3/4 pound fresh snow peas

In a bowl, combine cream cheese, mayonnaise and Worcestershire sauce until smooth. Add crab, bacon, onion and egg; stir until well mixed. Split the pea pods on the curved edge with a sharp knife. Spoon 1 teaspoon crab mixture into each pea pod. **Yield:** about 7 dozen.

ZESTY VEGETABLE DIP

Laura Mills, Liverpool, New York

There's an abundance of excellent cheeses made in our state, but sharp cheddar is our favorite. My mom used to make this dip for all of our family gatherings and it was so popular. Now I make it for get-togethers as well...it even gets my kids to eat vegetables!

1 cup mayonnaise
1 cup (4 ounces) shredded sharp cheddar cheese
1/2 cup sour cream
1 envelope Italian salad dressing mix
1 tablespoon dried minced onion
1 tablespoon dried parsley flakes
1 tablespoon lemon juice
1 teaspoon Worcestershire sauce
Assorted raw vegetables

In a small bowl, combine the first eight ingredients until well blended. Cover and refrigerate for 2 hours. Serve with vegetables. **Yield:** 2 cups.

TWO-FRUIT FROSTY

Angie Hansen, Gildford, Montana

(Pictured below)

This is a refreshing and colorful drink to serve for brunch. The cinnamon and nutmeg give it just the right amount of zing.

1-1/2 cups fresh *or* frozen blueberries *or* huckleberries
1 cup frozen unsweetened sliced peaches, thawed
1 cup milk
1 cup (8 ounces) vanilla yogurt
1/4 to 1/3 cup honey
1/2 teaspoon ground cinnamon
1/2 teaspoon ground nutmeg
Cinnamon sticks, optional

Combine blueberries, peaches and milk in a blender; cover and process on high. Add yogurt, honey, cinnamon and nutmeg; blend well. Pour into glasses. Garnish with cinnamon sticks if desired. Serve immediately. **Yield:** 4 (1-cup) servings.

HOT SPICED BEVERAGE

Ozela Haynes, Emerson, Arkansas

The tea lover on your Christmas list will delight in this sweet beverage. Present the mix in a bag with instructions for making the tea...or place all the ingredients (plus directions) in a pretty basket.

    3 cups packed brown sugar
  1/3 cup whole cloves
    1 tablespoon salt
ADDITIONAL INGREDIENTS (for each batch):
    3 cups pineapple juice
    3 cups water

Combine the first three ingredients; divide into six batches (about 1/2 cup each). Store in airtight containers. **Yield:** 6 batches (about 3 cups total). **To prepare beverage:** Pour pineapple juice and water into the water reserve of a coffeemaker; place one batch of spice mix in filter-lined basket of coffeemaker. Brew as you would coffee. Keep warm until serving. **Yield:** 1-1/2 quarts per batch.

EASY BLACK BEAN SALSA

Bettie Lake, Scottsdale, Arizona

(Pictured above)

This salsa is a staple at my house. I can make it in about 5 minutes, so it's great for quick meals or snacks.

    1 can (14-1/2 ounces) Mexican stewed tomatoes
    1 can (15 ounces) black beans, rinsed and drained
    1 can (4 ounces) chopped green chilies, undrained
  1/2 cup chopped onion
  1/4 cup minced fresh cilantro *or* parsley
  1/2 teaspoon salt
    1 can (2-1/4 ounces) sliced ripe olives, drained, optional
Tortilla chips

Drain tomatoes, reserving juice. Cut up tomatoes; place in a bowl. Add juice, beans, chilies, onion, cilantro or parsley, salt and olives; stir until combined. Cover and store in the refrigerator. Serve with tortilla chips or as an accompaniment to Mexican food. **Yield:** about 4 cups.

STRAWBERRY PUNCH

Luella Dirks, Emelle, Alabama

I've made this pleasing party punch for many get-togethers, and it's always a hit. The rosy color and sweet flavor of the strawberries come through in every sip.

☑ Uses less fat, sugar or salt. Includes Nutritional Analysis and Diabetic Exchanges.

    1 package (20 ounces) frozen unsweetened strawberries, thawed
    1 can (46 ounces) unsweetened pineapple juice
2-1/2 cups orange juice
  1/2 cup lemon juice
    2 liters diet lemon-lime soda

Place the strawberries in a blender or food processor; cover and puree until smooth. Transfer to a large freezer container; add pineapple, orange and lemon juices. Cover and freeze. Remove from the freezer 2-3 hours before serving. Just before serving, break up mixture with a wooden spoon or potato masher. Stir in soda. **Yield:** 22 servings. **Nutritional Analysis:** One 1/2-cup serving equals 59 calories, 14 mg sodium, 0 cholesterol, 15 gm carbohydrate, 1 gm protein, trace fat. **Diabetic Exchange:** 1 fruit.

JALAPENO CRANBERRY JELLY

Karen Bunzow, Saginaw, Michigan

The thing that inspires most of my recipes is getting an item that I don't know what to do with and trying to cobble together something to use it up. With this one, my brother giving me several jalapeno green peppers was the beginning.

3 cups cranberry juice
1 cup chopped seeded jalapeno peppers*
7 cups sugar
1 cup vinegar
2 pouches (3 ounces *each*) liquid fruit pectin
10 drops red food coloring, optional
Cream cheese, softened
Assorted crackers

Place cranberry juice and peppers in a blender; cover and process until peppers are fully chopped. Strain through a double thickness of cheesecloth. Pour the strained juice into a large kettle; add sugar. Bring to a full rolling boil, stirring constantly. Stir in vinegar and pectin; return to a full rolling boil. Boil for 1 minute, stirring constantly. Remove from the heat; skim foam. Add food coloring if desired. Pour into hot sterilized jars, leaving 1/4-in. headspace. Adjust caps. Process for 5 minutes in a boiling-water bath. Serve the jelly with cream cheese on crackers or use as a condiment with meat or poultry. **Yield:** 8 half-pints. ***Editor's Note:** When cutting or seeding hot peppers, use rubber or plastic gloves to protect your hands. Avoid touching your face.

CHEESY MUSHROOM APPETIZERS

Kathi Bloomer, Noblesville, Indiana

My husband loves mushrooms. Sometimes I think he makes up work functions just so I make a batch of these savory appetizers...and he can snack on them at his desk!

2 tubes (8 ounces *each*) refrigerated crescent rolls
2 packages (8 ounces *each*) cream cheese, softened
3 cans (4 ounces *each*) mushroom stems and pieces, drained and chopped
1-1/4 teaspoons garlic powder
1/2 teaspoon Cajun seasoning
1 egg
1 tablespoon water
2 tablespoons grated Parmesan cheese

Unroll crescent dough into two long rectangles; seal seams and perforations. In a mixing bowl, combine the cream cheese, mushrooms, garlic powder and Cajun seasoning. Spread over dough to within 1 in. of edges. Roll up each rectangle, jelly-roll style, starting with a long side; seal edges. Place seam side down on a greased baking sheet. Beat egg and water; brush over dough. Sprinkle with cheese. Bake at 375° for 20-25 minutes or until golden brown. Cut into slices. **Yield:** 16 appetizers.

FESTIVE APPETIZER SPREAD

Edith Howe, Woburn, Massachusetts

(Pictured above)

Our state is known for its cranberries, and there are many bogs in our area. I won first place with this recipe in a contest sponsored by our local newspaper.

1 cup water
1 cup sugar
1 package (12 ounces) fresh *or* frozen cranberries
1/2 cup apricot preserves
2 tablespoons lemon juice
1/3 cup slivered almonds, toasted
1 package (8 ounces) cream cheese
Assorted crackers

In a saucepan over medium heat, bring water and sugar to a boil without stirring; boil for 5 minutes. Add cranberries; cook until berries pop and sauce is thickened, about 10 minutes. Remove from the heat. Cut apricots in the preserves into small pieces; add to cranberry mixture. Stir in lemon juice. Cool. Add almonds. Spoon over cream cheese; serve with crackers. Store leftovers in the refrigerator. **Yield:** about 3 cups. **Editor's Note:** This sauce may also be served as an accompaniment to poultry or pork.

ROUND UP *the family for some*
mouth-watering main dishes guaranteed to
satisfy even the heartiest appetites.

CHOICE BEEF. Clockwise from top left: Old-Fashioned Pot Roast (p. 17), Tangy Beef Brisket (p. 18), Sesame Steaks (p. 17) and Chicken-Fried Cube Steaks (p. 17).

Main Dishes

OLD-FASHIONED POT ROAST

Georgia Edgington, Crystal, Minnesota

(Pictured at left)

Every time I fix this recipe for friends, it's asked for—and usually by the husbands! Some people I've shared the recipe with have used a beef brisket in place of the regular roast.

> 1 eye of round roast (3 to 4 pounds)
> 1 bottle (12 ounces) chili sauce
> 1 cup water
> 1 envelope onion soup mix
> 4 medium potatoes, cut into 1-inch pieces
> 5 medium carrots, cut into 1-inch pieces
> 2 celery ribs, cut into 1-inch pieces

Place roast in an ungreased roasting pan. Combine the chili sauce, water and onion soup mix; pour over roast. Cover and bake at 350° for 2 hours. Cut roast into 1/2-in. slices; return to pan. Top with potatoes, carrots and celery. Cover and bake 1 hour longer or until vegetables are tender, stirring the vegetables once. **Yield:** 8 servings.

CHICKEN-FRIED CUBE STEAKS

Toni Holcomb, Rogersville, Missouri

(Pictured at left)

Here in the Ozarks, country-fried steak is a staple. These are wonderful served with mashed potatoes and some freshly baked rolls. I developed the recipe to meet the spicy tastes of my family.

2-1/2 cups all-purpose flour, *divided*
> 2 tablespoons black pepper
> 1 to 2 tablespoons white pepper
> 2 tablespoons garlic powder
> 1 tablespoon paprika
1-1/2 teaspoons salt
> 1 teaspoon ground cumin
> 1/4 to 1/2 teaspoon cayenne pepper
> 2 cups buttermilk
> 2 cans (12 ounces *each*) evaporated milk
> 8 cube steaks (4 ounces *each*)
Oil for frying

> 1 teaspoon Worcestershire sauce
Dash hot pepper sauce

In a shallow bowl, combine 2 cups flour and seasonings; set aside. In another bowl, combine buttermilk and evaporated milk. Remove 3-1/2 cups for gravy and set aside. Dip cube steaks into buttermilk mixture, then into flour mixture, coating well. Repeat. In a skillet, heat 1/2 in. of oil on high. Fry steaks, a few at a time, for 5-7 minutes. Turn carefully and cook 5 minutes longer or until coating is crisp and meat is no longer pink. Remove steaks and keep warm. Drain, reserving 1/3 cup drippings in the skillet; stir remaining flour into drippings until smooth. Cook and stir over medium heat for 5 minutes or until golden brown. Whisk in reserved buttermilk mixture; bring to a boil. Cook and stir for 2 minutes. Add Worcestershire sauce and hot pepper sauce. Serve with steaks. **Yield:** 8 servings (4 cups gravy).

SESAME STEAKS

Elaine Anderson
Aliquippa, Pennsylvania

(Pictured at left and on the front cover)

I serve these flavorful steaks with baked potatoes, rice pilaf or another plain vegetable and salad.

> 1/2 cup soy sauce
> 2 tablespoons brown sugar
> 2 tablespoons vegetable oil
> 2 tablespoons sesame seeds
> 2 teaspoons onion powder
> 2 teaspoons lemon juice
> 1/4 teaspoon ground ginger
> 4 T-bone steaks (about 1 inch thick)

In a large resealable plastic bag or shallow glass container, combine the first seven ingredients; mix well. Add steaks and turn to coat. Cover and refrigerate for at least 4 hours. Drain and discard marinade. Grill steaks, uncovered, over medium heat for 5-7 minutes on each side or until meat reaches desired doneness (for rare, a meat thermometer should read 140°; medium, 160°; well-done, 170°). **Yield:** 4 servings.

Texas-Style Brisket's at Home on Any Range

GRAND PRIZE

"A CUT ABOVE" deliciously describes Tangy Beef Brisket from Jacque Watkins of Green River, Wyoming.

"Years ago," Jacque relates, "my husband Jerry's job took us here from our home state, Texas. Naturally, I brought along a number of Texas-style recipes.

"I was discouraged, though, when I first tried to make our favorite barbecued beef brisket out on the grill—the constant Wyoming wind just wouldn't let the coals cook hot enough."

Fortunately, Jacque resorted to her oven. "To my amazement, the brisket was better than ever!" she recalls.

The tangy taste came as a pleasant surprise to many neighbors, who were unfamiliar with brisket.

"Cooked this way, it's one of the best cuts of beef," Jacque assures. "The meat is so juicy and tender everyone requests seconds."

The secret's in the sauce. The sweetness of brown sugar and bite of horseradish don't disguise the flavor of the meat—in fact, they enhance it.

TANGY BEEF BRISKET

(Pictured on page 16)

1 large onion, diced
1/2 cup butter *or* margarine
1 bottle (28 ounces) ketchup
1-1/2 cups packed brown sugar
1/2 cup Worcestershire sauce
1/3 cup lemon juice
2 tablespoons chili powder
1-1/2 teaspoons hot pepper sauce
1 teaspoon prepared horseradish
1 teaspoon salt
1/2 teaspoon garlic powder
1 boneless beef brisket* (6 pounds)

In a saucepan, saute onion in butter until tender. Add the next nine ingredients; bring to a boil. Reduce heat; simmer, uncovered, for 30-40 minutes. Place brisket in a roasting pan. Add 3 cups of sauce. Cover and bake at 350° for 4 hours, basting occasionally. Skim fat. Remove brisket; thinly slice the beef and return to pan. Add remaining sauce if desired. **Yield:** 12-14 servings (6 cups sauce). ***Editor's Note:** This is a fresh beef brisket, not corned beef.

TURKEY SAUSAGE CASSEROLE

Nancy Arnold, Johnson City, Tennessee
This is a much-requested dish with my family. The blend of two kinds of meat with pasta and mushrooms is just fantastic.

✓ Uses less fat, sugar or salt. Includes Nutritional Analysis and Diabetic Exchanges.

1/2 cup finely chopped onion
2 teaspoons margarine, *divided*
1 pound low-fat smoked turkey sausage, cut into 1/4-inch slices
1 package (10 ounces) spiral noodles, cooked and drained
1/2 pound fresh mushrooms, sliced
1 can (10-3/4 ounces) low-fat condensed cream of chicken soup, undiluted
1 can (10-3/4 ounces) condensed cheddar cheese soup, undiluted
1 cup evaporated skim milk
1/2 cup crushed reduced-fat butter-flavored crackers

In a skillet, saute onion in 1 teaspoon margarine until tender. Add sausage, noodles, mushrooms, soups and milk; mix well. Transfer to a 13-in. x 9-in. x 2-in. baking dish that has been coated with nonstick cooking spray. Sprinkle with cracker crumbs; dot with remaining margarine. Bake, uncovered, at 375° for 20-25 minutes or until heated through. **Yield:** 8 servings. **Nutritional Analysis:** One 1-cup serving equals 344 calories, 1,128 mg sodium, 45 mg cholesterol, 43 gm carbohydrate, 18 gm protein, 11 gm fat. **Diabetic Exchanges:** 2-1/2 starch, 2 meat, 1 vegetable.

 ## TANGY RIBS AND ONIONS

Margaret Jestrab, Protivin, Iowa
We raised hogs on our farm when I was a child. This recipe was popular then...and it still is today.

4 pounds spareribs, cut into serving-size pieces
1 teaspoon salt

1/2 teaspoon pepper
2 medium onions, sliced
1 cup ketchup
3/4 cup water
2 tablespoons vinegar
2 tablespoons Worcestershire sauce
1 teaspoon chili powder
1 teaspoon paprika
1/2 teaspoon cayenne pepper

Place the ribs in a shallow roasting pan; sprinkle with salt and pepper. Top with onions. Cover and bake at 350° for 30 minutes; drain. Combine remaining ingredients; mix well. Pour over ribs. Cover and bake for 1 hour. Uncover and bake 15 minutes longer. **Yield:** 4 servings.

ASPARAGUS CHICKEN FRICASSEE

Lois Crissman, Mansfield, Ohio

Since we can hardly wait for asparagus to appear in the spring, this recipe is a real family favorite. If you get too impatient waiting for garden-fresh spears, you can substitute canned or frozen instead.

✓ Uses less fat, sugar or salt. Includes Nutritional Analysis and Diabetic Exchanges.

1/3 cup all-purpose flour
1 teaspoon salt, optional
1/2 teaspoon paprika
4 boneless skinless chicken breast halves (1 pound)
2 tablespoons vegetable oil
2 cups chicken broth, *divided*
1 teaspoon dill weed
3/4 pound fresh asparagus, trimmed and cut into 1-1/2-inch pieces
Hot cooked noodles, optional

In a bowl, combine flour, salt if desired and paprika; set 2 tablespoons aside. Coat chicken with remaining flour mixture. In a large skillet, brown chicken in oil. Combine 1-3/4 cups broth and dill; pour over chicken. Bring to a boil. Reduce heat; cover and simmer for 15 minutes. Add the asparagus; cover and simmer 8 minutes longer or until asparagus is almost tender. Meanwhile, combine remaining broth and reserved flour mixture until smooth. Remove chicken and keep warm. Stir flour mixture into asparagus mixture; bring to a boil. Cook and stir for 2 minutes. Serve the chicken and sauce over noodles if desired. **Yield:** 4 servings. **Nutritional Analysis:** One serving (prepared without salt and with low-sodium broth; calculated without noodles) equals 244 calories, 115 mg sodium, 65 mg cholesterol, 11 gm carbohydrate, 27 gm protein, 11 gm fat. **Diabetic Exchanges:** 3 lean meat, 1 vegetable, 1/2 starch.

STUFFED FLOUNDER

Cecil Nickerson, Somerville, Massachusetts

(Pictured below)

What's more New England than fish? I've grown up eating lots of fish, and this is one of my best recipes. I like to prepare this ahead of time when I'm expecting company. When my guests arrive, I just pop it in the oven and it's ready in 30 minutes.

1/2 cup butter *or* margarine, *divided*
1 medium tomato, chopped
1/2 cup finely chopped celery
1/4 cup minced fresh parsley
2-1/2 cups soft bread crumbs
2 ounces crumbled blue cheese
1 egg, lightly beaten
1/2 teaspoon salt
6 flounder *or* sole fillets (1-1/2 to 2 pounds)
1 tablespoon lemon juice

In a skillet, melt 1/4 cup of butter; add tomato, celery and parsley. Cook over low heat until vegetables are tender and juices evaporate, about 10 minutes. Remove from the heat; stir in the bread crumbs, blue cheese, egg and salt. Spread over fillets; roll up and secure with toothpicks. Place in a greased 11-in. x 7-in. x 2-in. baking dish. Melt remaining butter; add lemon juice. Pour over fillets. Cover and bake at 350° for 25-30 minutes or until fish flakes easily with a fork. Remove toothpicks before serving. **Yield:** 4-6 servings.

CHICKEN WITH CURRY DILL SAUCE

Barbara Kentfield, Wayne, Pennsylvania

(Pictured below)

This is one of my family's favorite recipes. Whenever I make chicken, this is the only way everyone wants it. It's so good and also easy to make.

2 tablespoons butter *or* margarine
2 tablespoons all-purpose flour
1/8 teaspoon salt
Dash pepper
1 cup milk
1/4 cup mayonnaise
1/2 teaspoon dill weed
1/4 teaspoon curry powder
6 bone-in chicken breast halves
1 tablespoon vegetable oil

In a saucepan over medium heat, melt butter. Add the flour, salt and pepper; stir until smooth. Gradually add milk and bring to a boil. Boil and stir for 2 minutes. Remove from the heat. Add the mayonnaise, dill and curry; stir until smooth. Set aside. In a skillet over medium heat, brown chicken in oil. Place in a greased shallow 3-qt. baking dish. Pour sauce over chicken. Bake, uncovered, at 350° for 50-60 minutes or until meat juices run clear. **Yield:** 6 servings.

SOUTHERN SUNDAY CHICKEN

Maurine Seavers, Oliver Springs, Tennessee

Southern fried chicken is a tradition here. I created this recipe as a substitute. My husband loves it.

☑ Uses less fat, sugar or salt. Includes Nutritional Analysis and Diabetic Exchanges.

1/2 cup all-purpose flour
1 teaspoon salt, optional
1 teaspoon paprika
1/4 to 1/2 teaspoon dried thyme
1/4 teaspoon celery seed
1/4 teaspoon pepper
1/8 teaspoon garlic powder
4 boneless skinless chicken breast halves (1 pound)
2 teaspoons butter *or* margarine
1/4 cup chopped onion
1/4 cup chopped celery
3 fresh mushrooms, sliced
1 can (14-1/2 ounces) chicken broth
3 tablespoons all-purpose flour
1 cup evaporated milk
Hot cooked noodles

In a large resealable bag, combine the first seven ingredients. Cut chicken pieces into thirds; place in the bag and shake to coat. In a large nonstick skillet, melt butter. Brown chicken on all sides; remove and keep warm. Add onion, celery and mushrooms; cook until tender. Return chicken to the pan; add broth. Cover and simmer for 15 minutes. In a small bowl, whisk flour and milk until smooth. Add to pan; cook and stir for 2 minutes or until thickened and bubbly. Serve over noodles. **Yield:** 4 servings. **Nutritional Analysis:** One serving (prepared with margarine, low-sodium broth and evaporated skim milk and without salt; calculated without noodles) equals 273 calories, 183 mg sodium, 67 mg cholesterol, 27 gm carbohydrate, 32 gm protein, 4 gm fat. **Diabetic Exchanges:** 3 very lean meat, 1-1/2 vegetable, 1 starch.

TENDERLOIN WITH CREAMY GARLIC SAUCE

Beth Taylor, Chapin, South Carolina

Served with green beans, mashed potatoes and salad, this is the main course at my family's annual Christmas gathering. Since garlic goes well with everything, the sauce would be good with pork or poultry, too.

1 jar (8 ounces) Dijon mustard, *divided*
10 garlic cloves, *divided*
2 tablespoons whole black peppercorns, coarsely crushed, *divided*

3 tablespoons vegetable oil, *divided*
1 beef tenderloin (4 to 5 pounds), halved
2 cups whipping cream
1 cup (8 ounces) sour cream

In a blender, combine half of the mustard, eight garlic cloves and 1 tablespoon peppercorns. Cover and process for 1 minute, scraping sides occasionally. Add 1 tablespoon oil; process until a paste forms. Spread over beef. In a large skillet, heat the remaining oil over medium-high heat. Brown beef on all sides. Transfer to an ungreased 13-in. x 9-in. x 2-in. baking dish. Cover and bake at 375° for 40-50 minutes or until meat reaches desired doneness (for rare, a meat thermometer should read 140°; medium, 160°; well-done, 170°). Remove to a warm serving platter. Let stand for 10-15 minutes. Meanwhile, mince remaining garlic. In a saucepan, combine garlic, whipping cream, sour cream and remaining mustard and peppercorns. Cook and stir over low heat until heated through. Slice beef; serve with the sauce. **Yield:** 12-15 servings.

✺✺✺✺✺✺✺✺✺✺✺✺

HERB-CRUSTED ROAST BEEF

Teri Lindquist, Gurnee, Illinois

(Pictured above right)

I used to be reluctant to cook a roast for fear of ruining a nice cut of meat. Then I started buying roasts on sale and experimenting. This recipe was the result. Now, my husband doesn't want a roast any other way.

1 boneless rump roast (4-1/2 to 5 pounds)
2 garlic cloves, minced
2 tablespoons Dijon mustard
2 tablespoons lemon juice
2 tablespoons olive *or* vegetable oil
2 tablespoons Worcestershire sauce
1 tablespoon dried parsley flakes
1 teaspoon dried basil
1 teaspoon salt
1 teaspoon coarsely ground pepper
1/2 teaspoon dried tarragon
1/2 teaspoon dried thyme
2-1/3 cups water, *divided*
2 teaspoons beef bouillon granules
1/4 to 1/3 cup all-purpose flour

Place roast with fat side up in an ungreased roasting pan. Combine the next five ingredients; pour over roast. Combine parsley, basil, salt, pepper, tarragon and thyme; rub over roast. Bake, uncovered, at 325° for 1-3/4 to 2-1/4 hours or until meat reaches desired doneness (for rare, a meat thermometer should read 140°; medium, 160°; well-done, 170°). Remove to a warm serving platter. Let stand for 10-15 minutes. Meanwhile, add

2 cups water and bouillon to pan drippings; bring to a boil. Combine flour and remaining water until smooth; gradually add to pan. Cook and stir until bubbly and thickened. Slice roast; serve with gravy. **Yield:** 10-12 servings.

✺✺✺✺✺✺✺✺✺✺✺✺

ASPARAGUS HAM BUNDLES

Barb Kopf, Wauwatosa, Wisconsin

A neighbor who grew his own asparagus gave me this recipe—along with much of his bounty—many years ago. The bundles are perfect for brunch or lunch.

3 tablespoons butter *or* margarine
3 tablespoons all-purpose flour
3/4 teaspoon salt
2 cups milk
1 cup (4 ounces) shredded Swiss cheese
2 cups cooked rice
8 slices fully cooked ham (about 1/8 inch thick)
24 fresh asparagus spears, cooked and drained
1/4 cup grated Parmesan cheese

In a saucepan, melt butter; stir in flour and salt until smooth. Gradually add milk; bring to a boil. Cook and stir until thickened and bubbly. Stir in Swiss cheese until melted. Combine 1 cup of cheese mixture with rice. Spread about 1/4 cup on the bottom third of each ham slice. Top with three asparagus spears; roll up. Place with seam side down in a greased 11-in. x 7-in. x 2-in. baking dish. Pour remaining cheese mixture over the bundles. Sprinkle with Parmesan cheese. Bake, uncovered, at 350° for 25-30 minutes or until heated through. **Yield:** 4 servings.

CHILI RELLENOS SANDWICHES

Gladys Hill, Qulin, Missouri

Since I retired over 20 years ago, I don't cook as much anymore, but I love to make these zippy sandwiches.

> 1 can (4 ounces) chopped green chilies, drained
> 6 slices bread
> 3 slices Monterey Jack cheese
> 2 eggs
> 1 cup milk
> 2 to 4 tablespoons butter *or* margarine
Salsa, optional

Mash chilies with a fork; spread on three slices of bread. Top with cheese and remaining bread. In a shallow bowl, beat eggs and milk; dip the sandwiches. Melt 2 tablespoons of butter in a large skillet. Cook sandwiches until golden brown on both sides and cheese is melted, adding additional butter if necessary. Serve with salsa if desired. **Yield:** 3 servings.

CHICK-A-RONI

Rosemary Fenton, West Salem, Illinois

I "invented" this dish one night with ingredients found in my pantry and fridge.

> 2 cups cubed cooked chicken
> 2 cups cooked macaroni
> 1 can (10-3/4 ounces) condensed cream of chicken soup, undiluted
> 1 jar (4 ounces) diced pimientos, drained
> 4 ounces process American cheese, cubed
> 1 cup (4 ounces) shredded cheddar cheese
> 1 package (3 ounces) cream cheese, cubed

In a large bowl, combine all ingredients. Transfer to a greased 3-qt. baking dish. Cover and bake at 350° for 20 minutes. Uncover; bake 20 minutes longer or until heated through. **Yield:** 6-8 servings.

COUNTRY-STYLE POT ROAST

Joan Best, Garrison, Montana

My husband goes deer hunting, so I have quite a few recipes for venison. This is his favorite.

> 2 cups water
> 2 cups vinegar
> 6 medium onions, thinly sliced
> 12 whole peppercorns
> 4 bay leaves
> 4 whole cloves
> 2 teaspoons salt

PORK CHOPS AND SAUERKRAUT

Delma Carretta, Wallingford, Connecticut

(Pictured above)

I make this hearty dish often for guests. I think the sauerkraut tastes very much like what we enjoyed in Munich restaurants when we visited Germany.

> 3 cups sauerkraut, well drained
> 2 cups applesauce
> 1/2 cup chicken broth
> 1/2 pound sliced bacon, cooked and crumbled
> 1 tablespoon brown sugar
> 1 teaspoon dried thyme
> 1/2 teaspoon ground mustard
> 1/2 teaspoon dried oregano
> 1/2 teaspoon salt
> 1/2 teaspoon pepper
> 6 pork chops (1 inch thick)
> 2 tablespoons vegetable oil
> 1/4 teaspoon paprika

In a large bowl, combine the sauerkraut, applesauce, broth, bacon, brown sugar and seasonings; spoon into an ungreased 13-in. x 9-in. x 2-in. baking dish. In a large skillet, brown pork chops in oil; drain. Place chops over the sauerkraut mixture. Sprinkle with paprika. Cover and bake at 350° for 1 to 1-1/4 hours or until meat is tender and juices run clear. **Yield:** 6 servings.

1 teaspoon Worcestershire sauce
1/2 teaspoon pepper
1/2 teaspoon garlic powder
1 boneless beef *or* venison rump *or* chuck roast (3-1/2 to 4 pounds)
2 tablespoons vegetable oil
10 medium carrots, cut into 1-inch chunks
5 to 7 tablespoons cornstarch
1/3 cup cold water

In a large resealable plastic bag or deep glass bowl, combine the first 10 ingredients; mix well. Add the roast. Cover and refrigerate for 24 hours. Remove roast, reserving the marinade. In a Dutch oven, brown roast in oil; drain. Add marinade and carrots; bring to a boil. Reduce heat; cover and simmer for 3-1/2 to 4 hours or until meat is tender. Remove roast and keep warm. Strain cooking juices; discard the vegetables and spices. Return juices to pan. Combine cornstarch and cold water until smooth; gradually add to pan juices. Bring to a boil; boil and stir for 2 minutes. Slice roast; serve with the gravy. **Yield:** 6-8 servings.

SOUR CREAM SWISS STEAK

Barb Benting, Grand Rapids, Michigan

One year, after we'd purchased half a beef, I searched for new and different recipes. This is one I found— my family loved it from the very first bite.

1/3 cup all-purpose flour
1-1/2 teaspoons *each* salt, pepper, paprika and ground mustard
3 pounds boneless round steak, cut into serving-size pieces
3 tablespoons vegetable oil
3 tablespoons butter *or* margarine
1-1/2 cups water
1-1/2 cups (12 ounces) sour cream
1 cup finely chopped onion
2 garlic cloves, minced
1/3 cup soy sauce
1/4 to 1/3 cup packed brown sugar
3 tablespoons all-purpose flour
Additional paprika, optional

In a shallow bowl, combine flour, salt, pepper, paprika and mustard; dredge the steak. In a large skillet, heat oil and butter. Cook steak on both sides until browned. Carefully add water; cover and simmer for 30 minutes. In a bowl, combine the sour cream, onion, garlic, soy sauce, brown sugar and flour; stir until smooth. Transfer steak to a greased 2-1/2-qt. baking dish; add sour cream mixture. Cover and bake at 325° for 1-1/2 hours or until tender. Sprinkle with paprika if desired. **Yield:** 6-8 servings.

SPICY ORANGE BEEF

Heather Ford, Pullman, Washington

(Pictured below)

When I first started out cooking, I did a lot of stir-frying. Although my menu has expanded, I still enjoy cooking and eating stir-fries. Oranges, ginger and pepper flakes give this dish a very distinctive flavor.

1/4 cup orange juice concentrate
3 tablespoons soy sauce
3 tablespoons water
1 tablespoon cornstarch
1 tablespoon finely grated orange peel
1 teaspoon sugar
5 tablespoons vegetable oil, *divided*
2 garlic cloves, minced
4 cups broccoli florets
12 green onions with tops, cut into 1-inch pieces
1/2 teaspoon ground ginger
1/4 teaspoon crushed red pepper flakes
1 pound boneless sirloin steak, cut into thin strips
3 medium oranges, sectioned
Hot cooked rice

In a small bowl, combine the first six ingredients; set aside. In a large skillet or wok, heat 3 tablespoons oil over medium heat; saute garlic for 30 seconds. Add broccoli, onions, ginger and pepper flakes; stir-fry for 2 minutes or until broccoli is crisp-tender. Remove vegetables and keep warm. Heat remaining oil in skillet; add beef. Stir-fry until no longer pink. Stir orange juice mixture; add to skillet. Cook and stir for 2 minutes or until sauce is thickened. Return vegetables to pan. Add oranges and heat through. Serve over rice. **Yield:** 6 servings.

STEW WITH CONFETTI DUMPLINGS

Lucile Cline, Wichita, Kansas

(Pictured below)

If you want a stew that will warm you to the bone, try this. My family particularly likes the dumplings.

  2 pounds boneless chuck roast, cut into
    1-inch cubes
  2 tablespoons vegetable oil
1/2 pound fresh mushrooms, halved
  1 large onion, thinly sliced
  1 garlic clove, minced
  2 cans (14-1/2 ounces *each*) beef broth
  1 teaspoon Italian seasoning
  1 teaspoon salt
1/4 teaspoon pepper
  1 bay leaf
1/3 cup all-purpose flour
1/2 cup water
  1 package (10 ounces) frozen peas
DUMPLINGS:
 1-1/2 cups biscuit/baking mix
  2 tablespoons diced pimientos, drained
  1 tablespoon minced chives
1/2 cup milk

In a Dutch oven, brown meat in oil. Add mushrooms, onion and garlic; cook until onion is tender, stirring occasionally. Stir in broth, Italian seasoning, salt, pepper and bay leaf; bring to a boil. Cover and simmer for 1-1/2 hours. Discard bay

leaf. Combine the flour and water until smooth; stir into stew. Bring to a boil; cook and stir for 1 minute. Reduce heat. Stir in peas. For dumplings, combine biscuit mix, pimientos and chives in a bowl. Stir in enough milk to form a soft dough. Drop by tablespoonfuls onto the simmering stew. Cover and simmer for 10-12 minutes or until dumplings test done (do not lift lid while simmering). Serve immediately. **Yield:** 10-12 servings (about 3 quarts).

BARBECUED PORK CHOPS

Karen Collins, Wauseon, Ohio

The best compliment a cook can receive is to be asked for the recipe of a dish she's served. That's happened almost every time I've made these pork chops. The sauce gives them a great barbecue flavor.

  2 cups soy sauce
  1 cup water
1/2 cup packed brown sugar
  1 tablespoon dark molasses
  6 pork chops (1 to 1-1/2 inches thick)
SAUCE:
1/2 cup ketchup
1/2 cup chili sauce
  2 tablespoons brown sugar
  1 tablespoon water
1/2 teaspoon ground mustard

In a saucepan, combine the soy sauce, water, brown sugar and molasses; bring to a boil. Remove from the heat and allow to cool. Pour into a shallow glass container or large resealable plastic bag; add pork chops and turn to coat. Cover or seal and refrigerate for 8 hours or overnight. Drain, discarding marinade; place chops in a shallow ungreased baking pan. Cover and bake at 375° for 30 minutes. Meanwhile, in a saucepan, combine sauce ingredients. Bring to a boil, stirring until smooth. Brush over both sides of the chops. Bake, uncovered, 30 minutes longer or until pork is no longer pink and glaze is lightly browned. **Yield:** 6 servings.

TUNA BAKE WITH CHEESE SWIRLS

Virginia Magee, Reene, New Hampshire

My family thinks this dish is a tasty alternative to regular tuna casserole. The proof is that there are never any leftovers.

  3 tablespoons chopped onion
  3 tablespoons chopped green pepper
1/3 cup butter *or* margarine
1/3 cup all-purpose flour

3 cups milk
1 can (10-3/4 ounces) condensed cream
    of mushroom soup, undiluted
1 can (12 ounces) tuna, drained and flaked
1 tablespoon lemon juice
1 teaspoon salt
DOUGH:
2 cups biscuit/baking mix
1/2 cup milk
1/2 cup shredded cheddar cheese
1/2 cup diced pimientos
1/4 cup minced fresh parsley
1 egg
2 teaspoons water

In a saucepan, saute onion and green pepper in butter. Blend in the flour until smooth. Gradually stir in milk; bring to a boil over medium heat. Cook and stir for 2 minutes. Remove from the heat; stir in soup, tuna, lemon juice and salt. Pour into an ungreased 13-in. x 9-in. x 2-in. baking dish. For dough, combine biscuit mix and milk until blended. On a lightly floured surface, roll dough into a 12-in. x 9-in. rectangle. Sprinkle with cheese, pimientos and parsley. Roll up, jelly-roll style, starting with a long side. Cut into 1-in. slices; place over tuna mixture. Beat egg and water; brush over the swirls. Bake, uncovered, at 400° for 20-25 minutes or until top is lightly browned. **Yield:** 6-8 servings.

Spicy Sausage Spaghetti

Nancy Rollag, Kewaskum, Wisconsin

(Pictured above right)

Served with crusty bread and a green salad, this is a good summer supper. It has lots of heat (my husband likes that) and it's colorful on the plate besides.

1 pound bulk Italian sausage
3 tablespoons olive *or* vegetable oil, *divided*
3 dried whole red chilies
1 can (28 ounces) plum tomatoes, drained
    and chopped
3 garlic cloves, minced
2 tablespoons minced fresh oregano *or* 2
    teaspoons dried oregano
1/2 teaspoon salt
1/4 teaspoon pepper
3 large sweet red peppers, thinly sliced
4 cups hot cooked spaghetti
1/2 cup minced fresh parsley
1/2 cup shredded Parmesan cheese

In a skillet over medium heat, cook sausage until no longer pink. Drain, discarding drippings. Set the sausage aside and keep warm. In a skillet, heat 2 tablespoons of oil; saute red chilies for 5-8

minutes or until they turn black. Discard chilies; cool oil slightly. Add the tomatoes, garlic, oregano, salt and pepper; simmer for 15 minutes. Stir in red peppers and sausage; heat through. Toss spaghetti with remaining oil. Add tomato sauce; toss to coat. Sprinkle with parsley and Parmesan cheese. **Yield:** 4 servings.

Bell Pepper Enchiladas

Melissa Cowser, Greenville, Texas

Peppers are probably the vegetable that gets used most frequently in my kitchen. My freezer's constantly stocked in case I discover a new recipe to try or want to whip up an old favorite again.

2 medium green peppers, chopped
1/2 cup shredded cheddar cheese
1/2 cup shredded Monterey Jack cheese
1/2 cup diced process American cheese
4 flour tortillas (8 inches)
1 small jalapeno pepper, minced,* optional
1 cup salsa, *divided*
Additional shredded cheese, optional

Sprinkle the green peppers and cheeses down the center of tortillas; add jalapeno if desired. Roll up. Spread 1/2 cup salsa in a shallow baking dish. Place tortillas seam side down over salsa. Top with remaining salsa. Bake at 350° for 20 minutes or until heated through. Sprinkle with additional cheese if desired. **Yield:** 4 enchiladas. ***Editor's Note:** When cutting or seeding hot peppers, use rubber or plastic gloves to protect your hands. Avoid touching your face.

Beef Recipes in Brief

THE FACT that beef's so satisfyingly filling doesn't mean it can't be fast besides...as these recipes—easy to make for everyday meals but special enough to serve company—prove. All can be on the table in around 30-45 minutes.

▪▪▪▪▪▪▪▪▪▪▪▪▪

SWEET AND SPICY STEAK

Marie Walter, Kaycee, Wyoming

The flavors of molasses and cayenne pepper blend beautifully in this steak stir-fry.

> 3 bunches green onions with tops
> 1-1/2 pounds boneless sirloin steak, cut into 1/2-inch cubes
> 1 tablespoon vegetable oil
> 1/2 cup molasses
> 1 teaspoon salt
> 1/4 teaspoon cayenne pepper
> Hot cooked rice

Cut onions into 3-in. pieces; cut white portion in half lengthwise. Set aside. In a large skillet or wok, stir-fry beef in oil for 4-5 minutes. Add onions, molasses, salt and cayenne. Stir-fry for 5 minutes or until heated through. Serve over rice. **Yield:** 6 servings.

▪▪▪▪▪▪▪▪▪▪▪▪▪

LEMON RIB EYES

Bill Huntington, Port Orchard, Washington

I never enjoyed cooking until I tried out this dish on my family with great success.

> 1-1/2 teaspoons dried basil
> 1-1/2 teaspoons dried oregano
> 1 teaspoon garlic powder
> 1/2 teaspoon salt
> 1/8 teaspoon pepper
> 2 rib eye steaks (8 ounces *each*)
> 1 tablespoon olive *or* vegetable oil

> 1 tablespoon lemon juice
> 2 tablespoons crumbled feta *or* blue cheese, optional
> 1 tablespoon sliced ripe olives, optional
> Lemon slices, optional

Combine basil, oregano, garlic powder, salt and pepper; rub over steaks. In a skillet, cook steaks in oil for 11-15 minutes or until meat reaches desired doneness (for rare, a meat thermometer should read 140°; medium, 160°; well-done, 170°). Transfer to a serving platter. Drizzle with lemon juice. If desired, top with cheese and olives and garnish with lemon. **Yield:** 2 servings.

▪▪▪▪▪▪▪▪▪▪▪▪▪

BEEF VEGETABLE BURRITOS

Ronda Jordan, Silver Lake, Oregon

I made up this recipe after trying a similar dish in a restaurant.

> 1 to 1-1/2 pounds boneless top round steak, cut into 1/4-inch cubes
> 2 medium red potatoes, cut into 1/2-inch cubes
> 1 medium turnip, peeled and cut into 1/4-inch cubes
> 1 small onion, chopped
> 2 tablespoons vegetable oil
> 1 teaspoon salt
> 1/2 teaspoon pepper
> 1/2 teaspoon ground cumin, optional
> 1-1/4 cups Spanish rice
> 10 flour tortillas (8 inches), warmed
> Salsa *or* sour cream, optional

In a large skillet, cook and stir beef, potatoes, turnip and onion in oil until meat and vegetables are tender. Season with salt, pepper and cumin if desired. Place about 1/2 cup beef mixture and rice down the center of each tortilla. Add salsa or sour cream if desired. Fold top and bottom of tortilla over filling and roll up. **Yield:** 10 servings.

Cheesy Beef Stroganoff

Gerrie Ferguson, Twining, Michigan

This easy-to-fix stroganoff has become a mainstay on our dinner table.

1 pound sirloin tips
2 tablespoons vegetable oil
1 can (4 ounces) mushroom stems and pieces, drained
1/2 teaspoon salt
1/4 teaspoon pepper
1 can (10-3/4 ounces) condensed cream of mushroom soup, undiluted
1/2 cup milk
1 cup (8 ounces) sour cream
1/2 cup shredded mozzarella cheese
1/2 cup shredded Monterey Jack cheese
Hot cooked noodles *or* rice

In a skillet over medium-high heat, cook beef in oil until no longer pink. Add the mushrooms, salt and pepper. Combine soup and milk; add to skillet. Reduce heat; stir in sour cream. Cook 30 minutes longer (do not boil). Add cheeses; heat for 5 minutes or until melted. Serve over noodles or rice. **Yield:** 4 servings.

Beefy Rice Supper

Bernadette Colvin, Houston, Texas

When I need to prepare a meal in a hurry, I can always depend on this beefy dish.

1 package (6.8 ounces) beef-flavored rice mix
1 pound boneless round steak, cut into 1/8-inch strips
1 tablespoon butter *or* margarine
2 cups broccoli florets
1 small onion, thinly sliced
1/2 cup julienned green *or* sweet red pepper

Prepare rice according to package directions. Meanwhile, in a skillet, saute beef in butter for 2-3 minutes. Add beef, broccoli, onion and green pepper to rice. Simmer, uncovered, for 10 minutes or until vegetables are crisp-tender. **Yield:** 4 servings.

Beef 'n' Cheese Wraps

Sue Sibson, Howard, South Dakota

(Pictured below)

During harvesttime, I make these wraps in advance for a quick lunch on the go.

4 flour tortillas (10 inches)
1 carton (8 ounces) onion and chive cream cheese spread
1 cup shredded carrots
1 cup (4 ounces) shredded Monterey Jack cheese
1 pound thinly sliced cooked roast beef
Leaf lettuce

Spread one side of each tortilla with cream cheese; top with the carrots and Monterey Jack cheese. Layer with beef and lettuce. Roll up tightly and wrap in plastic wrap. Refrigerate for at least 30 minutes. Cut in half or into 1-in. slices. **Yield:** 4 servings.

SPECIAL SHRIMP BAKE

Kathy Houchen, Waldorf, Maryland

(Pictured below)

My husband and I entertain most weekends, and to me the easiest way of serving a crowd is a buffet. This dish can be put together the night before, then baked the following day.

> 3 quarts water
> 1 tablespoon plus 1 teaspoon salt, *divided*
> 2-1/2 pounds uncooked medium shrimp, peeled and deveined
> 2 tablespoons vegetable oil
> 1 tablespoon lemon juice
> 1/4 cup finely chopped green pepper
> 1/4 cup finely chopped onion
> 2 tablespoons butter *or* margarine
> 1 can (10-3/4 ounces) condensed tomato soup, undiluted
> 1 cup whipping cream
> 2-1/4 cups cooked rice
> 1/8 teaspoon *each* ground mace, pepper and cayenne pepper
> 1/2 cup slivered almonds, toasted, *divided*

In a Dutch oven, bring water and 1 tablespoon salt to a boil. Add shrimp; cook for 3 minutes or until pink. Drain. Sprinkle shrimp with oil and lemon juice; set aside. In a skillet, saute green pepper and onion in butter for 5 minutes or until tender. Add soup, cream, rice, mace, pepper, cayenne, 1/4 cup of almonds and remaining salt. Set aside 1 cup of shrimp. Add remaining shrimp to the rice mixture. Transfer to a greased 2-qt. baking dish. Bake, uncovered, at 350° for 30-35 minutes. Top with reserved shrimp and remaining almonds; bake 20 minutes longer or until the shrimp are lightly browned. **Yield:** 8-10 servings.

BARBECUED SHORT RIBS

Cheryl Niemela, Cokato, Minnesota

People like the blending of many different flavors in this recipe. I consider it a very special one and generally fix it for company.

> 5 pounds bone-in short ribs, trimmed
> 2 medium onions, finely chopped
> 2 garlic cloves, minced
> 2 tablespoons olive *or* vegetable oil
> 1 can (14-1/2 ounces) diced tomatoes, undrained
> 1 cup chili sauce
> 1/3 cup soy sauce
> 1/3 cup honey
> 1/4 cup packed brown sugar
> 1/4 cup ketchup
> 2 teaspoons chili powder
> 1/2 teaspoon ground ginger
> 1/8 teaspoon cayenne pepper
> 1/8 teaspoon dried oregano
> 1/8 teaspoon liquid smoke, optional

Place ribs in a Dutch oven; add water to cover by 2 in. Bring to a boil. Reduce heat; simmer, uncovered, for 1-1/2 to 2 hours or until tender. Meanwhile, in a saucepan, saute onions and garlic in oil until tender. Add remaining ingredients; bring to a boil. Reduce heat; simmer, uncovered, for 30 minutes, stirring occasionally. Drain ribs. Arrange on a broiler pan and baste with barbecue sauce. Broil 4 to 5 in. from the heat for 5-10 minutes on each side or until sauce is bubbly. **Yield:** 6-8 servings.

HOME-STYLE ROAST BEEF

Sandra Furman-Krajewski, Amsterdam, New York

This moist roast gains richness from the gravy, and the bacon gives it a somewhat different taste. For variety, cube the roast and serve it over rice with gravy.

> 1 bottom round beef roast (10 to 12 pounds)
> 1 can (14-1/2 ounces) chicken broth
> 1 can (10-1/4 ounces) beef gravy

1 can (10-3/4 ounces) condensed cream
   of celery soup, undiluted
1/4 cup water
1/4 cup Worcestershire sauce
1/4 cup soy sauce
3 tablespoons dried parsley flakes
3 tablespoons dill weed
2 tablespoons dried thyme
4-1/2 teaspoons garlic powder
1 teaspoon celery salt
Pepper to taste
1 large onion, sliced 1/4 inch thick
8 bacon strips
1/4 cup butter *or* margarine, cut into cubes

Place roast in a large roasting pan with fat side up. Prick meat in several places with a meat fork. Combine broth, gravy, soup, water, Worcestershire sauce and soy sauce; pour over roast. Sprinkle with seasonings. Arrange onion slices over roast. Place bacon strips diagonally over onion. Dot with butter. Bake, uncovered, at 325° for 2-1/2 to 3-1/2 hours or until the meat reaches desired doneness (for rare, a meat thermometer should read 140°; medium, 160°; well-done, 170°). Let stand for 15 minutes before slicing. **Yield:** 25-30 servings.

stantly. Reduce heat; simmer for 25-30 minutes or until thickened. Stir in almonds. Slice ham; serve with the relish. **Yield:** 8-10 servings (4 cups relish).

SPICED HAM WITH APPLE RELISH

Vicki Tasker, Oakland, Maryland

(Pictured above right)

If you think Thanksgiving turkey tastes good as a leftover, try this. The ham's wonderful served cold on a bun with hot or cold relish spooned on the top. The meat can be sliced and cooked up in a soup as well or added to a green bean casserole.

1 teaspoon ground cloves
1 teaspoon ground allspice
1 boneless fully cooked ham (3 to 4 pounds)
APPLE RELISH:
4 medium tart apples, peeled and chopped
2 cups sugar
1 cup chopped dried apricots
1 cup golden raisins
1/4 cup vinegar
2 tablespoons grated orange peel
1/2 cup slivered almonds, toasted

Combine cloves and allspice; rub over ham. Wrap tightly in foil and place in a shallow baking pan. Bake at 325° for 1 to 1-1/2 hours or until a meat thermometer reads 140° and the ham is heated through. In a large saucepan, combine the first six relish ingredients. Bring to a boil, stirring con-

PEPPER STEAK

Cindy Gerber, Ayr, Ontario

I sometimes like to add mushrooms and water chestnuts to this savory steak as well.

1-1/4 cups beef broth, *divided*
1/4 cup soy sauce
1-1/4 teaspoons ground ginger
1/2 teaspoon sugar
1/4 teaspoon pepper
1-1/2 pounds boneless round steak, cut into strips
1 garlic clove, minced
1/4 cup olive *or* vegetable oil
4 medium green peppers, julienned
2 large tomatoes, peeled and chopped
3 tablespoons cornstarch
Hot cooked rice

In a small bowl, combine 3/4 cup broth, soy sauce, ginger, sugar and pepper; set aside. In a skillet or wok over medium-high heat, brown beef and garlic in oil. Add peppers and tomatoes. Cook and stir until peppers are crisp-tender, about 3 minutes. Stir the soy sauce mixture and add to pan. Cover and cook until the meat is tender, about 15 minutes. Combine cornstarch with the remaining broth until smooth; add to pan. Bring to a boil; cook and stir for 2 minutes. Serve over rice. **Yield:** 8 servings.

CHICKEN CROQUETTES

Carleen Mullins, Wise, Virginia

Here's a different recipe to try with leftover chicken. It really has a good flavor. These croquettes make a fun meal.

  2 tablespoons butter *or* margarine
  3 tablespoons all-purpose flour
  2 teaspoons ground mustard
  1/4 teaspoon salt
  1/8 teaspoon pepper
  1 cup milk
  2 cups chopped cooked chicken
  1/4 cup chopped green pepper
  1 tablespoon minced fresh parsley
  1 tablespoon finely chopped onion
  1 teaspoon lemon juice
  1/4 teaspoon paprika
  1/8 teaspoon cayenne pepper
1-1/2 cups dry bread crumbs
  1 egg
  2 tablespoons water
Oil for deep-fat frying

In a saucepan over medium heat, melt butter. Add flour, mustard, salt and pepper; stir until smooth. Gradually add milk; bring to a boil. Cook and stir for 2 minutes; remove from the heat. Add chicken, green pepper, parsley, onion, lemon juice, paprika and cayenne; mix well. Refrigerate for at least 2 hours. Shape into six 4-in. x 1-in. logs. Place bread crumbs in a shallow dish. In another dish, beat egg and water. Roll logs in bread crumbs, then in egg mixture, then again in crumbs. Heat oil in an electric skillet or deep-fat fryer to 350°. Drop logs, a few at a time, into hot oil. Fry for 1-2 minutes on each side or until golden brown. Drain on paper towels. Serve immediately. **Yield:** 6 croquettes. **Editor's Note:** This recipe may easily be doubled.

PEPPER-TOPPED PIZZA

Sonia Speh, Gordonsville, Virginia

(Pictured above)

We prefer this recipe over regular pizza. Its tomato and pepper topping is irresistible.

  1 tube (12 ounces) refrigerated flaky
    buttermilk biscuits
  1 tablespoon olive *or* vegetable oil
1/2 cup chopped green pepper
1/2 cup chopped sweet yellow pepper
1/2 cup chopped tomato
1/4 cup chopped onion
1/2 teaspoon garlic powder
1/4 teaspoon dried basil
1/4 teaspoon dried oregano
1/4 cup shredded Parmesan cheese

Split biscuits in half horizontally. Arrange on a lightly greased 12-in. round pizza pan; press dough together to seal the edges. Brush with oil. Sprinkle with peppers, tomato, onion, garlic powder, basil and oregano. Bake at 400° for 15-20 minutes or until crust is golden brown. Cover edges with foil to prevent overbrowning if necessary. Sprinkle with Parmesan cheese. Serve immediately. **Yield:** 4-6 servings.

COLORFUL APRICOT CHUTNEY

Lucile Cline, Wichita, Kansas

Serve this chutney as an accompaniment to pork or chicken. The recipe earned me first prize in a "Pepper Day" recipe contest.

  3 large sweet red peppers, diced
 12 ounces dried apricots, diced
  1 cup raisins
  1 cup sugar
  1 large onion, finely chopped
3/4 cup cider *or* red wine vinegar
  5 garlic cloves, minced

1-1/2 teaspoons salt
1-1/2 teaspoons crushed red pepper flakes
1/4 teaspoon ground ginger
1/4 teaspoon ground cumin
1/4 teaspoon ground mustard

In a large heavy saucepan, combine all ingredients; bring to a boil. Reduce heat; simmer, uncovered, for 25-30 minutes or until thickened, stirring occasionally. Cover and refrigerate. Serve as an accompaniment to pork or chicken. Chutney may be stored in the refrigerator for up to 1 month. **Yield:** 4 cups.

***

MARINATED PORK ROAST

Rita Berube, Lewiston, Maine

Because almost all of the preparation is done ahead of time, this recipe is perfect for get-togethers. It's one of our family's favorite dishes.

1 liter ginger ale
1/2 cup soy sauce
1/4 cup finely chopped green pepper
4 garlic cloves, minced
1 tablespoon lemon juice
1 tablespoon sugar
1 bone-in center-cut pork roast (3 to 4 pounds)
1/4 cup all-purpose flour
1/3 cup water

In a large heavy-duty resealable plastic bag or shallow glass dish, combine the first six ingredients. Add pork roast. Seal or cover and refrigerate overnight, turning once. Place roast and marinade in a shallow roasting pan. Bake at 325° for 1 hour and 45 minutes or until a meat thermometer reads 160°-170°. Let stand for 10 minutes. Meanwhile, measure 2 cups pan drippings. Skim fat; pour into a saucepan. Combine the flour and water until smooth; add to drippings. Bring to a boil; cook and stir for 2 minutes. Serve with the roast. **Yield:** 6-8 servings.

***

PICANTE PEPPER RELISH

Olivia Abrams, Canton, Texas

In addition to being served with different meats or fajitas, this zippy relish tastes terrific with corn chips.

1 can (11-1/2 ounces) picante V-8 juice
1 medium onion, chopped
1 medium tomato, seeded and chopped
1 cup minced fresh cilantro *or* parsley
4 to 5 serrano peppers, seeded and minced*

3 tablespoons lemon juice
1 teaspoon salt

In a bowl, combine all ingredients; mix well. Cover and refrigerate. Serve as an accompaniment to meat or fajitas. **Yield:** 3 cups. ***Editor's Note:** When cutting or seeding hot peppers, use rubber or plastic gloves to protect your hands. Avoid touching your face.

***

SAVORY BEEF SANDWICHES

Lynn Williamson, Hayward, Wisconsin

(Pictured below)

Before heading to work in the morning, I'll get this going in the slow cooker. Then it's all ready to serve as soon as my husband and I get home.

1 tablespoon dried minced onion
2 teaspoons salt
2 teaspoons garlic powder
2 teaspoons dried oregano
1 teaspoon dried rosemary, crushed
1 teaspoon caraway seeds
1 teaspoon dried marjoram
1 teaspoon celery seed
1/4 teaspoon cayenne pepper
1 boneless chuck roast (3 to 4 pounds), halved
8 to 10 sandwich rolls, split

Combine seasonings; rub over roast. Place in a slow cooker. Cover and cook on low for 6-8 hours or until meat is tender. Shred with a fork. Serve on rolls. **Yield:** 8-10 servings. **Editor's Note:** No liquid is added to the slow cooker. The moisture comes from the roast.

BASIL-STUFFED STEAK
Linda Gronewaller, Hutchinson, Kansas

(Pictured below)

This is a recipe I developed. We love beef, and grilling is an easy way to add variety to our meals. My mom and grandma taught me how to cook. I've entered several cooking competitions and have won some awards.

     1 boneless sirloin steak (2 to 2-1/2
        pounds and about 1-1/2 inches thick)
 1/2 teaspoon salt
 1/4 teaspoon pepper
 1/4 teaspoon dried parsley flakes
 1-1/2 cups lightly packed fresh basil
 1/4 cup finely chopped onion
     4 garlic cloves, minced
 1-1/2 teaspoons minced fresh rosemary *or* 1/2
        teaspoon dried rosemary, crushed
 1/8 teaspoon minced fresh thyme *or* pinch
        dried thyme
     1 teaspoon olive *or* vegetable oil

With a sharp knife, make five lengthwise cuts three-fourths of the way through the steak. Combine salt, pepper and parsley; rub over steak. Coarsely chop the basil; add onion, garlic, rosemary and thyme. Stuff into pockets in steak; using heavy-duty string, tie the steak at 2-in. intervals, closing the pockets. Drizzle with oil. Grill, covered, over indirect medium heat for 35-45 minutes or until the meat reaches desired doneness (for rare, a meat thermometer should read 140°; medium, 160°; well-done, 170°). Cover and let stand for 5-10 minutes. Remove string before slicing. **Yield:** 6-8 servings. **Editor's Note:** Steak can also be baked, uncovered, at 400° for 45 minutes or until meat reaches desired doneness.

SHRIMP PUFFS
Maudry Ramsey, Sulphur, Louisiana

Shrimp and rice are two foods that are abundant in our area. These shrimp puffs are my family's favorite.

     2 eggs, *separated*
 3/4 cup milk
     1 tablespoon vegetable oil
     1 cup all-purpose flour
 1-1/2 teaspoons baking powder
 1-1/2 teaspoons onion powder
     1 teaspoon salt
 1/2 teaspoon pepper
     3 cups cooked rice
     1 pound uncooked shrimp, peeled,
        deveined and chopped *or* 2 cans (4-1/2
        ounces *each*) small shrimp, drained
 1/4 cup minced fresh parsley
 1/2 teaspoon hot pepper sauce
Oil for deep-fat frying

In a large bowl, beat egg yolks, milk and oil. Combine flour, baking powder, onion powder, salt and pepper; add to yolk mixture and mix well. Stir in rice, shrimp, parsley and hot pepper sauce. In a mixing bowl, beat the egg whites until soft peaks form; fold into shrimp mixture. In an electric skillet or deep-fat fryer, heat oil to 350°. Drop batter by tablespoons into hot oil. Fry puffs, a few at a time, for 1-1/2 minutes on each side or until browned and puffy. Drain on paper towels. Serve warm. **Yield:** about 4 dozen.

THE PERFECT HAMBURGER
Shirley Kidd, New London, Minnesota

The chili sauce and horseradish add some zip to these hamburgers. We think they're perfect!

     1 egg, lightly beaten
     2 tablespoons chili sauce
     1 teaspoon dried minced onion
     1 teaspoon prepared horseradish
     1 teaspoon Worcestershire sauce
 1/2 teaspoon salt
Pinch pepper
     1 pound lean ground beef
     4 hamburger buns, split
Optional toppings: sliced tomato, onion,
     pickles and condiments

In a large bowl, combine the first seven ingredients. Add beef and mix well. Shape into four 3/4-in. thick patties. Grill, uncovered, over medium-hot heat for 5-6 minutes on each side or until juices run clear. Serve on buns with desired toppings. **Yield:** 4 servings.

Prime Beef Pointers

• When making a marinade, before adding the meat, reserve a little to pour over noodles or rice you plan to serve alongside. —*Nancy Spradley Hemingway, South Carolina*

• If you're out of sour cream, add plain yogurt to your favorite Stroganoff recipe (it also provides extra nutrition). —*Dianne Senecal Bracebridge, Ontario*

• To avoid heating up your kitchen in summer, try cooking pot roast in a slow cooker. All you lose is extra heat! —*Caroline Christensen Richfield, Utah*

• Roll-up-style steaks are great frozen dinners. I love to make extras and send them home with my grown kids. —*Edith Landinger, Longview, Texas*

• When making soup, skim as much fat as possible off the beef broth before adding vegetables. —*Evelyn Plyler Apple Valley, California*

• One way to tenderize flank steak is to score it: Make shallow crisscrossed diamond-shaped cuts on both sides of the meat before cooking it. —*Margaret Herz, Hastings, Nebraska*

• A sprig of fresh dill adds fun flavor to beef stew. —*Frances Preszler Braddock, North Dakota*

• For a fast meal, freeze barbecued sliced or shredded beef in individual or large resealable freezer bags. Then you can heat up enough for one sandwich …or a dinner for all! —*Paula Conkle Severn, Maryland*

• I often use a steak pinwheel recipe when I'm unsure about the number of dinner guests to expect. You can feed as few or as many as you like simply by adjusting the number you prepare. —*Ellen Baird Kennewick, Washington*

• For a super-easy slow-cooker recipe, try adding a couple envelopes of Italian salad dressing mix to the roast …and nothing else. —*Sharon Wilging Mountain, Wisconsin*

• Rub butter on each side of a steak before placing it on a hot grill to sear and lock in flavor (discard any remaining butter). Never pierce beef with a fork while turning or checking for doneness—all the juices will escape! —*Wanda Quiggins Horse Cave, Kentucky*

• Want a nice evenly sliced brisket? Put the meat in the refrigerator after cooking to cool completely. Then slice diagonally across the grain. Serve cold or hot with your favorite sauce. —*Charlotte Thompson Palm Bay, Florida*

• You'll add richness and flavor to beef roast by browning it in butter (add a little garlic salt, too, if you wish) before oven-baking or slow-cooking it. —*Lisa Seaba, Muscatine, Iowa*

• It's much easier to slice uncooked beef (for stir-fry, etc.) when it's partially frozen and you use a sharp knife.
For a tasty new twist to plain white sauce, sprinkle in some dill weed. —*Elfrieda Neufeld Leamington, Ontario*

APPLE-HAM CONFETTI LOAF

Gloria Snyder, Gastonia, North Carolina

(Pictured below)

One day I had some ground ham and pork in the refrigerator and was thinking about how to use them together in a recipe. I looked outside at my loaded apple tree and decided to combine the three ingredients into one dish. This is what I came up with. My husband thought it was good.

>   3 eggs
>   1/4 cup packed brown sugar
>   2 tablespoons prepared mustard
>   1 tablespoon soy sauce
>   1/8 teaspoon pepper
>   3 cups crushed cornflakes
>   2/3 cup *each* chopped green, sweet red and
>   yellow peppers
>   2 cups diced peeled apples
>   1/2 cup chopped onion
> 1-1/2 pounds ground ham
> 1-1/2 pounds ground pork
> **Orange marmalade *or* apricot preserves**

In a bowl, combine eggs, brown sugar, mustard, soy sauce and pepper; stir in cornflakes, peppers, apples and onion. Add ham and pork; mix well. Divide between two ungreased 8-in. x 4-in. x 2-in. loaf pans. Bake, uncovered, at 350° for 45 minutes. Spoon marmalade or preserves over loaves. Bake 20-30 minutes longer or until a meat thermometer reads 170°. **Yield:** 10-12 servings.

FILLETS WITH MUSHROOM SAUCE

Carolyn Brinkmeyer, Aurora, Colorado

I serve this dish to company because it's simple to make, but looks as if I spent hours in the kitchen.

> ☑ Uses less fat, sugar or salt. Includes Nutritional Analysis and Diabetic Exchanges.

>   4 beef tenderloin fillets (4 ounces *each*)
>   1 large onion, cut into 1/2-inch slices
>   1/2 pound fresh mushrooms, thickly sliced
>   2 tablespoons margarine
>   1 can (14-1/2 ounces) diced tomatoes,
>   undrained
>   1/4 cup water
>   1/2 teaspoon dried basil
>   1/2 teaspoon low-sodium beef bouillon
>   granules
>   1/8 teaspoon pepper

Broil or grill fillets, turning once, for 15-25 minutes or until meat reaches desired doneness (for rare, a meat thermometer should read 140°; medium, 160°; well-done, 170°). Meanwhile, in a skillet, saute onion and mushrooms in margarine until tender. Stir in tomatoes, water, basil, bouillon and pepper. Cook and stir over medium heat for 5 minutes or until thickened. Serve over beef. **Yield:** 4 servings. **Nutritional Analysis:** One serving equals 278 calories, 299 mg sodium, 70 mg cholesterol, 10 gm carbohydrate, 26 gm protein, 14 gm fat. **Diabetic Exchanges:** 3 meat, 2 vegetable.

MARINATED OSTRICH STEAK

Jennie Schmidt, Sudlersville, Maryland

We raise ostriches on our farm on the eastern shore of Maryland, so we have an abundance of meat on hand to use for a variety of dishes.

>   3/4 cup vegetable oil
>   1/3 cup soy sauce
>   1/4 cup cider *or* white wine vinegar
>   3 tablespoons lemon juice
>   2 tablespoons Worcestershire sauce
>   1 tablespoon ground mustard
>   1 teaspoon salt
>   1 teaspoon pepper
>   1 teaspoon dried parsley flakes
>   1/2 teaspoon garlic powder
>   4 ostrich *or* beef tenderloin fillets (about
>   1/4 pound *each*)

In a resealable plastic bag or shallow glass container, combine the first 10 ingredients; mix well. Add meat to marinade and turn to coat. Seal bag or cover container; refrigerate overnight, turning meat occasionally. Drain and discard marinade.

Broil or grill, covered, over medium heat for 5 minutes. Turn and cook 6-8 minutes longer or until meat reaches desired doneness (for rare, a meat thermometer should read 140°; medium, 160°; and well-done, 170°). **Yield:** 4 servings.

BACON-CHEESE PUFF PIE

Sherry Lee, Sheridan, Indiana

This pie is great for brunch any time of year. My family loves the combination of bacon, tomatoes and cheese.

  1 unbaked pastry shell (9 inches)
  1 pound sliced bacon, cooked and
     crumbled
  1 large tomato, peeled and sliced
  1 cup (4 ounces) shredded cheddar cheese
  3 eggs, *separated*
3/4 cup sour cream
1/2 cup all-purpose flour
1/2 teaspoon salt
Paprika

Line unpricked pastry shell with a double thickness of heavy-duty foil. Bake at 450° for 5 minutes. Remove foil. Bake 5 minutes longer. Cool completely. Sprinkle bacon over the crust. Top with tomato and cheese. In a bowl, beat egg yolks, sour cream, flour and salt until smooth. In another bowl, beat egg whites until stiff. Fold into sour cream mixture; spread over cheese. Sprinkle with paprika. Bake at 350° for 45 minutes or until a knife inserted near the center comes out clean. Let stand 5-10 minutes before cutting. **Yield:** 6 servings.

PEPPERY PHILLY STEAKS

Edie Fitch, Clifton, Arizona

(Pictured above right)

Since we love to cook and eat, my husband and I are always developing new recipes. This is one we especially enjoy when we have fresh peppers.

1-1/2 pounds boneless sirloin steak, cut into
    1/4-inch strips
  1 *each* medium green and sweet red
    peppers, julienned
  1 large onion, thinly sliced
  3 tablespoons vegetable oil
  2 tablespoons butter *or* margarine
  5 to 6 French *or* Italian sandwich rolls,
    split
  2 cans (4 ounces *each*) whole green
    chilies, drained and halved
  5 to 6 slices Swiss cheese

In a large skillet, cook steak, peppers and onion in oil until meat reaches desired doneness and vegetables are soft. Spread butter on rolls; top with meat mixture, chilies and cheese. Wrap in heavy-duty foil. Bake at 350° for 10-12 minutes or until heated through and cheese is melted. **Yield:** 5-6 servings.

CRANBERRY CHICKEN

Sandy Brooks, Tacoma, Washington

Cooking with cranberries is a happy habit. I like to include them because the fruit is filled with vitamin C— and because my husband and son love the flavor.

  1 cup fresh *or* frozen cranberries
3/4 cup chopped onion
1/2 teaspoon salt
1/4 teaspoon ground cinnamon
1/4 teaspoon ground ginger
  1 broiler/fryer chicken (about 3-1/2
    pounds), quartered and skin removed
  1 cup orange juice
  1 teaspoon grated orange peel
  3 tablespoons butter *or* margarine, melted
  3 tablespoons all-purpose flour
  2 to 3 tablespoons brown sugar
Hot cooked noodles

In a slow cooker, combine the first five ingredients; top with chicken. Pour orange juice over chicken and sprinkle with orange peel. Cover and cook on low for 5-6 hours or until meat juices run clear. Remove chicken; debone and cut up the meat. Set aside and keep warm. Combine butter and flour until smooth; add to slow cooker. Cook on high until thickened, about 20 minutes. Stir in chicken and brown sugar; heat through. Serve over noodles. **Yield:** 4-6 servings.

▪▪▪▪▪▪▪▪▪▪▪▪▪

CHICKEN-STUFFED GREEN PEPPERS

Shelley Armstrong, Buffalo Center, Iowa

(Pictured above)

Both for a family meal and for entertaining, this is a dish I serve frequently. It's very appealing to the eye, and people like the wild rice and the peppers. What I learned about cooking came from an expert—my husband! He's the real chef in the family.

4 large green peppers
1/3 cup chopped onion
1 garlic clove, minced
2 tablespoons butter *or* margarine
3 cups diced cooked chicken
2 cups chicken broth
1 package (6 ounces) long grain brown and wild rice blend
1/3 cup sliced celery
1/4 cup finely chopped carrot
1/4 teaspoon dried basil
1/4 teaspoon dried thyme
1 can (14-1/2 ounces) diced tomatoes, undrained
1 cup chopped fresh mushrooms
1/2 cup chopped zucchini
1/4 cup grated Parmesan cheese

Cut tops off peppers; remove seeds. In a large kettle, cook peppers in boiling water for 3 minutes. Drain and rinse in cold water; set aside. In a large saucepan, saute onion and garlic in butter until tender. Add chicken, broth, rice with contents of seasoning packet, celery, carrot, basil and thyme; bring to a boil. Reduce heat; cover and simmer for 25 minutes or until the rice is almost tender. Remove from the heat; stir in tomatoes, mushrooms and zucchini. Spoon rice mixture into the peppers; place in a greased 2-qt. baking dish. Spoon the remaining rice mixture around peppers. Cover and bake at 350° for 25-30 minutes or until the peppers are tender and filling is heated through. Uncover and sprinkle with Parmesan cheese; bake 5 minutes longer. **Yield:** 4 servings.

▪▪▪▪▪▪▪▪▪▪▪▪▪

TENDER BEEF AND NOODLES

Nancy Peterson, Farmington, British Columbia

This convenient main dish cooks by itself. If you like, substitute stew meat for the roast. Either way, it's a hearty everyday meal with a special tasty twist.

1 boneless chuck roast (2 to 2-1/2 pounds), cut into 1-inch cubes
2 large onions, chopped
3 tablespoons butter *or* margarine
1 can (8 ounces) tomato sauce
2 teaspoons sugar
2 teaspoons paprika
2 teaspoons Worcestershire sauce
1 to 2 teaspoons salt

1-1/2 teaspoons caraway seeds
1 teaspoon dill weed
1/4 teaspoon pepper
1/8 teaspoon garlic powder
1 cup (8 ounces) sour cream
Hot cooked noodles

In a large saucepan or Dutch oven, cook beef and onions in butter until the meat is browned. Add the next nine ingredients; bring to a boil. Reduce heat; cover and simmer for 1-3/4 to 2 hours or until meat is tender. Remove from the heat; stir in sour cream. Serve over noodles. **Yield:** 4-6 servings.

SPINACH-STUFFED SALMON

Janice Bell, Sumner, Washington

Some of the best salmon can be found here in western Washington. Whenever I serve this delicious recipe to guests, it never fails to impress.

2 celery ribs, chopped
1 large onion, chopped
1/2 cup butter *or* margarine
5 slices bread, cubed
1 package (10 ounces) frozen chopped spinach, thawed and drained
1-1/4 teaspoons salt, *divided*
1/8 teaspoon pepper
1 teaspoon olive *or* vegetable oil
2 salmon fillets (2-1/2 to 3 pounds *each*)
1 teaspoon chicken bouillon granules
1 cup boiling water
LEMON-DIJON BUTTER:
1 cup water
1/4 cup Dijon mustard
2 tablespoons lemon juice
1 teaspoon chicken bouillon granules
3 green onions, cut into 1-inch pieces
1/4 cup whipping cream
1 cup cold butter (no substitutes)

In a skillet, saute celery and onion in butter until tender. Remove from heat; add bread, spinach, 1/4 teaspoon salt and pepper. Combine oil and remaining salt; rub over salmon skin. Place one fillet, skin side down, in a greased roasting pan. Top with stuffing. Place second fillet over stuffing, skin side up. Tie with string if desired. Dissolve bouillon in water; pour around salmon. Bake, uncovered, at 350° for 45 minutes or until fish flakes easily with fork. In a saucepan, combine first five sauce ingredients. Bring to a boil; boil for 5 minutes or until sauce is reduced to 1/2 cup. Discard onions. Add cream; return to a boil. Remove from heat. Whisk in butter, 2 tablespoons at a time, until sauce thickens slightly. Serve with the salmon. **Yield:** 8-10 servings.

BRAISED BEEF WITH BARLEY

June Formanek, Belle Plaine, Iowa

(Pictured below)

I love the combination of beef and barley, so I was delighted when I saw this recipe in our newspaper. It's one dish I've served often.

1 boneless chuck roast (2 to 2-1/2 pounds)
1 tablespoon vegetable oil
1 medium onion, chopped
1/2 pound fresh mushrooms, sliced
3 garlic cloves, minced
1 can (14-1/2 ounces) beef broth
1 bay leaf
1-1/2 teaspoons salt
1/4 teaspoon pepper
1/2 cup pearl barley
1 cup frozen peas
1/3 cup sour cream, optional

In a Dutch oven over medium heat, brown roast in oil. Remove roast and set aside. Drain, reserving 1 tablespoon of drippings. Saute onion, mushrooms and garlic in drippings until tender. Return roast to the pan. Add broth, bay leaf, salt and pepper; bring to a boil. Reduce heat; cover and simmer for 1-1/2 hours. Add barley. Cover and simmer for 45 minutes or until meat and barley are tender. Add peas; cover and simmer for 5-10 minutes or until peas are tender. Discard bay leaf. Set the roast and barley aside; keep warm. If desired, add sour cream to the pan juices; stir until heated through. Slice roast; serve with barley and gravy. **Yield:** 4-6 servings.

APPLE SAUSAGE BAKE

Lynn McAllister, Mt. Ulla, North Carolina

This recipe is one of my favorite dishes. It tastes great and is usually the talk of the party.

    2 eggs
    1/2 cup milk
    1-1/2 cups crushed saltines (about 45 crackers)
    1 cup finely chopped peeled tart apple
    1/4 cup finely chopped onion
    2 pounds bulk pork sausage

In a large bowl, beat eggs; add milk, saltines, apple and onion. Add the sausage and mix well. Lightly press into a greased 6-cup ring mold or other mold. Invert onto a lightly greased 15-in. x 10-in. x 1-in. baking pan; remove mold. Bake, uncovered, at 350° for 1 hour or until a meat thermometer reads 170°; drain. **Yield:** 8 servings.

WINTER GARDEN SCRAMBLED EGGS

Carol Ice, Burlingham, New York

(Pictured below)

I like to serve hearty country breakfasts, so I'm always searching for different ways to cook eggs. I created this recipe and make it often on Sundays.

    8 eggs
    1 cup finely chopped fully cooked ham
    1/4 cup chopped sweet red pepper
    1/4 cup chopped green pepper

    1/4 cup sliced canned mushrooms
    1/4 cup chopped onion
    1/4 cup butter *or* margarine
    1/4 teaspoon garlic salt
Pinch pepper
Pinch celery seed

In a bowl, beat eggs; add ham, peppers, mushrooms and onion. Melt butter in a large skillet; add the egg mixture. Cook and stir gently over medium heat until the eggs are completely set. Add garlic salt, pepper and celery seed. **Yield:** 4 servings.

SLOW-COOKED STEW

Diane Delaney, Harrisburg, Pennsylvania

I often depend on this stew to put a hot, nutritious meal on the table after a long day at work.

✓ Uses less fat, sugar or salt. Includes Nutritional Analysis and Diabetic Exchanges.

    2 cups frozen French-style green beans
    2 cups fresh baby carrots, halved
    2 celery ribs, thinly sliced
    1 small onion, chopped
    1-1/2 pounds beef stew meat, cut into 1-inch cubes
    4 cups reduced-sodium V-8 juice
    3 tablespoons quick-cooking tapioca
    1 tablespoon sugar
    1/4 teaspoon pepper
Hot cooked noodles

In a slow cooker, combine beans, carrots, celery and onion. Top with beef. Combine V-8, tapioca, sugar and pepper; add to slow cooker. Cover and cook on low for 9-10 hours or until beef is tender. Serve over noodles. **Yield:** 10 servings. **Nutritional Analysis:** One 1-cup serving (calculated without noodles) equals 166 calories, 210 mg sodium, 42 mg cholesterol, 15 gm carbohydrate, 15 gm protein, 5 gm fat. **Diabetic Exchanges:** 1-1/2 meat, 1 starch.

HAM WITH MAPLE GRAVY

Sue Ward, Thunder Bay, Ontario

Watch out when you make this dish, because the delicious aroma that comes from your kitchen will be sure to create some big appetites.

    1 fully cooked boneless ham (6 pounds)
    30 whole cloves
    3/4 cup maple syrup, *divided*
    4 teaspoons ground mustard
    2 cups apple juice
    3 tablespoons cornstarch

Main Dishes

3 tablespoons water
2 tablespoons butter *or* margarine
6 medium tart apples, cored and cut into
1/2-inch slices

Place ham on a rack in a shallow roasting pan. With a sharp knife, make diagonal cuts in a diamond pattern about 1/2 in. deep in the surface of the ham. Push a clove into each diamond. Combine 1/2 cup maple syrup and mustard; pour over ham. Pour apple juice into the roasting pan. Bake at 325° for 1-1/2 to 2 hours or until a meat thermometer reads 140°, basting frequently. Remove ham and keep warm. Transfer the pan juices to a saucepan. Combine cornstarch and water until smooth; add to saucepan. Bring to a boil over medium heat; boil for 1 minute or until thickened. Meanwhile, in a skillet, melt butter over medium heat. Add apples and remaining syrup. Cover and cook for 10-15 minutes, stirring occasionally. Slice ham; serve with the apples and gravy. **Yield:** 12-14 servings.

SURF 'N' TURF TENDERLOIN

Colleen Gonring, Brookfield, Wisconsin

Here's a new version of "surf and turf"—succulent steaks stuffed with shrimp. Don't be fooled...this hearty main-course pleaser only looks tricky. It's actually a cinch to prepare.

1 tablespoon finely chopped onion
1 garlic clove, minced
2 tablespoons olive *or* vegetable oil, *divided*
2 tablespoons butter *or* margarine, *divided*
1/4 cup beef broth
16 uncooked medium shrimp (about 1/2 pound), peeled and deveined
1 tablespoon minced fresh parsley *or* 1 teaspoon dried parsley flakes
4 beef tenderloin steaks (1-1/2 to 2 inches thick)

In a small skillet, saute onion and garlic in 1 tablespoon oil and 1 tablespoon butter until tender. Add broth; cook and stir for 1 minute. Add the shrimp; cook and stir until shrimp turn pink, about 3-5 minutes. Add parsley. Meanwhile, make a lengthwise cut three-fourths of the way through each steak. Place three shrimp in each pocket. Cover remaining shrimp and sauce for garnish; set aside and keep warm. In a large skillet, heat remaining oil and butter over medium-high heat. Add steaks; cook until meat reaches desired doneness (about 10-13 minutes for medium), turning once. Top with remaining shrimp and sauce. **Yield:** 4 servings.

WILD RICE SHRIMP SAUTE

Judy Robinette Ommert, Sebring, Florida

(Pictured above)

The seafood is so good here in Florida, and shrimp is at the top of our list of favorites. Shrimp and wild rice make a delicious combination.

2-1/3 cups water
4 tablespoons butter *or* margarine, *divided*
1 teaspoon lemon juice
1/2 teaspoon Worcestershire sauce
1/2 teaspoon ground mustard
1/4 teaspoon pepper
1 package (6 ounces) long grain and wild rice mix
1 pound uncooked shrimp, peeled and deveined
2 tablespoons chopped green pepper
2 tablespoons chopped green onions

In a saucepan over medium heat, combine water, 1 tablespoon butter, lemon juice, Worcestershire sauce, mustard and pepper; bring to a boil. Add rice with seasoning packet; return to a boil. Reduce heat; cover and simmer for 25-30 minutes or until rice is tender and liquid is absorbed. Meanwhile, in a skillet over medium heat, melt remaining butter. Add shrimp, green pepper and onions. Cook and stir for 7-9 minutes or until shrimp turn pink and are cooked through. Add rice; heat through. **Yield:** 4 servings.

COOKING can't get much more "country" than hearty, homemade soups. And soups can't get much more satisfying than the filling fare here.

SOUP-ER! Clockwise from top left: Neighborhood Bean Soup (p. 44), Chunky Beef Noodle Soup (p. 43), Marvelous Mushroom Soup (p. 43) and Chicken 'n' Dumpling Soup (p. 44).

Satisfying Soups

MARVELOUS MUSHROOM SOUP

Beverly Rafferty, Winston, Oregon

(Pictured at left)

Soup is tops on the list of things I love to cook. I've used this one as the beginning course to a meal...and as a Sunday supper with hot rolls and butter.

    1/2 pound fresh mushrooms, sliced
      1 large onion, finely chopped
      1 garlic clove, minced
    1/2 teaspoon dried tarragon
    1/4 teaspoon ground nutmeg
      3 tablespoons butter *or* margarine
    1/4 cup all-purpose flour
      2 cans (14-1/2 ounces *each*) beef broth
      1 cup (8 ounces) sour cream
    1/2 cup half-and-half cream
    1/2 cup evaporated milk
      1 teaspoon lemon juice
Dash hot pepper sauce
Salt and pepper to taste

In a Dutch oven or soup kettle, saute the mushrooms, onion, garlic, tarragon and nutmeg in butter until vegetables are tender. Stir in flour until smooth. Gradually add broth; bring to a boil, stirring constantly. Reduce heat to low; slowly add sour cream. Cook and stir until smooth. Stir in cream and milk. Add lemon juice, hot pepper sauce, salt and pepper. Heat through but do not boil. **Yield:** 6 servings.

CHUNKY BEEF NOODLE SOUP

Lil Morris, Emerald Park, Saskatchewan

(Pictured at left)

We lived for 11 years in the Arctic, where there was very little fresh produce. This hearty soup became a staple since it requires ingredients I could easily find.

      1 pound boneless round steak, cut into
        1/2-inch cubes
      1 medium onion, chopped
      2 garlic cloves, minced

      1 tablespoon vegetable oil
      2 cups water
      1 can (14-1/2 ounces) diced tomatoes,
        undrained
      1 can (10-1/2 ounces) condensed beef
        consomme, undiluted
      1 to 2 teaspoons chili powder
      1 teaspoon salt
    1/2 teaspoon dried oregano
      1 cup uncooked spiral pasta
      1 medium green pepper, chopped
    1/4 cup minced fresh parsley

In a large saucepan, cook round steak, onion and garlic in oil until the meat is browned and the onion is tender, about 5 minutes. Stir in water, tomatoes, consomme and seasonings; bring to a boil. Reduce heat; cover and simmer until meat is tender, about 1-1/2 hours. Stir in pasta and green pepper. Simmer, uncovered, until noodles are tender, about 8 minutes. Add parsley. **Yield:** 8 servings (2 quarts).

CHILLED STRAWBERRY SOUP

Ellen Lohrenz, Enid, Oklahoma

A neighbor gave this recipe to my young daughter after she went to visit with a bowl and spoon in hand!

      1 quart fresh strawberries
      1 cup orange juice
    1/8 teaspoon ground cinnamon
  1-1/2 teaspoons quick-cooking tapioca
      1 cup buttermilk
    1/2 cup sugar
      2 teaspoons lemon juice
      1 teaspoon grated lemon peel
Whipped cream *or* yogurt and fresh mint,
    optional

In a blender, combine strawberries, orange juice and cinnamon; cover and process until smooth. Transfer to a medium saucepan; add the tapioca and let stand for 5 minutes. Bring to a boil; boil and stir for 2 minutes. Remove from the heat; stir in buttermilk, sugar, lemon juice and peel. Refrigerate. Garnish with whipped cream or yogurt and mint if desired. **Yield:** 4-6 servings.

Neighbors Agree—Her Bean Soup Is Best

RICH AND SUBSTANTIAL, Neighborhood Bean Soup from Cheryl Trowbridge is truly a meal in a bowl. "Served with half a sandwich or some bread, it'll satisfy the heartiest appetite," she assures from Windsor, Ontario.

Cheryl's delicious, beany blend indeed is aptly named. "Several neighbor ladies really enjoy this soup, and I love sharing it with them," she explains.

"In fact, each leaves her own personal container in my pantry so I can ladle it full when I make a batch. After that's done, there are just a couple of servings left for me and my father!"

It was her dad, Cheryl adds, who inspired her with his own soup recipe.

"When I first tasted his bean soup, I liked it immediately," she recollects. "But, as usual, I decided to 'tinker' with the ingredients a bit myself.

"I mixed in some more unusual spices—savory and marjoram. They go together beautifully and blend well with the taste of the ham."

In addition to her father and friends, this cheerful Canadian enjoys feeding her two cats and two dogs. She recently remodeled her kitchen with country-style cupboards, providing more room for her neighbors' empty soup containers.

Prepare a pot of her soup soon, and you'll know why it's in demand. Better be sure, though, to make a big batch—in case the neighbors catch a whiff!

NEIGHBORHOOD BEAN SOUP

(Pictured on page 42)

2 cups dry great northern beans
5 cups chicken broth
3 cups water
1 large meaty ham bone
2 to 3 tablespoons chicken bouillon granules
1 teaspoon dried thyme
1/2 teaspoon dried marjoram
1/2 teaspoon pepper
1/4 teaspoon rubbed sage
1/4 teaspoon dried savory
2 medium onions, chopped
3 medium carrots, chopped
3 celery ribs, chopped
1 tablespoon vegetable oil

Place beans in a Dutch oven or soup kettle; add water to cover by 2 in. Bring to a boil; boil for 2 minutes. Remove from the heat; cover and let stand for 1 hour. Drain. Add broth, water, ham bone, bouillon and seasonings; bring to a boil. Reduce heat; cover and simmer for 2 hours. Saute onions, carrots and celery in oil; add to soup. Cover and simmer 1 hour longer. Debone ham and cut into chunks; return to soup. Skim fat. **Yield:** 10 servings (2-3/4 quarts).

CHICKEN 'N' DUMPLING SOUP

Rachel Hinz, St. James, Minnesota

(Pictured on page 42)

This recipe's one I had to learn to marry into my husband's family! It is the traditional Hinz Christmas Eve meal, served before going to church.

1 broiler/fryer chicken (3 to 3-1/2 pounds)
3 quarts water
1/4 cup chicken bouillon granules
1 bay leaf
1 teaspoon whole peppercorns
1/8 teaspoon ground allspice
6 cups uncooked wide noodles
4 cups sliced carrots
3/4 cup sliced celery
1/2 cup chopped onion
1 package (10 ounces) frozen mixed vegetables
1/4 cup uncooked long grain rice
2 tablespoons minced fresh parsley
DUMPLINGS:
1-1/3 cups all-purpose flour
2 teaspoons baking powder
1 teaspoon dried thyme
1/2 teaspoon salt
2/3 cup milk
2 tablespoons vegetable oil

In a Dutch oven or soup kettle, combine the first six ingredients; bring to a boil. Reduce heat; cover and simmer for 1-1/2 hours. Remove chicken; allow to cool. Strain broth; discard bay leaf and peppercorns. Skim fat. Debone chicken and cut into chunks; return chicken and broth to pan. Add noodles, vegetables, rice and parsley; bring to a simmer. For dumplings, combine flour, baking powder, thyme and salt in a bowl. Combine milk and oil; stir into dry ingredients. Drop by teaspoonfuls onto simmering soup. Reduce heat; cover and simmer for 15 minutes (do not lift the cover). **Yield:** 20 servings (5 quarts).

MIXED VEGETABLE SOUP

Lucille Franck, Independence, Iowa

I received this recipe from my sister who worked as a dietitian for years. I always make a batch when my family gathers for the holidays.

✓ Uses less fat, sugar or salt. Includes Nutritional Analysis and Diabetic Exchanges.

  2 small carrots, grated
  2 celery ribs, chopped
  1 small onion, chopped
  1/2 cup chopped green pepper
  1/4 cup margarine
  2 cans (14-1/2 ounces *each*) low-sodium chicken broth, *divided*
  2 cans (14-1/2 ounces *each*) no-salt-added diced tomatoes, undrained
  1 tablespoon sugar
  1/4 teaspoon pepper
  1/4 cup all-purpose flour

In a 3-qt. saucepan, saute carrots, celery, onion and green pepper in margarine until tender. Reserve 1/2 cup chicken broth. Add tomatoes, sugar, pepper and remaining broth to pan; bring to a boil. Reduce heat; cover and simmer for 20 minutes. Combine flour and reserved broth until smooth; gradually add to soup. Bring to a boil; cook and stir for 2 minutes. **Yield:** 8 servings (2 quarts). **Nutritional Analysis:** One 1-cup serving equals 116 calories, 170 mg sodium, 2 mg cholesterol, 13 gm carbohydrate, 3 gm protein, 7 gm fat. **Diabetic Exchanges:** 1 starch, 1 fat.

SPICY SPLIT PEA SOUP

Cathy Dobbins, Rio Rancho, New Mexico

(Pictured at right)

I like to bake a ham just so I can use the leftover bone to make my split pea soup. After moving to New Mexico a few years ago, I discovered folks here put peppers or chilies in almost everything. So I decided to add some to this soup.

  1 package (1 pound) dry split peas
  6 cups water

  1 meaty ham bone *or* 2 smoked ham hocks *or* shanks
  4 chicken bouillon cubes
  3 to 5 medium Anaheim peppers, roasted, peeled, seeded and chopped* *or* 2 to 3 cans (4 ounces *each*) chopped green chilies
  2 medium carrots, sliced
  2 celery ribs, sliced
  1 medium onion, chopped
  1 garlic clove, minced
1-1/2 teaspoons dried oregano
  1/4 teaspoon pepper
  1/8 teaspoon ground cumin

In a Dutch oven or soup kettle, combine peas, water, ham bone and bouillon; bring to a boil. Reduce heat; cover and simmer for 1-1/2 hours. Add the remaining ingredients; bring to a boil. Reduce heat; cover and simmer 1 hour longer. Remove ham bone and cut meat from bone. Return to the soup and heat through. **Yield:** 8-10 servings (about 2-1/2 quarts). ***Editor's Note:*** When cutting or seeding hot peppers, use rubber or plastic gloves to protect your hands. Avoid touching your face. To roast peppers, place whole peppers on a broiler pan. Broil 4 in. from the heat, rotating often, until skins are blistered and blackened. Immediately place in a brown paper bag; close bag and let stand for 15-20 minutes. Peel off and discard charred skin.

HEARTY LENTIL SOUP

Suzanne Prince, Spokane, Washington

(Pictured below)

Served with biscuits and a tossed salad, this soup is simply delicious on a chilly autumn evening. It's one of my family's favorites.

    2 celery ribs, thinly sliced
    1 medium onion, chopped
    1 garlic clove, minced
    2 tablespoons butter *or* margarine
    6 cups water
    1 can (28 ounces) diced tomatoes,
      undrained
    3/4 cup dry lentils, rinsed
    3/4 cup pearl barley
    2 tablespoons chicken bouillon granules
    1/2 teaspoon dried oregano
    1/2 teaspoon dried rosemary, crushed
    1/4 teaspoon pepper
    1 cup thinly sliced carrots
    1 cup (4 ounces) shredded Swiss cheese,
      optional

In a Dutch oven or soup kettle, saute the celery, onion and garlic in butter until tender. Add water, tomatoes, lentils, barley, bouillon, oregano, rosemary and pepper; bring to a boil. Reduce heat; cover and simmer for 40 minutes or until lentils and barley are almost tender. Add carrots; simmer for 15 minutes or until carrots, lentils and barley are tender. Sprinkle each serving with cheese if desired. **Yield:** 8-10 servings (about 2-1/2 quarts).

MUSHROOM BARLEY SOUP

Patricia Maly, Mokena, Illinois

This is one of our foods to eat while watching football games. It really warms us up!

✓ Uses less fat, sugar or salt. Includes Nutritional Analysis and Diabetic Exchanges.

    1 can (49 ounces) low-sodium chicken
      broth
    2 medium carrots, thinly sliced
    1 medium onion, chopped
    2 garlic cloves, minced
    1/2 teaspoon dried basil
    1/2 teaspoon dried oregano
    1/2 teaspoon pepper
    1-1/2 cups medium pearl barley
    2 cups low-sodium tomato juice
    1 can (14-1/2 ounces) no-salt-added diced
      tomatoes, undrained
    1/2 pound fresh mushrooms, thinly sliced

In a Dutch oven or soup kettle, combine broth, carrots, onion, garlic, basil, oregano and pepper; bring to a boil. Add barley. Reduce heat; cover and simmer for 45-55 minutes or until barley is tender. Add remaining ingredients; cook for 10-15 minutes or until mushrooms are tender. **Yield:** 11 servings (about 2-3/4 quarts). **Nutritional Analysis:** One 1-cup serving equals 140 calories, 85 mg sodium, 3 mg cholesterol, 29 gm carbohydrate, 6 gm protein, 2 gm fat. **Diabetic Exchanges:** 1-1/2 starch, 1 vegetable.

BEST CHICKEN NOODLE SOUP

Cheryl Rogers, Ames, Iowa

(Pictured on page 48)

For years, I worked at making a chicken soup that tasted just like my mother's. When I couldn't, I came up with my own recipe. It was an immediate hit!

    1 tablespoon dried rosemary, crushed
    2 teaspoons garlic powder
    2 teaspoons pepper
    2 teaspoons seasoned salt
    2 broiler/fryer chickens (3 to 3-1/2
      pounds *each*)
    1-1/2 quarts chicken broth
    2-1/4 cups sliced fresh mushrooms
    1/2 cup chopped celery
    1/2 cup sliced carrots
    1/2 cup chopped onion
    1/4 teaspoon pepper
NOODLES:
    2-1/2 cups all-purpose flour, *divided*
    1 teaspoon salt

2 eggs
1 can (5 ounces) evaporated milk
1 tablespoon olive *or* vegetable oil

Combine the first four ingredients; rub over chickens. Place in an ungreased 13-in. x 9-in. x 2-in. baking pan. Cover and bake at 350° for 1-1/4 hours or until tender. Drain and reserve drippings. Skim fat. Cool chicken; debone and cut into chunks. Cover and refrigerate chicken. In a Dutch oven or soup kettle, bring chicken broth and reserved drippings to a boil. Add mushrooms, celery, carrots, onion and pepper; simmer for 30 minutes. Meanwhile, for noodles, set aside 1/3 cup of flour. Combine salt and remaining flour in a bowl. Beat eggs, milk and oil; stir into dry ingredients. Sprinkle kneading surface with reserved flour; knead dough until smooth. Divide into thirds. Roll out each portion to 1/8-in. thickness; cut to desired width. Freeze two portions to use at another time. Bring soup to a boil. Add one portion of noodles; cook for 7-9 minutes or until almost tender. Add chicken; heat through. **Yield:** 10 servings (2-3/4 quarts).

SAVORY TOMATO BEEF SOUP

Edna Tilley, Morganton, North Carolina

(Pictured on page 49)

This soup's one my mother taught me to make. It makes a nice lunch with a side salad or homemade corn bread.

1 pound beef stew meat, cut into 1/2-inch cubes
1 small meaty beef soup bone
2 tablespoons vegetable oil
4 cups water
1 can (28 ounces) diced tomatoes, undrained
1 cup chopped carrots
1 cup chopped celery
1/4 cup chopped celery leaves
1 tablespoon salt
1/2 teaspoon dried marjoram
1/2 teaspoon dried basil
1/4 teaspoon dried savory
1/4 teaspoon dried thyme
1/8 teaspoon ground mace
1/8 teaspoon hot pepper sauce

In a Dutch oven or soup kettle, brown the stew meat and soup bone in oil. Add the remaining ingredients; bring to a boil. Reduce heat; cover and simmer for 4-5 hours or until meat is tender. Skim fat. Remove meat from bone; cut into 1/2-in. cubes. Return to soup; heat through. **Yield:** 6-8 servings (about 2 quarts).

MONTEREY JACK CHEESE SOUP

Susan Salenski, Copemish, Michigan

(Pictured on page 48)

I love cheese and our kids like anything with Mexican flavor, so this soup is popular at our house.

1 cup chicken broth
1 large tomato, peeled, seeded and diced
1/2 cup finely chopped onion
2 tablespoons chopped green chilies
1 garlic clove, minced
2 tablespoons butter *or* margarine
2 tablespoons all-purpose flour
Salt and pepper to taste
3 cups milk, *divided*
1-1/2 cups (6 ounces) shredded Monterey Jack cheese

In a 3-qt. saucepan, combine the first five ingredients; bring to a boil. Reduce heat; cover and simmer for 10 minutes or until vegetables are tender. Remove from the heat and set aside. In another saucepan, melt butter. Stir in flour, salt and pepper. Cook and stir over medium heat until smooth. Gradually stir in 1-1/2 cups milk; bring to a boil. Boil for 1 minute, stirring constantly. Slowly stir into vegetable mixture. Add cheese and remaining milk. Cook and stir over low heat until cheese is melted. Serve immediately. **Yield:** 5 servings.

SPLIT PEA SAUSAGE SOUP

Donna Mae Young, Menomonie, Wisconsin

(Pictured on page 49)

When my husband and I eat out and enjoy a dish, I go home and try to duplicate it. That's how I came up with this recipe.

1 pound smoked kielbasa
1 pound dry split peas
6 cups water
1 cup chopped carrots
1 cup chopped onion
1 cup chopped celery
1 tablespoon minced fresh parsley
1 teaspoon salt
1/2 teaspoon coarse black pepper
2 bay leaves

Cut sausage in half lengthwise; cut into 1/4-in. pieces. Place in a Dutch oven or soup kettle; add remaining ingredients. Bring to a boil. Reduce heat; cover and simmer for 1-1/4 to 1-1/2 hours or until peas are tender. Remove bay leaves. **Yield:** 8 servings (2 quarts).

WHETHER *your family favors soup that's robust with meat or creamy and a bit more delicate, they'll warm up to this soup-erior spread.*

SOUP'S ON. Clockwise from top right: Savory Tomato Beef Soup (p. 47), Swedish Meatball Soup (p. 50), Stir-Fried Pork Soup (p. 51), Split Pea Sausage Soup (p. 47), Monterey Jack Cheese Soup (p. 47), Best Chicken Noodle Soup (p. 46), Lentil Barley Soup (p. 50) and Cream of Cabbage Soup (p. 50).

SWEDISH MEATBALL SOUP

Debora Taylor, Inkom, Idaho

(Pictured on page 49)

To me, this is a very comforting, filling, homey soup. I especially like cooking it during winter months and serving it with hot rolls, bread or muffins.

>   1 egg
>   2 cups half-and-half cream, *divided*
>   1 cup soft bread crumbs
>   1 small onion, finely chopped
> 1-3/4 teaspoons salt, *divided*
> 1-1/2 pounds ground beef
>   1 tablespoon butter *or* margarine
>   3 tablespoons all-purpose flour
> 3/4 teaspoon beef bouillon granules
> 1/2 teaspoon pepper
> 1/8 to 1/4 teaspoon garlic salt
>   3 cups water
>   1 pound red potatoes, cubed
>   1 package (10 ounces) frozen peas, thawed

In a bowl, beat egg; add 1/3 cup cream, bread crumbs, onion and 1 teaspoon of salt. Add beef; mix well. Shape into 1/2-in. balls. In a Dutch oven or soup kettle, brown meatballs in butter, half at a time. Remove from the pan; set aside. Drain fat. To pan, add flour, bouillon, pepper, garlic salt and remaining salt; stir until smooth. Gradually stir in water; bring to a boil, stirring often. Add potatoes and meatballs. Reduce heat; cover and simmer for 25 minutes or until the potatoes are tender. Stir in peas and remaining cream; heat through. **Yield:** 9 servings (about 2 quarts).

LENTIL BARLEY SOUP

Anita Warner, Mt. Crawford, Virginia

(Pictured on page 48)

Soups are among my favorite things to prepare. They're so easy, and nothing is better on a chilly evening with some homemade bread or biscuits.

>   1 medium onion, chopped
> 1/2 cup chopped green pepper
>   3 garlic cloves, minced
>   1 tablespoon butter *or* margarine
>   1 can (49-1/2 ounces) chicken broth
>   3 medium carrots, chopped
> 1/2 cup dry lentils
> 1-1/2 teaspoons Italian seasoning
>   1 teaspoon salt
> 1/4 teaspoon pepper
>   1 cup cubed cooked chicken *or* turkey

> 1/2 cup quick-cooking barley
>   2 medium fresh mushrooms, chopped
>   1 can (28 ounces) crushed tomatoes, undrained

In a Dutch oven or soup kettle, saute the onion, green pepper and garlic in butter until tender. Add broth, carrots, lentils, Italian seasoning, salt and pepper; bring to a boil. Reduce heat; cover and simmer for 25 minutes. Add chicken, barley and mushrooms; return to a boil. Reduce heat; cover and simmer for 10-15 minutes or until the lentils, barley and carrots are tender. Add tomatoes; heat through. **Yield:** 8-10 servings (about 2-1/2 quarts).

CREAM OF CABBAGE SOUP

Helen Riesterer, Kiel, Wisconsin

(Pictured on page 49)

People love this soup's flavor and creamy cheesy consistency. I've given the recipe to friends, who've varied it a little. One substituted summer squash and zucchini for the rutabaga. She said it tasted just great that way, too.

>   4 cups water
>   2 tablespoons chicken bouillon granules
>   3 cups diced peeled potatoes
>   1 cup finely chopped onion
>   1 cup diced peeled rutabaga
> 1/2 cup diced carrots
>   6 cups chopped cabbage
>   1 cup chopped celery
> 1/2 cup chopped green pepper
>   1 garlic clove, minced
>   1 teaspoon salt
>   1 teaspoon dill weed
>   1 cup butter *or* margarine
>   1 cup all-purpose flour
>   2 cups milk
>   2 cups chicken broth
> 1/2 pound process American cheese, cubed
> 1/2 teaspoon dried thyme

Pepper to taste
Additional milk, optional

In a Dutch oven or soup kettle, bring water and bouillon to a boil. Add potatoes, onion, rutabaga and carrots. Reduce heat; cover and simmer for 5 minutes. Add cabbage, celery and green pepper; simmer, uncovered, for 5 minutes or until vegetables are crisp-tender. Add garlic, salt and dill. In a saucepan, melt butter. Stir in flour; cook and stir over medium heat until golden brown. Gradually add milk and broth, stirring until smooth. Add cheese, thyme and pepper; cook on low until cheese is melted. Stir into vegetable mixture; simmer for 5 minutes. Thin with milk if needed. **Yield:** 12-14 servings (about 3-1/2 quarts).

STIR-FRIED PORK SOUP

Louise Johnson, Harriman, Tennessee

(Pictured on page 49)

This soup is a treat—especially to guests who enjoy the variety of Chinese cooking. I like serving it with fried noodles or rice as a side dish.

- 2/3 pound boneless pork loin, cut into thin strips
- 1 cup sliced fresh mushrooms
- 1 cup chopped celery
- 1/2 cup diced carrots
- 2 tablespoons vegetable oil
- 6 cups chicken broth
- 1/2 cup chopped fresh spinach
- 2 tablespoons cornstarch
- 3 tablespoons cold water
- 1 egg, lightly beaten

Pepper to taste

In a 3-qt. saucepan, stir-fry pork, mushrooms, celery and carrots in oil until pork is browned and vegetables are tender. Add broth and spinach. Combine cornstarch and water to make a thin paste; stir into soup. Return to a boil; boil for 1 minute. Quickly stir in egg. Add pepper. Serve immediately. **Yield:** 4-6 servings.

CURRIED ACORN SQUASH SOUP

Marilou Robinson, Portland, Oregon

(Pictured below)

This is an easy soup to make and it keeps well. I came up with this recipe as a change of pace from ordinary baked squash. The curry powder gives it a unique taste.

- 3 medium acorn squash, halved and seeded
- 1/2 cup chopped onion
- 3 to 4 teaspoons curry powder
- 2 tablespoons butter *or* margarine
- 3 cups chicken broth
- 1 cup half-and-half cream
- 1/2 teaspoon ground nutmeg

Salt and pepper to taste
Crumbled cooked bacon, optional

Place the squash, cut side down, in a greased shallow baking pan. Bake at 350° for 35-40 minutes or until the squash is almost tender. In a saucepan, saute onion and curry powder in butter until onion is tender. Remove from the heat; set aside. Carefully scoop out squash; add pulp to saucepan. Gradually add broth. Cook over medium heat for 15-20 minutes or until squash is very tender. In a food processor or blender, process the squash mixture until smooth; return to saucepan. Stir in cream, nutmeg, salt and pepper. Cook over low heat until heated through (do not boil). Garnish with bacon if desired. **Yield:** 4-6 servings.

RED PEPPER SOUP

Barb Nelson, Victoria, British Columbia

(Pictured below)

While I don't have scientific proof of it, Red Pepper Soup works for me as a head cold remedy! It is a good gift to take when visiting a sick friend, too. For a pretty touch, top the soup with grated cheese and parsley. We enjoy it with jalapeno cheese buns. You can also serve it with warm garlic bread.

> 6 medium sweet red peppers, chopped
> 2 medium carrots, chopped
> 2 medium onions, chopped
> 1 celery rib, chopped
> 4 garlic cloves, minced
> 1 tablespoon olive *or* vegetable oil
> 2 cans (one 49-1/2 ounces, one 14-1/2 ounces) chicken broth
> 1/2 cup uncooked long grain rice
> 2 tablespoons minced fresh thyme *or* 2 teaspoons dried thyme
> 1-1/2 teaspoons salt
> 1/4 teaspoon pepper
> 1/8 to 1/4 teaspoon cayenne pepper
> 1/8 to 1/4 teaspoon crushed red pepper flakes

In a large Dutch oven or soup kettle, saute red peppers, carrots, onions, celery and garlic in oil until tender. Stir in the broth, rice, thyme, salt, pepper and cayenne; bring to a boil. Reduce heat; cover and simmer for 20-25 minutes or until the vegetables and rice are tender. Cool for 30 minutes. Puree in small batches in a blender; return to pan. Add red pepper flakes; heat through. **Yield:** 10-12 servings (about 3 quarts).

VEGETABLE BEEF SOUP

Marie Freigang, Rocky Mountain House, Alberta

My husband and I love this beef and vegetable-packed soup. Broccoli, turnips or peas also make a nice addition.

> ✓ Uses less fat, sugar or salt. Includes Nutritional Analysis and Diabetic Exchanges.

> 2 quarts water
> 3 tablespoons low-sodium beef bouillon granules
> 1 tablespoon onion soup mix
> 2 cans (14-1/2 ounces *each*) no-salt-added tomatoes, undrained and chopped
> 1-1/2 cups cubed cooked roast beef
> 2 celery ribs, chopped

Thrifty Soup Doesn't Skimp on Taste

NOTHING GOES to waste at Jan Setterlund's Omaha, Nebraska place. The proof's in her home-made soup that gets its start with chicken gizzards.

"My mom believed in using every part of the bird," relates Jan, whose family enjoyed this truly "from scratch" soup when she was growing up. Now, her husband, Virgil, and their two children—Sam and Carly—often ask for steaming bowls of seconds.

If your family likes meat, Jan suggests, add more gizzards. If they prefer noodles, put in oodles. Whichever way you serve this tasty Gizzard Soup, prepare for a blizzard…of compliments!

GIZZARD SOUP

1/2 cup all-purpose flour
1 tablespoon seasoned salt
1-1/2 pounds chicken gizzards, trimmed and halved
1/4 cup vegetable oil

2 cans (49-1/2 ounces *each*) chicken broth
5 cups uncooked wide egg noodles

Combine flour and seasoned salt in a large resealable plastic bag. Add gizzards; shake to coat. In a Dutch oven or soup kettle, brown gizzards in oil. Add chicken broth. Cover and simmer for 2-3 hours or until the gizzards are tender. Add noodles; simmer, uncovered, for 30 minutes. **Yield:** 12-14 servings (about 3-1/2 quarts).

---

1 medium onion, chopped
1 cup shredded cabbage
3/4 cup dry lentils, rinsed
1/2 cup frozen mixed vegetables
1/4 cup no-salt-added ketchup
1 tablespoon uncooked wild rice
2 garlic cloves, minced
1/2 teaspoon hot pepper sauce
1/2 teaspoon pepper

In a Dutch oven or large saucepan, combine all ingredients. Bring to a boil. Reduce heat; cover and simmer for 50-60 minutes or until rice is tender. **Yield:** 12 servings. **Nutritional Analysis:** One 1-cup serving equals 98 calories, 82 mg sodium, 9 mg cholesterol, 15 gm carbohydrate, 7 gm protein, 1 gm fat. **Diabetic Exchanges:** 1 starch, 1/2 meat.

TOMATO BEAN SOUP

Diane Antonioli, Marmora, New Jersey
This filling soup will fit nicely into almost any event. It's a big hit at our house. In fact, my husband and our three children request it all year-round.

1 pound dry great northern beans
4 cups chicken broth
2 cups water
2 bay leaves

7 bacon strips, diced
3 cups thinly sliced onion
2 cups thinly sliced celery
2 large carrots, thinly sliced
1/2 pound fully cooked smoked sausage, diced
4 garlic cloves, minced
2 teaspoons sugar
2 cans (28 ounces *each*) diced tomatoes, drained
1/2 teaspoon salt
1/2 teaspoon pepper
1/4 teaspoon hot pepper sauce

Place beans in a Dutch oven or soup kettle; add water to cover by 2 in. Bring to a boil; boil for 2 minutes. Remove from the heat; cover and let stand for 1 hour. Drain beans and discard liquid; return beans to Dutch oven. Add broth, water and bay leaves; bring to a boil. Reduce heat; cover and simmer for 1-1/4 hours or until the beans are tender. Meanwhile, in a large skillet, cook bacon, onion, celery and carrots until vegetables are crisp-tender, about 12 minutes. Add sausage, garlic and sugar; cook for 5 minutes. Remove with a slotted spoon to Dutch oven. Stir in tomatoes; bring to a boil. Reduce heat; simmer, uncovered, for 45 minutes or until beans begin to break apart and soup thickens, stirring occasionally. Add salt, pepper and hot pepper sauce. Discard bay leaves before serving. **Yield:** 12-14 servings (3-1/2 quarts).

A Bowlful of Soup Secrets

• To make a thicker and creamier black bean soup without adding cream, pour some of the cooled soup into a blender and process until smooth. Return it to the saucepan and heat through. —*Tonya Grell*
Seattle, Washington

• I save ham bones, leftover meat and vegetable liquid to use in flavorful (and economical!) soup stock.
—*Linda Mervyn*
Delta, British Columbia

• The "secret ingredient" in my broccoli soup is the instant mashed potato flakes I add with the milk and butter to thicken it. —*Jane Lee Boyd*
Cameron, West Virginia

• When making soup with link sausage, use your kitchen scissors to cut the links into smaller pieces so they're easier to eat. —*Dorothy Dylong*
Boston, New York

• Instead of cheddar cheese, shred 3/4 cup of carrots over cauliflower soup for a tasty and colorful topper.
—*Joy Smith, Winnipeg, Manitoba*

• Homemade tomato soup provides a wonderful base for spaghetti or vegetable soup, as well as a tasty addition to meat loaf. —*Juanita Pardue*
Heath Springs, South Carolina

• The night before I prepare a big kettle of soup, I chop and measure all the vegetables and refrigerate them in resealable plastic bags or in covered bowls. Next day, assembling the soup is a breeze! —*Rose Boudreaux*
Bourg, Louisiana

• To make a creamy potato soup special, top with crumbled cooked bacon, shredded cheese and/or herbed croutons. —*Kelly Parsons, Seale, Alabama*

• Crushed red pepper flakes add extra zing to minestrone.
—*Nancy Solberg, Madison, Wisconsin*

• To save time, I brown ground beef in advance, then freeze it. I can quickly make taco soup by adding the remaining ingredients. —*Sherry Abrams*
Broken Bow, Oklahoma

• My husband loves this fast, easy soup: Combine 1 can *each* of tomato and cream of mushroom soup with 2 cans of milk. Heat through.
—*Mary Ann Flieg*
Ste. Genevieve, Missouri

• I make and freeze several batches of basic chicken soup in two-serving and four-serving containers. Then for a quick supper, I simply reheat the soup, add rice or pasta and cook for 20 to 30 minutes. —*Coral Smith, Mt. Ayr, Iowa*

• Vegetable soups are so versatile! I often substitute combinations of vegetables that suit my family's tastes for those listed in recipes.
—*Mary Nell Ruhenkoenig*
Burleson, Texas

• I keep containers in the freezer for beef soup and chicken soup so that I can regularly add small leftover amounts of cooked vegetables or even gravy. On soup day, I make the stock, then add my variety of "recycled" vegetables. —*Betty Anderson*
Lothian, Maryland

▟▞▟▞▟▞▟▞▟▞
SWEET POTATO MINESTRONE

Helen Vail, Glenside, Pennsylvania

I don't cook as much now that our daughters are on their own. But when I do, this is the recipe I reach for.

☑ Uses less fat, sugar or salt. Includes Nutritional Analysis and Diabetic Exchanges.

4 cans (14-1/2 ounces *each*) low-sodium beef broth
3 cups water
2 medium sweet potatoes, peeled and cubed
1 medium onion, chopped
4 garlic cloves, minced
2 teaspoons Italian seasoning
6 cups shredded cabbage
1 package (7 ounces) small pasta shells
2 cups frozen peas

In a Dutch oven or soup kettle, combine beef broth, water, potatoes, onion, garlic and Italian seasoning; bring to a boil. Reduce heat; cover and simmer for 10 minutes. Return to a boil. Add the cabbage, pasta and peas; cook for 8-10 minutes or until the pasta and vegetables are tender. **Yield:** 14 servings (about 3-1/2 quarts). **Nutritional Analysis:** One 1-cup serving equals 127 calories, 67 mg sodium, 0 cholesterol, 23 gm carbohydrate, 6 gm protein, 1 gm fat. **Diabetic Exchanges:** 1-1/2 starch, 1 vegetable.

▟▞▟▞▟▞▟▞▟▞
CLASSIC CHILI MIX

Bernice Morris, Marshfield, Missouri

This full-flavored chili seasoning will heat up your holiday gift-giving. The mix is on the mild side, which is nice for those who aren't partial to extra-spicy food. To raise the "temperature", add more chili powder!

1 cup plus 2 tablespoons all-purpose flour
3/4 cup dried minced onion
4 to 6 tablespoons chili powder
1/4 cup paprika
2 tablespoons salt
1 tablespoon ground cumin
1 tablespoon dried minced garlic
1 tablespoon sugar

ADDITIONAL INGREDIENTS (for each batch):
1 pound ground beef
1 can (15 ounces) pinto beans, rinsed and drained
1 small green pepper, chopped
1 can (14-1/2 ounces) diced tomatoes, undrained
1/2 to 3/4 cup water

Combine the first eight ingredients; divide into six batches (a little less than 1/2 cup each). Store in airtight containers. **Yield:** 6 batches (2-3/4 cups total). **To prepare chili:** Brown beef in a large saucepan; drain. Stir in one batch of chili mix, beans, green pepper, tomatoes and water; bring to a boil. Reduce heat; simmer for 30 minutes. **Yield:** 4 servings per batch.

▟▞▟▞▟▞▟▞▟▞
GOLDEN STATE MUSHROOM SOUP

Dave Patton, San Jose, California

(Pictured below)

Mushrooms have become very popular in my area, but they've long been a favorite of mine. After years of searching for a good mushroom soup recipe, I gave up and created my own.

1 pound fresh mushrooms, sliced
1 medium onion, chopped
1/4 cup butter *or* margarine
1/4 cup all-purpose flour
1/2 teaspoon salt
1/8 teaspoon pepper
1-1/2 cups milk
1 can (14-1/2 ounces) chicken broth
1 teaspoon chicken bouillon granules
1 cup (8 ounces) sour cream
Minced fresh parsley, optional

In a large saucepan, saute mushrooms and onion in butter until tender. Sprinkle with flour, salt and pepper; mix well. Gradually stir in milk, broth and bouillon; bring to a boil. Cook and stir for 2 minutes. Reduce heat. Stir in the sour cream; heat through (do not boil). Garnish with parsley if desired. **Yield:** 4-6 servings.

Time-Saving Soups

WHEN you want the comforting taste of home-made soup, but time seems too tight, turn to this page. Every super-convenient recipe here takes less than 30 minutes from beginning to bowl.

━━━━━━━━━━━━━━

SPICY FISH SOUP

Linda Murray, Allenstown, New Hampshire

The addition of salsa packs a punch in this simple soup recipe. We enjoy eating it with oven-fresh bread and dessert.

> 2 cans (14-1/2 ounces *each*) chicken broth
> 2-1/2 cups water
> 2/3 cup uncooked instant rice
> 1-1/2 cups salsa
> 1 package (10 ounces) frozen corn
> 1 pound frozen cod, thawed and cut into 2-inch pieces
> Fresh lime wedges, optional

In a large saucepan, bring broth, water and rice to a boil. Reduce heat; cover and simmer for 5 minutes. Add the salsa and corn; return to a boil. Add fish. Reduce heat; cover and simmer for 5 minutes or until fish flakes easily with a fork. Serve with lime if desired. **Yield:** 8 servings (about 2-1/4 quarts).

━━━━━━━━━━━━━━

QUICK BEAN SOUP

Dorothy Anderson, Woodstock, Illinois

A co-worker of mine brought this soup for everyone to sample at lunch one day. I ended up eating a heaping bowlful even though I don't normally care for soup. It's that good!

> 1 medium onion, chopped
> 2 medium carrots, chopped
> 2 celery ribs, chopped

> 2 cups water
> 2 cans (15 ounces *each*) navy *or* great northern beans
> 1 can (28 ounces) diced tomatoes, undrained
> 1 pound smoked sausage, cut into 1/4-inch slices and halved
> 1 teaspoon salt
> 1/2 teaspoon garlic salt
> 1/2 teaspoon paprika
> 1/2 teaspoon dried marjoram
> 1/2 teaspoon dried thyme
> 1/2 teaspoon pepper

In a 3-qt. saucepan, combine onion, carrots, celery and water. Bring to a boil; boil for 5 minutes. Add the remaining ingredients; mix well. Heat through. **Yield:** 6-8 servings (about 2-1/4 quarts).

━━━━━━━━━━━━━━

ZIPPY TOMATO SOUP

Ardith Morton, Merriman, Nebraska

I'll often add cooked macaroni, vegetables or cooked ground beef to this soup to make an easy one-pot meal. It's a zesty change of pace from regular tomato soup.

> 2 quarts tomato juice
> 1 beef bouillon cube
> 1 tablespoon dried minced onion
> 1/2 teaspoon dried basil
> 1/4 teaspoon dried oregano
> 1/4 teaspoon garlic powder
> 1/8 teaspoon cayenne pepper
> 2 tablespoons minced fresh parsley *or* cilantro

Combine the first seven ingredients in a 3-qt. saucepan; bring to a boil. Reduce heat; cover and simmer for 5 minutes. Add parsley. Serve immediately. **Yield:** 8 servings (2 quarts).

CREAMY CARROT SOUP

Anneliese Deising, Plymouth, Michigan

Every time I make a pot of this creamy soup, everyone comments on its appealing taste and eye-catching color. It's irresistible.

> 3 leeks (white part only), thinly
>   sliced
> 2 tablespoons butter *or* margarine
> 3 medium carrots, grated
> 6 cups chicken broth
> 3/4 cup cooked long grain rice
> 1/4 teaspoon ground mace
> Dash pepper
> 3/4 cup whipping cream
> Additional grated carrots, optional

In a 3-qt. saucepan, saute leeks in butter for 1 minute. Add carrots and cook 1 minute longer. Stir in broth, rice, mace and pepper; bring to a boil. Reduce heat; cover and cook for 15 minutes or until rice and carrots are tender. Cool slightly. Puree in batches in a blender; return to pan. Add cream; heat through but do not boil. Garnish with carrots if desired. **Yield:** 6 servings.

SPINACH BISQUE

Patricia Tuckwiller, Lewisburg, West Virginia

(Pictured below)

Not only is this soup healthy and filling, it's easy to prepare and elegant besides.

> 1/2 cup chopped onion
> 2 tablespoons butter *or* margarine
> 1/3 cup all-purpose flour
> 1/2 to 1 teaspoon salt
> 1/8 teaspoon ground nutmeg
> 2-1/2 cups milk
> 1 cup water
> 3/4 cup cubed process American cheese
> 1 package (10 ounces) frozen chopped
>   spinach, thawed and drained
> Oyster crackers, optional

In a 3-qt. saucepan, saute onion in butter until tender. Stir in the flour, salt and nutmeg until smooth. Gradually whisk in milk and water. Add cheese; cook and stir over medium heat until melted. Add spinach; cover and simmer for 4-5 minutes or until heated through. Serve with oyster crackers if desired. **Yield:** 5-6 servings.

CALICO SOUP MIX

Rhonda Letendre, Epsom, New Hampshire

Loaded with beans of all shapes and sizes, this colorful combination cooks up into a satisfying soup that'll stand by itself or serve as a side dish. Not only do I give the mix away as a gift, I keep it on hand to make for my family, too. They love it!

BEAN MIX:
1-1/2 cups *each* dry lentils, baby lima beans, yellow split peas, red kidney beans, great northern beans, pinto beans, green split peas and navy beans

ADDITIONAL INGREDIENTS (for each batch):
2-1/4 quarts water
2 cups cubed fully cooked ham
1 can (14-1/2 ounces) stewed tomatoes
1 medium onion, sliced
1 medium green pepper, chopped
1 garlic clove, minced
2 teaspoons salt
1 teaspoon *each* dried marjoram, oregano, parsley flakes and Italian seasoning

Combine beans; divide into six batches (2 cups each). Store in airtight containers. **Yield:** 6 batches (12 cups total). **To prepare soup:** Place one batch of bean mix in a Dutch oven or soup kettle; add water to cover by 2 in. Bring to a boil; boil for 2 minutes. Remove from the heat; cover and let stand for 1 hour. Drain. Add 2-1/4 qts. water; bring to a boil. Reduce heat; cover and simmer for 1-1/2 to 2 hours or until beans are tender. Add ham, tomatoes, onion, green pepper, garlic and seasonings; return to a boil. Reduce heat; simmer for 45-50 minutes. **Yield:** 16 servings (about 4 quarts) per batch.

SOUTHWESTERN TURKEY DUMPLING SOUP

Lisa Williams, Steamboat Springs, Colorado

(Pictured at far right)

Here's a Western twist on traditional turkey dumpling soup. I especially like this recipe because it's fast, easy and uses up leftover turkey or chicken.

1 can (15 ounces) tomato sauce
1 can (14-1/2 ounces) diced tomatoes, undrained
1-3/4 cups water
1 envelope chili seasoning
3 cups diced cooked turkey *or* chicken
1 can (16 ounces) kidney beans, rinsed and drained

1 can (15 ounces) black beans, rinsed and drained
1 can (15-1/4 ounces) whole kernel corn, drained
1-1/2 cups biscuit/baking mix
1/2 cup cornmeal
3/4 cup shredded cheddar cheese, *divided*
2/3 cup milk

In a Dutch oven, combine the first five ingredients; bring to a boil. Reduce heat; cover and simmer for 10 minutes, stirring occasionally. Add beans and corn. In a bowl, combine biscuit mix, cornmeal and 1/2 cup of cheese; stir in milk. Drop by heaping tablespoonfuls onto the simmering soup. Cover and cook for 12-15 minutes or until dumplings are firm. Sprinkle with remaining cheese; cover and simmer 1 minute longer or until the cheese is melted. Serve immediately. **Yield:** 6-8 servings (2-1/2 quarts).

CAJUN SHRIMP SOUP

Mrs. Ollie Jameson, Jefferson, Louisiana

(Pictured at right)

My mom used to cut the corn off the cob to make this soup, but I just use convenient, canned cream-style corn. This is a very good dish to come home to on a chilly day.

2 tablespoons vegetable oil
2 tablespoons all-purpose flour
3 celery ribs, thinly sliced
1 medium onion, chopped
1 small green pepper, chopped
2 green onions, thinly sliced
2 garlic cloves, minced
4 cans (14-3/4 ounces *each*) cream-style corn
1 can (10 ounces) diced tomatoes and green chilies, undrained
1 bay leaf
1/8 to 1/4 teaspoon white pepper
1/8 to 1/4 teaspoon cayenne pepper
Dash hot pepper sauce
3 cups cooked small shrimp
1/3 cup minced fresh parsley

Heat oil in a heavy saucepan over medium heat. Carefully add flour; cook and stir until golden brown, about 6-8 minutes. Reduce heat to low. Add celery, onion, green pepper, green onions and garlic; cook and stir for 5 minutes. Add corn, tomatoes, bay leaf, peppers and hot pepper sauce; bring to a boil. Reduce heat; cover and simmer for 30-40 minutes. Stir in shrimp and parsley; heat through. Remove bay leaf before serving. **Yield:** 8-10 servings (2-3/4 quarts).

LADLE UP brimming bowls of Southwestern Turkey Dumpling Soup, Cajun Shrimp Soup and Slow-Cooked Sauerkraut Soup (shown above, clockwise from top right) for your friends and family.

SLOW-COOKED SAUERKRAUT SOUP

Linda Lohr, Lititz, Pennsylvania

(Pictured above)

We live in Lancaster County, which has a rich heritage of German culture. Dishes like this that include sauerkraut, potatoes and sausage abound here. This soup is so convenient since it's made in a slow cooker.

1 medium potato, cut into 1/4-inch cubes
1 pound smoked kielbasa, cut into
   1/2-inch cubes
1 can (32 ounces) sauerkraut, rinsed and
   drained
4 cups chicken broth

1 can (10-3/4 ounces) condensed cream
   of mushroom soup, undiluted
1/2 pound fresh mushrooms, sliced
1 cup cubed cooked chicken
2 medium carrots, cut into 1/4-inch slices
2 celery ribs, sliced
2 tablespoons vinegar
2 teaspoons dill weed
1/2 teaspoon pepper
3 to 4 bacon strips, cooked and crumbled

In a 5-qt. slow cooker, combine the first 12 ingredients. Cover and cook on high for 5-6 hours or until the vegetables are tender. Skim fat. Garnish individual servings with bacon. **Yield:** 10-12 servings (about 3 quarts).

COUNTRY-STYLE *salads and side dishes—featuring fresh fruits and vegetables, pasta or rice—make perfect complements to your main dishes.*

FINISHING TOUCHES. Top to bottom: Wilted Endive Salad, Summertime Strawberry Gelatin Salad and Special Baked Potatoes (all recipes on p. 61).

Salads & Side Dishes

SPECIAL BAKED POTATOES

Tressa Surdick, Bethel Park, Pennsylvania

(Pictured at left)

For a nifty way to spice up plain old potatoes, try this recipe. Our guests always rave about them.

    4 medium baking potatoes
    2 tablespoons butter *or* margarine, melted
    2 teaspoons Italian seasoning
    1 teaspoon salt
    1/4 cup finely shredded cheddar cheese
    2 tablespoons grated Parmesan cheese
    2 tablespoons minced fresh parsley *or* 2
      teaspoons dried parsley flakes

With a sharp knife, slice potatoes thinly but not all the way through, leaving slices attached at the bottom. Fan potatoes slightly. Place in an ungreased 13-in. x 9-in. x 2-in. baking dish. Drizzle with butter. Sprinkle with Italian seasoning and salt. Bake, uncovered, at 425° for 50 minutes. Sprinkle with cheeses and parsley; bake 10-15 minutes longer or until lightly browned. **Yield:** 4 servings.

SUMMERTIME STRAWBERRY GELATIN SALAD

Janet England, Chillicothe, Missouri

(Pictured at left)

For years, this pretty salad has been a "must" at family dinners and special occasions.

    1 package (3 ounces) strawberry gelatin
    1 cup boiling water
    1 cup cold water
MIDDLE LAYER:
    1 envelope unflavored gelatin
    1/2 cup cold water
    1 cup half-and-half cream
    1 package (8 ounces) cream cheese,
      softened
    1 cup sugar
    1/2 teaspoon vanilla extract
TOP LAYER:
    1 package (6 ounces) strawberry gelatin

    1 cup boiling water
    1 cup cold water
    3 to 4 cups sliced fresh strawberries

In a bowl, dissolve strawberry gelatin in boiling water; stir in cold water. Pour into a 13-in. x 9-in. x 2-in. dish; chill until set. Meanwhile, place unflavored gelatin and cold water in a small bowl; let stand until softened. In a saucepan over medium heat, heat cream (do not boil). Add softened gelatin; stir until gelatin is dissolved. Cool to room temperature. In a mixing bowl, beat cream cheese, sugar and vanilla until smooth. Gradually add the unflavored gelatin mixture; mix well. Carefully pour over the bottom layer. Refrigerate until set, about 1 hour. For top layer, dissolve strawberry gelatin in boiling water; stir in cold water. Cool to room temperature. Stir in strawberries; carefully spoon over middle layer. Refrigerate overnight. **Yield:** 12-16 servings. **Editor's Note:** This salad takes time to prepare since each layer must be set before the next layer is added.

WILTED ENDIVE SALAD

Mildred Davis, Hagerstown, Maryland

(Pictured at left)

The blend of seasonings, greens and warm bacon dressing makes this salad a sure hit.

    2 bacon strips, diced
    1 tablespoon olive *or* vegetable oil
    2 garlic cloves, minced
    2 tablespoons finely chopped green onion
    2 tablespoons tarragon *or* cider vinegar
    2 tablespoons minced fresh tarragon *or* 2
      teaspoons dried tarragon
    1 teaspoon salt
    1/4 teaspoon pepper
    1 bunch curly endive *or* romaine, torn
    4 slices bread, cubed and toasted

In a skillet, cook bacon until crisp. Remove to paper towels to drain. Add oil to drippings; saute garlic and onion until tender. Stir in vinegar, tarragon, salt and pepper. In a large bowl, toss the endive, bread cubes and bacon. Pour warm dressing over salad and serve. **Yield:** 4-6 servings.

STRAWBERRY CHICKEN SALAD

Mirien Church, Aurora, Colorado

I like to serve this colorful salad with warm rolls for lunch or a light dinner. The combination of flavors is fantastic.

    4 cups cubed cooked chicken
    3/4 cup chopped celery
    1/3 cup mayonnaise
    2 tablespoons lemon juice
    1 tablespoon minced fresh mint
    3/4 teaspoon salt
    1/8 teaspoon pepper
    2 cups sliced fresh strawberries
    1/3 cup slivered almonds, toasted

In a bowl, combine chicken and celery. In a small bowl, combine mayonnaise, lemon juice, mint, salt and pepper; pour over chicken and toss. Refrigerate. Just before serving, fold in strawberries and almonds. **Yield:** 6 servings.

AVOCADO CITRUS SALAD

Dorothy Kostas, Escondido, California

(Pictured below)

We have a 2-1/2-acre avocado grove. It's located on a high slope just north of town. In the distance, we see foothills covered with avocado and citrus groves. Those two crops make a great combination in this salad. Friends always request it.

    1/2 cup vegetable oil
    3 tablespoons cider vinegar

    2 tablespoons sugar
    1/2 teaspoon salt
    2 medium ripe avocados, peeled and sliced
    8 to 10 cups torn salad greens
    2 medium oranges, peeled and sectioned
    1 large grapefruit, peeled and sectioned
    1 medium pear, cored and thinly sliced
    1 cup green grapes
    1/4 cup chopped walnuts

In a small bowl, combine oil, vinegar, sugar and salt. Add avocados. In a large salad bowl, toss remaining ingredients. Pour the dressing over salad and gently toss to coat. Serve immediately. **Yield:** 8-10 servings.

FESTIVE POTATO SALAD

Gloria Warczak, Cedarburg, Wisconsin

Every member of my family likes creamy-type potato salads. So I make mine often for many occasions.

    8 medium red potatoes, cooked and cubed
    2 celery ribs with leaves, thinly sliced
    2 green onions with tops, chopped
    4 hard-cooked eggs, chopped
    1/2 cup chopped peeled cucumber
    1/4 cup chopped sweet red pepper
    1/4 cup chopped green pepper
  1-1/4 cups mayonnaise
    1/4 cup sour cream
    1/4 cup plain yogurt
    1 tablespoon *each* minced fresh basil,
      marjoram and dill *or* 1 teaspoon *each*
      dried basil, marjoram and dill weed
    1 teaspoon sugar
    1/2 teaspoon salt
    1/2 teaspoon pepper
    4 plum tomatoes, coarsely chopped
    1 cup frozen peas, thawed
    1 cup (4 ounces) shredded cheddar cheese

In a large bowl, combine the first seven ingredients. In another bowl, combine the mayonnaise, sour cream, yogurt and seasonings. Pour over potato mixture; toss to coat. Gently stir in tomatoes, peas and cheese. Cover and refrigerate until serving. **Yield:** 14 servings.

HERBED VEGETABLE MEDLEY

Deborah Ereth, Salem, Oregon

This scrumptious side dish features an unusual way to serve a variety of well-flavored veggies—you bundle and bake the produce in parchment or foil packets. The squash, zucchini, carrots and leeks have such wonderful aroma and taste that even the pickiest eaters dig right in.

    2 cups julienned carrots
    1 cup julienned yellow summer squash
    1 cup julienned zucchini
    2 leeks (white part only), thinly sliced
    1 teaspoon lemon juice
    2 teaspoons minced fresh basil *or* 1/2
        teaspoon dried basil
    1 teaspoon minced fresh thyme *or* 1/4
        teaspoon dried thyme
    1/2 teaspoon salt
    1/8 to 1/4 teaspoon white pepper

In a bowl, toss the vegetables and lemon juice; set aside. Fold four 12-in. pieces of parchment paper or heavy-duty foil in half to form triangles; unfold. Coat with nonstick cooking spray. Place 1/2 cup vegetable mixture in the center of each square. Combine basil, thyme, salt and pepper; sprinkle over vegetables. Fold parchment over vegetables and seal edges tightly. Place packets on an ungreased baking sheet. Bake at 350° for 20-25 minutes or until tender. Carefully open packets and transfer vegetables to plates. **Yield:** 4 servings.

▟▟▟▟▟▟▟▟▟▟▟▟

SWISS POTATO KUGEL

Judy Wilson, Placentia, California

(Pictured at right)

I've enjoyed cooking and baking ever since I was small. I'd rather read a cookbook than a best-selling novel. I thoroughly enjoy planning a sumptuous dinner for my family. We have a daughter who loves potatoes of any kind. I believe she could eat this dish and pass over all the other goodies on the table.

    1 cup finely chopped onion
    2 tablespoons butter *or* margarine
    4 cups shredded *or* diced cooked peeled
        potatoes (about 4 medium)
    2 cups (8 ounces) shredded Swiss cheese
    1/4 cup all-purpose flour
    1 teaspoon salt
    1/4 teaspoon pepper
    3 eggs
    3/4 cup half-and-half cream
Tomato slices and fresh thyme, optional

In a large skillet, saute onion in butter until tender. Remove from the heat; add potatoes. Toss cheese with flour, salt and pepper; add to skillet and blend well. In a small bowl, combine the eggs and cream. Stir into the potato mixture. Spoon into a greased 9-in. square baking dish. Bake, uncovered, at 350° for 20-30 minutes or until golden brown. Cool for 5 minutes; cut into

squares. Garnish with tomato and thyme if desired. **Yield:** 9 servings. **Editor's Note:** This recipe can be prepared the day before, covered and refrigerated overnight. Remove from the refrigerator 30 minutes before baking. Bake for 30-40 minutes.

▟▟▟▟▟▟▟▟▟▟▟▟

HOLIDAY GREEN SALAD

Rita Farmer, Houston, Texas

The combination of crisp veggies, a seasoned dressing and dried cranberries can't be beat. It's a refreshing salad to make for a luncheon or an evening meal.

    6 cups torn iceberg lettuce
    6 cups torn romaine
    3 green onions, thinly sliced
    1 celery rib, thinly sliced
    1/4 cup vegetable oil
    1/4 cup vinegar
    1/4 cup sugar
    1 tablespoon minced fresh parsley
    1/2 to 1 teaspoon hot pepper sauce
    1/4 teaspoon salt
    3/4 to 1 cup dried cranberries
    1/4 cup sliced almonds, toasted

In a large bowl, combine greens, onions and celery. In a small bowl, combine the oil, vinegar, sugar, parsley, hot pepper sauce and salt; mix well. Pour over salad and toss to coat. Add cranberries and almonds. Serve immediately. **Yield:** 10-12 servings.

🔲🔲🔲🔲🔲🔲🔲🔲🔲🔲

CRANBERRY RELISH SALAD

Edna Means, Iola, Kansas

(Pictured above)

My three grown daughters and their families are very fond of this festive-looking salad. It's on our buffet table every Christmas.

- 1 package (3 ounces) strawberry gelatin
- 1 cup boiling water
- 1/2 cup orange juice concentrate
- 1 package (12 ounces) fresh *or* frozen cranberries, chopped
- 1 medium apple, peeled and chopped
- 1-1/2 cups sugar
- 1/2 cup chopped pecans

In a bowl, dissolve gelatin in boiling water. Stir in concentrate. Combine cranberries, apple and sugar; add to gelatin mixture. Stir in pecans. Pour into a 1-1/2-qt. serving dish. Refrigerate for 4 hours or overnight. **Yield:** 6-8 servings.

🔲🔲🔲🔲🔲🔲🔲🔲🔲🔲

ASPARAGUS STRAWBERRY SALAD

Elissa Armbruster, Medford Lakes, New Jersey

This simple salad's one of the best I've tasted—and it's so pretty, too! A friend served it at a baby shower…all of us were raving over it and asking for the recipe.

✓ Uses less fat, sugar or salt. Includes Nutritional Analysis and Diabetic Exchanges.

- 1/4 cup sugar
- 2 tablespoons cider vinegar
- 1 tablespoon poppy seeds
- 1-1/2 teaspoons sesame seeds
- 3/4 teaspoon grated onion
- 1/4 teaspoon salt, optional
- 1/8 teaspoon paprika
- 1/8 teaspoon Worcestershire sauce
- 1/4 cup vegetable oil
- 1 pound fresh asparagus, trimmed
- 1 pint fresh strawberries, sliced
- 1/4 cup crumbled blue cheese, optional

In a jar with tight-fitting lid, combine the sugar, vinegar, poppy seeds, sesame seeds, onion, salt if desired, paprika and Worcestershire sauce; shake until sugar is dissolved. Add the oil; shake well. Cover and refrigerate for 1 hour. In a skillet, cook the asparagus in a small amount of water until crisp-tender, about 6-8 minutes; drain well. Cover and refrigerate at least 1 hour. Arrange the asparagus and strawberries on a serving plate; sprinkle with blue cheese if desired. Pour the dressing over all. Serve with a slotted spoon. **Yield:** 8 servings. **Nutritional Analysis:** One serving (prepared without salt and blue cheese) equals 108 calories, 5 mg sodium, 0 cholesterol, 10 gm carbohydrate, 1 gm protein, 8 gm fat. **Diabetic Exchanges:** 1 vegetable, 1 fat, 1/2 fruit.

🔲🔲🔲🔲🔲🔲🔲🔲🔲🔲

LEMONADE SALAD

Karen Dougherty, Freeport, Illinois

This refreshing concoction will spark up any event! To make it extra festive, arrange cherries and oranges on top in the shapes of flowers. The salad can also be made with orange juice concentrate instead of lemonade, if you like.

- 2-1/4 cups butter-flavored cracker crumbs (about 64 crackers)
- 1/2 cup butter *or* margarine, melted
- 3 tablespoons sugar
- 2 cans (14 ounces *each*) sweetened condensed milk
- 1 can (12 ounces) frozen lemonade concentrate, thawed
- 1 carton (12 ounces) frozen whipped topping, thawed
- 1 can (11 ounces) mandarin oranges, drained
- 6 to 8 maraschino cherries

Combine cracker crumbs, butter and sugar. Press into an ungreased 13-in. x 9-in. x 2-in. dish; set aside. In a bowl, combine milk and lemonade concentrate until smooth (mixture will begin to thicken). Gently fold in whipped topping. Pour over crust. Cover and refrigerate for 3-4 hours. Garnish with oranges and cherries. **Yield:** 12-16 servings.

Time-Proven Pepper Tips

• To get stuffed peppers to stand upright, shave a thin slice from the bottom so they will sit level, taking care not to cut into the pepper's interior.
—*Edith Delaronde, Naples, Florida*

• For an attractive side dish, I fill green pepper halves (uncooked) with canned kernel corn that's been heated and seasoned with salt, pepper and butter. One large can will fill about four halves. It's not only pretty, but nutritious, too!   —*Thelma Pugh*
Monroe, Ohio

• To easily roast 10 to 12 peppers at a time, rub them with vegetable oil and place over the highest heat on an outdoor grill until skins blacken completely. Remove from grill and place in a brown bag to cool. Peel and seed cooled peppers.   —*Bronwyn Morgan*
Blytheville, Arkansas

• To roast peppers in the broiler, put pepper halves in a foil-lined baking pan. Broil them until they are blackened; cover with foil immediately and seal tight. Once they cool, remove skins. Transfer the peppers and their juice to an airtight container and refrigerate.   —*Diana Payne*
East Sandwich, Massachusetts

• It's best to be safe in preparing and eating peppers. Consider any pepper to be hot if you don't know what kind it is. You can always add more the next time you use it.   —*Martha Dawson*
Squaw Valley, California

• Since many of my casserole recipes call for finely chopped peppers, I freeze them that way! After chopping peppers, I place them in a metal mesh strainer, blanch for 1 minute in a pot of boiling water, drain, then put them into ice cube trays (each cube contains around 2 tablespoons).

Once they are frozen, I transfer the cubes to freezer bags. That allows me to quickly and easily pick the color and amount that's needed for a recipe.
—*Ann McKellips, Lynchburg, Virginia*

• While peppers are still in season, I wash, halve, seed and freeze them in freezer bags. Then all winter long, I'll use them for my stuffed peppers.
—*Barbara Cashen*
Lafayette, New Jersey

• To avoid odor in the freezer, cut peppers and lightly freeze them on a baking sheet, then place in glass jars. Frozen peppers usually are not as crisp as fresh ones. But if you run very cold water over them instead of completely thawing them in the refrigerator, they will be firm enough for a salad.
—*Alisa Bos*
Abbotsford, British Columbia

• Try making chili vinegar to lend zing to a salad dressing. Place freshly washed jalapeno peppers in a jar; cover with vinegar. Shake every day for 2 weeks, then strain and refrigerate. Use in place of vinegar in any salad dressing recipe.   —*Phyllis Clinehens*
Maplewood, Ohio

• We buy large amounts of roasted green chili peppers at a roadside stand. Then I freeze them whole, six to eight to a bag. When I need them, I simply defrost, peel, remove seeds and chop.
—*Phyllis Watters, El Paso, Texas*

Hearty Black-Eyed Pea Salad

Karen McElroy, Warrenton, Virginia

(Pictured below)

This recipe is great any time of the year. It's easy to make and tastes so good. I often take it along on family picnics.

   3 cans (15 ounces *each*) black-eyed peas,
      rinsed and drained
   1/2 pound fully cooked ham, diced
   3 medium tomatoes, seeded and diced
   1/2 cup chopped green onions
   1 medium carrot, chopped
DRESSING:
   5 tablespoons olive *or* vegetable oil
   3 tablespoons cider *or* red wine vinegar
   1 tablespoon Dijon mustard
   1 tablespoon lemon juice
   2 garlic cloves, minced
   1 tablespoon minced fresh basil *or* 1
      teaspoon dried basil
   1 teaspoon soy sauce
   1/2 teaspoon dried oregano
   1/2 teaspoon sugar
   1/4 teaspoon Worcestershire sauce
   1/4 teaspoon salt
   1/8 teaspoon pepper
   1/8 teaspoon hot pepper sauce

In a large bowl, toss peas, ham, tomatoes, onions and carrot; set aside. Combine dressing ingredients in a jar with a tight-fitting lid; shake well. Pour over the salad and toss to coat. Cover and refrigerate for at least 1 hour. **Yield:** 10-12 servings.

Strawberry Spinach Salad

Pat Brune, Ridgecrest, California

This is an especially good salad to take to summer potluck dinners.

   3 tablespoons lemon juice
   1/4 cup sugar
   6 tablespoons vegetable oil
   1 package (10 ounces) fresh spinach
   2 cups sliced fresh strawberries

Place the lemon juice and sugar in a blender. With blender running, add oil in a slow steady stream; process until slightly thickened. Just before serving, combine spinach and strawberries in a large salad bowl or individual bowls or plates; drizzle with dressing. **Yield:** 6-8 servings.

Asparagus Ham Salad

Lorrie Donald, Nepean, Ontario

Our entire family loves asparagus! This recipe is among our very favorites. The salad has such a fresh taste, while the Dijon mustard adds a bit of tartness to the dressing.

   1 pound fresh asparagus, trimmed
   1/2 cup olive *or* vegetable oil
   1/4 cup cider *or* white wine vinegar
   1 tablespoon Dijon mustard
   1/2 teaspoon salt
   1/4 teaspoon pepper
   1/2 teaspoon sugar, optional
   1 cup diced fully cooked ham
   2 green onions, thinly sliced

In a skillet, cook asparagus in a small amount of water until crisp-tender, about 6-8 minutes; drain well. Cover and refrigerate for at least 1 hour. Meanwhile, in a jar with tight-fitting lid, combine the oil, vinegar, mustard, salt, pepper and sugar if desired; shake well. Cover and refrigerate for at least 1 hour. Place asparagus in a serving bowl. Top with ham, onions and dressing. Serve with a slotted spoon. **Yield:** 6-8 servings.

Corn Bread Salad

Charlene McKenzie, DeLeon Springs, Florida

This salad is so tasty it brings everyone back asking for seconds. I serve it with roast chicken and vegetables to round out a satisfying meal.

   1 package (8-1/2 ounces) corn bread/
      muffin mix
   1 egg, beaten

1/3 cup milk
4 medium tomatoes, peeled and chopped
1 medium green pepper, chopped
1 medium onion, chopped
1/2 pound bacon, cooked and crumbled
1/2 cup chopped sweet pickles
1 cup mayonnaise
1/4 cup sweet pickle juice
Shredded Parmesan cheese

In a bowl, combine corn bread mix, egg and milk; mix well. Spoon into a greased 8-in. square baking pan. Bake at 400° for 15-20 minutes or until golden brown. Cool; cut into cubes and set aside. In a bowl, combine tomatoes, green pepper, onion, bacon and pickles; toss gently. Combine mayonnaise and pickle juice; mix well. Layer half of the corn bread, tomato mixture and mayonnaise mixture in a large glass bowl; repeat layers. Sprinkle with Parmesan cheese. Cover and chill for 2 hours. **Yield:** 8-10 servings.

CRANBERRY-APPLE BUTTERNUT SQUASH

Pat Waymire, Yellow Springs, Ohio

This casserole is a wonderful accompaniment for fall and winter dinners. The preserves and marmalade give the dish a fine fruitiness.

2 pounds butternut squash, peeled, seeded and cubed (about 6 cups)
4 cups water
1 can (21 ounces) apple pie filling
3/4 cup whole-berry cranberry sauce
2 tablespoons orange marmalade
2 tablespoons apricot preserves

In a large saucepan, combine squash and water; bring to a boil. Reduce heat; cover and simmer until squash is tender, about 25 minutes. Drain. Spread the pie filling in a greased 8-in. square baking dish. Top with squash. Combine cranberry sauce, marmalade and preserves; spoon over squash. Bake, uncovered, at 350° for 25 minutes or until heated through. **Yield:** 8 servings.

HOT GERMAN RICE SALAD

Lyn Rhein, Stuttgart, Arkansas

(Pictured above right)

This area has a long rice-growing history. In fact, our town has two of the largest farmer-owned rice mills in the country, so I like to use rice in lots of recipes.

8 bacon strips
1/3 cup sugar

1/3 cup cider vinegar
3/4 teaspoon celery seed
1/8 teaspoon pepper
1/4 cup chopped pimientos
1/4 cup chopped green pepper
1 tablespoon chopped onion
3-1/2 cups hot cooked rice
1 hard-cooked egg, sliced

In a skillet over medium heat, cook bacon until crisp. Drain, reserving 1/3 cup drippings. Crumble bacon and set aside. Add the sugar, vinegar, celery seed and pepper to drippings. Bring to a boil; cook and stir for 1 minute. Stir in pimientos, green pepper, onion, rice and bacon. Garnish with egg. Serve warm. **Yield:** 4-6 servings.

PEPPERED CORN

Kim Garner, Batesville, Arkansas

This peppy side dish is always the first to disappear whenever I take it to a potluck.

1 package (8 ounces) cream cheese, cubed
1/3 cup butter *or* margarine
2 cans (11 ounces *each*) Mexicorn, drained
2 to 4 medium jalapeno peppers, seeded and minced*

In a saucepan over low heat, cook and stir the cream cheese and butter until smooth. Stir in corn and jalapenos. Pour into an ungreased 8-in. square baking dish. Bake, uncovered, at 350° for 15-20 minutes or until bubbly. **Yield:** 6-8 servings. ***Editor's Note:** When cutting or seeding hot peppers, use rubber or plastic gloves to protect your hands. Avoid touching your face.

smooth; cook and stir until bubbly. Gradually add milk, salt and pepper; cook and stir over medium heat until thick, about 3 minutes. Stir in vegetables; pour into the crust. Sprinkle with cheese. Bake at 350° for 30-40 minutes or until crust edges begin to brown. Let stand for 10 minutes before serving. **Yield:** 6-8 servings. ***Editor's Note:** Light or fat-free mayonnaise may not be substituted for regular mayonnaise.

CARROT CASSEROLE

Vivian Herrington, Florien, Louisiana

This recipe originally called for sweet potatoes, but I've substituted carrots. I think it tastes wonderful and others do as well, because I've received many compliments on it.

> 2 pounds medium carrots, cooked and
>   mashed
> 1/2 cup milk
> 1/2 cup sugar
> 1/3 cup butter *or* margarine, melted
> 2 eggs, beaten
> 1 teaspoon vanilla extract

TOPPING:
> 2/3 cup packed brown sugar
> 1/3 cup all-purpose flour
> 2 tablespoons cold butter *or* margarine
> 2/3 cup chopped pecans
> 2/3 cup flaked coconut

Combine the first six ingredients; place in a greased 1-1/2-qt. baking dish. Combine brown sugar and flour; cut in butter until crumbly. Stir in nuts and coconut. Sprinkle over carrot mixture. Bake, uncovered, at 350° for 30 minutes or until heated through. **Yield:** 6-8 servings.

ARTICHOKE SPINACH CASSEROLE

Judy Johnson, Missoula, Montana

Although he isn't a fan of spinach, my husband loves this dish. The combination of ingredients may sound unusual, but the flavors meld well. It's an excellent side vegetable for a formal dinner.

> 1 pound fresh mushrooms, sliced
> 1/3 cup chicken broth
> 1 tablespoon all-purpose flour
> 1/2 cup evaporated milk
> 4 packages (10 ounces *each*) frozen
>   chopped spinach, thawed and well
>   drained
> 2 cans (14-1/2 ounces *each*) diced
>   tomatoes, drained

VEGETABLE RICE PIE

Debbie Christensen, Milton-Freewater, Oregon

(Pictured above)

I like all kinds of rice dishes, so I was pleased when I found this recipe. My husband, Stan, and I have a small country farm, where we grow three kinds of apples.

CRUST:
> 1-1/2 cups cooked long grain rice
> 1/2 cup grated Parmesan cheese
> 1/4 cup mayonnaise*
> 1/4 cup finely chopped onion

FILLING:
> 1 cup chopped fresh broccoli
> 1 cup chopped fresh cauliflower
> 1 cup chopped carrots
> 1/4 cup chopped onion
> 1/4 cup mayonnaise*
> 3 tablespoons all-purpose flour
> 1 cup milk
> 1/4 teaspoon salt

Pinch pepper
> 1/2 cup grated Parmesan cheese

Combine the crust ingredients; press onto the bottom and up the sides of a greased 9-in. pie plate; set aside. In a saucepan, cook broccoli, cauliflower, carrots and onion in a small amount of water until crisp-tender; drain well. In another saucepan, combine mayonnaise and flour until

2 cans (14 ounces *each*) water-packed
artichoke hearts, drained and thinly
sliced
1 cup (8 ounces) sour cream
1/2 cup mayonnaise
3 tablespoons lemon juice
1/2 teaspoon garlic powder
1/4 teaspoon salt
1/4 teaspoon pepper
Paprika, optional

In a large skillet, cook mushrooms and broth
over medium heat until tender, about 3 minutes.
Remove mushrooms with a slotted spoon and set
aside. Whisk flour and milk until smooth; add to
skillet. Bring to a boil; cook and stir for 2 minutes.
Remove from the heat; stir in spinach, tomatoes
and mushrooms. Place half of the artichokes in an
ungreased 13-in. x 9-in. x 2-in. baking dish. Top
with half of the spinach mixture. Repeat layers.
Combine sour cream, mayonnaise, lemon juice,
garlic powder, salt and pepper; dollop over casserole. Sprinkle with paprika if desired. Bake, uncovered, at 350° for 25-30 minutes or until bubbly. **Yield:** 12-14 servings.

SUMMER SALAD WITH CITRUS VINAIGRETTE

Carolyn Williams, Costa Mesa, California

(Pictured below right)

*I live in Orange County and, as you might guess by
our county's name, there are plenty of orange trees
here. This salad is one of my favorite ways to use this
fruit. It's a nice light salad for a hot day.*

☑ Uses less fat, sugar or salt. Includes Nutritional
Analysis and Diabetic Exchanges.

VINAIGRETTE:
3 tablespoons orange juice
3 tablespoons cider *or* red wine vinegar
2 teaspoons honey
1-1/2 teaspoons Dijon mustard
1 teaspoon olive *or* vegetable oil
SALAD:
1 pound boneless sirloin steak, cut into
thin strips
1 tablespoon vegetable oil
1/2 teaspoon salt, optional
4 cups torn romaine
2 large oranges, peeled and sectioned
1/2 cup sliced fresh strawberries
1/4 cup chopped walnuts, toasted, optional

In a small bowl, whisk the vinaigrette ingredients;
set aside. In a large skillet, stir-fry steak in oil for
1-2 minutes. Sprinkle with salt if desired. In a
large bowl, toss romaine, oranges, strawberries and

steak. Add vinaigrette and toss. Top with walnuts if desired. **Yield:** 4 servings. **Nutritional
Analysis:** One serving (prepared without salt and
walnuts) equals 291 calories, 110 mg sodium, 77
mg cholesterol, 19 gm carbohydrate, 28 gm protein, 12 gm fat. **Diabetic Exchange:** 3 lean meat.

FOUR-CHEESE MACARONI

Darlene Marturano, West Suffield, Connecticut

*I adapted this recipe from one a friend gave to me. It
has a distinctive blue cheese taste and is very filling. I
like to serve it with chicken.*

1 package (16 ounces) elbow macaroni
1/4 cup butter *or* margarine
1/4 cup all-purpose flour
1/2 teaspoon salt
1/8 teaspoon pepper
3 cups milk
2 cups (8 ounces) shredded cheddar
cheese
1-1/2 cups (6 ounces) shredded Swiss cheese
1/2 cup crumbled blue cheese
1/2 cup grated Parmesan cheese

Cook macaroni according to package directions.
Meanwhile, in a 5-qt. Dutch oven over medium
heat, melt butter. Stir in flour, salt and pepper until smooth. Bring to a boil; boil and stir for 2
minutes. Gradually add milk, stirring constantly.
Reduce heat to low; add cheeses and stir until
melted. Drain macaroni; add to cheese sauce and
stir until well coated. **Yield:** 12 servings.

CRAN-APPLE SAUCE

Anita Aungst, McVeytown, Pennsylvania

Not content with plain old applesauce, I found a fun way to jazz it up—by adding cranberries! This version is really zippy. It tastes great topped with fresh whipped cream.

- 1 package (12 ounces) fresh *or* frozen cranberries
- 1 to 1-1/2 cups sugar
- 1 teaspoon grated orange peel
- 3 cups unsweetened applesauce
- Whipped cream, optional

Place cranberries in a saucepan; add water just to cover. Bring to a boil. Reduce heat; simmer until the berries pop. Stir in the sugar until dissolved. Add orange peel. Refrigerate for 2 hours. Place in a blender or food processor; process until coarsely chopped. Pour into a bowl; stir in applesauce. Refrigerate until serving. Garnish with whipped cream if desired. **Yield:** 6-8 servings.

CHRISTMAS FRUIT SALAD

Ina Vickers, Dumas, Arkansas

(Pictured above)

I first tasted this salad at the first Thanksgiving I spent with my husband's family. My mother-in-law shared

the recipe. Now I serve it for special occasions, plus it's a mainstay at the potlucks we have at work.

- 3 egg yolks, beaten
- 3 tablespoons water
- 3 tablespoons vinegar
- 1/2 teaspoon salt
- 2 cups whipping cream, whipped
- 3 cups miniature marshmallows
- 2 cups halved green grapes
- 1 can (20 ounces) pineapple tidbits, drained
- 1 can (11 ounces) mandarin oranges, drained
- 1 jar (10 ounces) red maraschino cherries, drained and sliced
- 1 cup chopped pecans
- 3 tablespoons lemon juice

In a large saucepan, combine egg yolks, water, vinegar and salt. Cook over medium heat, stirring constantly, until mixture thickens and reaches 160°. Remove from the heat and cool; fold in whipped cream. In a large bowl, combine remaining ingredients. Add dressing; toss to coat. Cover and refrigerate for 24 hours. **Yield:** 12-14 servings.

SPRINGTIME SPINACH SALAD

Kathryn Anderson, Casper, Wyoming

This crisp classic is sure to be a favorite at your next affair. Since all you need to do is mix the tangy dressing ingredients, then toss with fresh produce, you'll want to keep the recipe handy for family meals, too.

- 3 unpeeled garlic cloves
- 4 bacon strips, diced
- 1/2 cup mayonnaise
- 1/2 cup sour cream
- 1/2 cup buttermilk
- 2 teaspoons ranch salad dressing mix
- 2 teaspoons lemon juice
- 1 teaspoon cider vinegar
- 1/2 teaspoon pepper
- 4 cups torn fresh spinach
- 1/4 cup shredded red cabbage
- 2 medium oranges, peeled and sliced
- 1/2 cup sliced fresh mushrooms
- Sliced onion

Pierce garlic cloves with a knife; place in a small baking dish. Bake, uncovered, at 350° for 20 minutes. Cool. Mash with a fork to remove pulp; discard skins and set pulp aside. In a skillet, cook bacon until crisp. Remove bacon to paper towel to drain; reserve 2 teaspoons drippings. In a bowl, whisk mayonnaise, sour cream and buttermilk. Add salad dressing mix, lemon juice, vinegar, pepper, garlic pulp and reserved bacon drip-

Toss Some Heat...on Summer Salads

SALAD DAYS for Vicky Paulson of Zimmerman, Minnesota get fired up with Hot Pepper Dressing.

"This recipe was given to me by a friend who was a chef," pens Vicky, a wife, mother and grandmother. "I've always grown peppers in my garden. So I was looking for ways to use them.

"The dressing is very easy to prepare—and everyone who tries it loves it! It's wonderful tossed over mixed greens...but you can also serve it on steamed vegetables or use it as a meat marinade."

Vicky shares her zippy dressing so you can try topping off your next summer salad with it. See if it doesn't rate as "hot stuff" at your table, too!

HOT PEPPER DRESSING

2 small fresh cherry peppers, seeded and minced*
2 tablespoons olive or vegetable oil
2 tablespoons lemon juice
1 garlic clove, minced
1/2 teaspoon salt
1/8 to 1/4 teaspoon pepper

In a jar with tight-fitting lid, combine peppers, oil, lemon juice, garlic, salt and pepper; shake until blended. Store in the refrigerator. **Yield:** about 1/4 cup. ***Editor's Note:** When cutting or seeding hot peppers, use rubber or plastic gloves to protect your hands. Avoid touching your face.

---

pings; mix well. Cover and refrigerate for at least 30 minutes. Toss spinach and cabbage in a large salad bowl. Add oranges, mushrooms and onion. Sprinkle with bacon. Drizzle with dressing or serve on the side. **Yield:** 6 servings.

PICKLED PEPPERS

Heather Prendergast, Sundre, Alberta
Well received at potlucks, this colorful, tasty dish adds zest to the menu. I also make it as a salad or accompaniment for a luncheon or dinner at home.

2 *each* medium green, sweet red and yellow peppers, cut into 1-inch pieces
1 large red onion, halved and thinly sliced
1 cup cider vinegar
1 cup sugar
1/3 cup water
2 teaspoons mixed pickling spices
1/2 teaspoon celery seed

In a large glass bowl, combine peppers and onion; set aside. In a saucepan, combine the vinegar, sugar and water. Place the pickling spices and celery seed in a double thickness of cheesecloth; bring up the corners of cloth and tie with string to form a bag. Add to saucepan. Bring to a boil; boil for 1 minute. Transfer spice bag to pepper mixture. Pour the vinegar mixture over all. Cover and refrigerate for 24 hours, stirring occasionally. Discard spice bag. Peppers may be stored in the refrigerator for up to 1 month. **Yield:** 4 cups.

MAKE-AHEAD VEGETABLE SALAD

Rozelle Garrigus, Carrollton, Texas
This is a wonderful salad to make for parties because you prepare it ahead of time. I also like the dressing served over fruit.

5 cups broccoli florets
4 cups thinly sliced cauliflower
1 medium green pepper, chopped
1 medium red onion, thinly sliced
DRESSING:
1 cup mayonnaise *or* salad dressing
1/2 cup vegetable oil
1/3 cup sugar
1/3 cup cider *or* red wine vinegar
1 teaspoon ground mustard
1/2 teaspoon salt
1/2 teaspoon pepper

In a serving bowl, combine broccoli, cauliflower and green pepper; place the onion rings on top. In a small bowl, whisk dressing ingredients; pour over salad (do not stir). Cover and refrigerate for 12 hours or overnight. Toss just before serving. **Yield:** 12-14 servings.

BISCUITS AND SAUSAGE GRAVY

Sue Baker, Jonesboro, Arkansas

(Pictured above)

This is an old Southern recipe I've adapted. Maybe you'd like to try it and take a "trip" to the South.

- 1/4 pound bulk pork sausage
- 2 to 3 tablespoons all-purpose flour
- 2 tablespoons butter *or* margarine
- 1/4 teaspoon salt
- 1/8 teaspoon pepper
- 1-1/4 to 1-1/3 cups milk
- Warm biscuits

In a skillet over medium heat, cook the sausage until no longer pink; drain if necessary. Stir in flour, butter, salt and pepper; cook and stir until butter is melted. Gradually add the milk, stirring constantly. Bring to a boil; boil and stir for 2 minutes. Serve over biscuits. **Yield:** 2 servings.

GREEN SALAD WITH ONION DRESSING

Cara Bonnema, Painesville, Ohio

This is such an elegant salad. It will dress up any table. The caramelized onion in the dressing tastes fantastic.

- 1 large onion, peeled and cut into eighths
- 8 tablespoons olive *or* vegetable oil, *divided*

- 1-1/2 teaspoons sugar
- 1/4 cup chicken broth
- 2 tablespoons cider *or* white wine vinegar
- 1/4 teaspoon salt
- 14 cups torn salad greens
- 1 cup chopped walnuts, toasted
- 1/2 cup thinly sliced red onion

Place onion in a baking dish. Drizzle with 1 tablespoon oil; sprinkle with sugar. Bake, uncovered, at 400° for 30 minutes. Turn and bake 25-30 minutes longer, stirring several times, until the onion is tender and lightly browned. Cool for 30 minutes. Place onion in a blender or food processor; add broth, vinegar, salt and remaining oil. Cover and process until smooth (mixture will be thick). Chill. Just before serving, toss greens, walnuts, red onion and dressing in a large salad bowl. **Yield:** 12 servings.

PASTA SALAD WITH STEAK

Julie DeRuwe, Oakville, Washington

While there are quite a few ingredients in this recipe, it doesn't take too long to make—and cleanup afterward's a snap.

- 3/4 cup olive oil
- 2 tablespoons lemon juice
- 1 tablespoon Dijon mustard
- 2 teaspoons dried oregano
- 2 teaspoons cider *or* red wine vinegar
- 1 teaspoon sugar
- 1/2 teaspoon salt

1/2 teaspoon pepper
3 cups cooked small shell pasta
1 sirloin steak (1 pound)
RUB:
1 tablespoon olive oil
3 garlic cloves, minced
2 teaspoons dried oregano
2 teaspoons pepper
1 teaspoon sugar
SALAD:
2/3 cup diced cucumber
1/2 cup crumbled blue *or* feta cheese
1/4 cup sliced ripe olives
1/4 cup chopped red onion
1/4 cup minced fresh parsley
1 jar (2 ounces) diced pimientos, drained
Iceberg *or* romaine lettuce

Combine the first eight ingredients; set half of the dressing aside. Place pasta in a bowl; add remaining dressing. Toss to coat; cover and refrigerate. Pierce steak with a fork. Combine the rub ingredients; rub over steak. Cover and refrigerate for at least 15 minutes. Grill steak, uncovered, over medium heat for 9-10 minutes on each side or until meat reaches desired doneness (for rare, a meat thermometer should read 140°; medium, 160°; well-done, 170°). Let stand for 10 minutes. Meanwhile, add the cucumber, cheese, olives, onion, parsley and pimientos to pasta; mix well. Spoon onto a lettuce-lined platter. Slice steak and arrange over salad. Serve with the reserved dressing. **Yield:** 4 servings.

GARLIC CHEESE GRITS

Bobbie Jo Yokley, Franklin, Kentucky

My dad prepared this family favorite every Christmas morning. Grits are a true Southern specialty. The garlic and cheese add a tasty touch.

1 cup quick-cooking grits
1 cup (4 ounces) shredded process American cheese
1/2 cup butter *or* margarine
1 teaspoon garlic salt
1 egg
1/4 to 1/3 cup milk
Additional cheese, optional

Cook grits according to package directions. Add cheese, butter and garlic salt; stir until cheese and butter are melted. In a measuring cup, beat egg; add milk to measure 1/2 cup. Stir into grits. Pour into a greased 1-1/2-qt. baking dish. Bake, uncovered, at 350° for 20-25 minutes or until bubbly around the edges. Sprinkle with additional cheese if desired. **Yield:** 4-6 servings.

SUNSHINE STATE SALAD

Doris Wendling, Palm Harbor, Florida

(Pictured below)

My husband and I retired from Illinois to Florida over 13 years ago. Several times, a friend gave us grapefruit from his backyard tree. One day I was going to make a lemon pineapple gelatin salad and discovered I didn't have pineapple. So, I cut up a fresh grapefruit and used it in the salad. It was good, and I tried adding other fruits until I came up with this recipe.

☑ Uses less fat, sugar or salt. Includes Nutritional Analysis and Diabetic Exchanges.

1 package (3 ounces) lemon gelatin
1 cup boiling water
1 can (8 ounces) pineapple chunks, undrained
1 large grapefruit, peeled, sectioned and diced
1 medium apple, peeled and chopped
1/4 cup chopped pecans

In a bowl, dissolve gelatin in boiling water. Drain pineapple, reserving juice; set pineapple aside. Add cold water to juice to measure 1 cup; stir into gelatin mixture. Chill until partially set. Stir in grapefruit, apple, pecans and pineapple; pour into a 1-1/2-qt. bowl. Chill until firm. **Yield:** 8 servings. **Nutritional Analysis:** One 1/2-cup serving (prepared with sugar-free gelatin and unsweetened pineapple) equals 65 calories, 24 mg sodium, 0 cholesterol, 10 gm carbohydrate, 1 gm protein, 3 gm fat. **Diabetic Exchanges:** 1/2 fruit, 1/2 fat.

ASPARAGUS PASTA SALAD

Teresa Kokx, Hart, Michigan

For 6 weeks each June and early July, my husband, Eugene, and I eat, sleep and breathe asparagus. Farming with his parents, we harvest 350 acres of the tasty spears. Carrots and radishes add crunch to this tasty pasta salad in which asparagus stars.

- 3 cups cut fresh asparagus (1-inch pieces)
- 3 cups medium pasta shells, cooked and drained
- 1 small red onion, chopped
- 1 small cucumber, sliced
- 1 cup sliced carrots
- 1/2 cup sliced radishes
- 1/2 cup Italian salad dressing
- 1/2 cup shredded Parmesan cheese

Cook asparagus in a small amount of water until crisp-tender, about 4 minutes. Rinse in cold water; drain and cool. Place asparagus in a large bowl; add pasta, onion, cucumber, carrots and radishes. Combine salad dressing and Parmesan cheese; pour over pasta mixture and toss to coat. Cover and refrigerate for at least 2 hours. **Yield:** 8-10 servings.

SPRING SPINACH SALAD

Cyndi Trenery, Middletown, California

(Pictured below)

My mom gave me this recipe. I make it often when strawberries are in season. The combination of greens and fruit surprises people. The clincher is the dressing—a hit every time I prepare it.

- 1/2 cup vegetable oil
- 2 to 3 tablespoons cider *or* white wine vinegar
- 2 to 3 tablespoons sugar
- 1 tablespoon lemon juice
- 1 tablespoon poppy seeds
- 1/2 teaspoon salt
- 1/2 teaspoon ground mustard
- 10 cups torn spinach
- 2 cups sliced fresh strawberries
- 1 cup chopped pecans, toasted
- 1/2 cup chopped Vidalia *or* sweet onion

In a jar with a tight-fitting lid, combine the first seven ingredients; shake well. Just before serving, combine spinach, strawberries, pecans and onion in a large salad bowl. Add dressing and toss to coat. **Yield:** 8-10 servings.

FRUITED CRANBERRY SALAD

Edna Havens, Wann, Oklahoma

Whenever we have a special-occasion family gathering, I'm always asked to bring along this cool and fruity salad. Everyone loves the combination of tart cranberries and sweet oranges, grapes and pineapple.

✓ Uses less fat, sugar or salt. Includes Nutritional Analysis and Diabetic Exchanges.

- 2 cups fresh *or* frozen cranberries
- 1 medium unpeeled orange, cut into wedges and seeds removed
- **Artificial sweetener equivalent to 3/4 cup sugar**
- 1 package (.3 ounce) sugar-free cherry gelatin
- 1 cup boiling water
- 1 cup red seedless grapes, halved
- 1 cup unsweetened crushed pineapple, drained
- 1/2 cup diced celery
- 1/4 cup finely chopped pecans

In a blender or food processor, combine the first three ingredients. Cover and process until the fruit is coarsely chopped; let stand for 30 minutes. Meanwhile, in a large bowl, dissolve gelatin in water. Refrigerate for 15-20 minutes or until mixture begins to thicken. Add cranberry mixture, grapes, pineapple, celery and pecans. Pour into a 2-qt. serving bowl or individual dishes. Refrigerate for several hours or overnight. **Yield:** 12 servings. **Nutritional Analysis:** One 1/2-cup serving equals 49 calories, 5 mg sodium, 0 cholesterol, 9 gm carbohydrate, 1 gm protein, 2 gm fat. **Diabetic Exchanges:** 1/2 fruit, 1/2 fat.

Corn Relish in Pepper Cups

Lola Lance, Zirconia, North Carolina

This colorful easy-to-fix side dish featuring flavorful veggies is a favorite at my house. I've made it on many special occasions for more than 30 years now. What I like best about the recipe is that I can prepare it ahead of time and keep it in the fridge until company comes.

- 1/2 cup vinegar
- 1/4 cup sugar
- 1/2 teaspoon salt
- 1/4 teaspoon pepper
- 1/4 teaspoon celery seed
- 2 cans (15-1/4 ounces *each*) whole kernel corn, drained
- 3 tablespoons vegetable oil
- 2 tablespoons chopped sweet red pepper
- 4 bacon strips, cooked and crumbled
- 4 medium sweet red peppers, halved lengthwise and seeded

In a small saucepan, combine the first five ingredients; bring to a boil. Reduce heat; cover and simmer for 2 minutes. Cool. Transfer to a bowl. Add corn, oil and chopped red pepper; toss to coat. Cover and refrigerate for 2 hours. Drain; stir in bacon. Spoon into pepper halves. **Yield:** 8 servings.

Herbed Rice-Vermicelli Mix

Brenda Hagemann, Paola, Kansas

This savory rice pilaf is an ideal companion to broiled chicken, beef or fish. It stores very well.

- 6 cups uncooked long grain rice
- 3 cups broken thin spaghetti (2-inch pieces)
- 7 tablespoons chicken *or* beef bouillon granules
- 1/4 cup dried parsley flakes
- 2 tablespoons lemon-pepper seasoning
- 1 tablespoon garlic powder

ADDITIONAL INGREDIENTS (for each batch):
- 2-3/4 cups water
- 1 tablespoon butter *or* margarine, optional

Combine the first six ingredients; divide into six batches (about 1-2/3 cups each). Store in airtight containers in a cool dry place. **Yield:** 6 batches (about 9-3/4 cups total). **To prepare rice:** Place water and butter if desired in a medium saucepan; bring to a boil. Stir in one batch of rice mix; return to a boil. Reduce heat; cover and simmer for 15-20 minutes or until rice is tender. **Yield:** 4-6 servings per batch.

Ranch Beans

Wilma Ruth James, Ranger, Texas

(Pictured above)

This recipe is served at all of our barbecues. It seems most people who live here like spicy flavorful food, and this fits the bill just right.

- 1 package (16 ounces) dry pinto beans
- 1 quart water
- 1 can (6 ounces) tomato paste
- 1/2 cup chopped onion
- 1 garlic clove, minced
- 1 to 2 tablespoons chili powder
- 2 to 3 teaspoons crushed red pepper flakes
- 1 teaspoon salt
- 1 teaspoon ground cumin
- 1/2 teaspoon dried marjoram

Place beans in a Dutch oven or soup kettle; add water to cover by 2 in. Bring to a boil; boil for 2 minutes. Remove from the heat; cover and let stand for 1 hour. Drain, discarding liquid. Return beans to pan; add 1 qt. water. Bring to a boil. Reduce heat; cover and simmer for 1-1/4 to 1-1/2 hours or until beans are tender. Add remaining ingredients; bring to a boil. Reduce heat; cover and simmer 1-1/2 hours longer. **Yield:** 6-8 servings.

1/2 cup diced sweet red pepper
2 teaspoons low-sodium chicken bouillon granules
1/2 cup skim milk
2 cans (4 ounces *each*) chopped green chilies
1 teaspoon chili powder
1/2 teaspoon ground cumin
1/8 teaspoon cayenne pepper
1 cup (4 ounces) shredded reduced-fat Monterey Jack cheese, *divided*

In a skillet coated with nonstick cooking spray, saute zucchini, corn, onion and red pepper. Cover and simmer for 8 minutes. Combine bouillon and milk; add to vegetables with chilies, chili powder, cumin and cayenne. Cover and simmer for 5 minutes. Stir in half of the cheese. Pour into a 1-1/2-qt. baking dish that has been coated with nonstick cooking spray. Top with remaining cheese. Cover and bake at 350° for 20 minutes. Uncover; bake 10 minutes longer or until cheese is bubbly. **Yield:** 4 servings. **Nutritional Analysis:** One 1/2-cup serving equals 168 calories, 461 mg sodium, 21 mg cholesterol, 16 gm carbohydrate, 14 gm protein, 6 gm fat. **Diabetic Exchanges:** 1 starch, 1 meat, 1 vegetable.

▪▪▪▪▪▪▪▪▪▪▪▪

COUNTRY PINEAPPLE CASSEROLE

Margaret Lindemann, Kenvil, New Jersey

(Pictured above)

My family enjoyed this dish at a church ham supper, so I asked for the recipe. I've made it for many covered-dish meals since and have received many compliments. It really is delicious.

1/2 cup butter *or* margarine, softened
2 cups sugar
8 eggs
2 cans (20 ounces *each*) crushed pineapple, drained
3 tablespoons lemon juice
10 slices day-old white bread, cubed

In a mixing bowl, cream butter and sugar. Add the eggs, one at a time, beating well after each addition. Stir in pineapple and lemon juice. Fold in the bread cubes. Pour into a greased 13-in. x 9-in. x 2-in. baking dish. Bake, uncovered, at 325° for 35-40 minutes or until set. **Yield:** 12-16 servings.

▪▪▪▪▪▪▪▪▪▪▪▪

ZUCCHINI CORN CASSEROLE

Nanci Keatley, Salem, Oregon

I depend on fast and healthy meals that my whole family can enjoy—this is one of their favorites!

☑ Uses less fat, sugar or salt. Includes Nutritional Analysis and Diabetic Exchanges.

1-1/2 cups coarsely chopped zucchini
1-1/2 cups fresh *or* frozen corn
1 medium onion, finely chopped

▪▪▪▪▪▪▪▪▪▪▪▪

SCALLOPED CELERY

Peg Cooper, Union, Michigan

A lot of celery is grown in this area, and this recipe is one of my favorites that features our "star crop". It's a very colorful dish and is perfect for get-togethers.

4 cups thinly sliced celery
6 tablespoons butter *or* margarine, *divided*
3 tablespoons all-purpose flour
1/2 teaspoon salt
1 cup milk
1 can (4 ounces) mushroom stems and pieces, drained
2 tablespoons finely chopped green pepper
2 tablespoons diced pimientos
1 cup (4 ounces) shredded sharp cheddar cheese
1 cup soft bread crumbs

In a large skillet, saute celery in 4 tablespoons butter until tender, about 5 minutes. Remove celery with a slotted spoon and set aside. Stir flour and salt into skillet until smooth. Gradually add milk; bring to a boil. Cook and stir for 2 minutes. Add mushrooms, green pepper, pimientos and cheese. Stir until cheese is melted. Return celery to pan; stir to coat. Pour into a greased 1-qt. baking dish. Melt remaining butter; toss with bread crumbs. Sprinkle over the celery mixture. Bake, uncovered, at 350° for 20-25 minutes or until bubbly. **Yield:** 4-6 servings.

✦✦✦✦✦✦✦✦✦✦✦✦✦

GRILLED THREE-PEPPER SALAD

Ruth Wickard, York, Pennsylvania

(Pictured on the front cover)

I've been cooking since my mom taught me at an early age. I'm always trying new recipes. This one's both flavorful and colorful.

> 2 *each* large green, sweet red and yellow peppers, cut into 1-inch pieces
> 1 large red onion, halved and thinly sliced
> 1 pound bulk mozzarella cheese, cut into bite-size cubes
> 1 can (6 ounces) pitted ripe olives, drained and halved

VINAIGRETTE:
> 2/3 cup olive *or* vegetable oil
> 1/3 cup cider *or* red wine vinegar
> 2 tablespoons lemon juice
> 2 tablespoons Dijon mustard
> 1 tablespoon minced fresh basil *or* 1 teaspoon dried basil
> 1/2 teaspoon cayenne pepper
> 1/2 teaspoon garlic powder

Thread peppers onto metal or soaked wooden skewers; grill or broil for 10-12 minutes or until edges are browned. Remove from skewers and place in a large bowl. Add onion, mozzarella and olives; toss gently. Cover and refrigerate. Combine vinaigrette ingredients in a jar with tight-fitting lid; shake well. Pour over the pepper mixture just before serving; toss to coat. **Yield:** 10-12 servings.

✦✦✦✦✦✦✦✦✦✦✦✦✦

SWEET POTATO SALAD

Lorene Cox, Bozeman, Montana

(Pictured below)

When I served this salad to relatives visiting from the Midwest, I was surprised to find it was something they'd never tried before. It's popular in our area.

> 2 pounds sweet potatoes
> 1-1/2 cups mayonnaise
> 2 teaspoons Dijon mustard
> 1/4 teaspoon salt
> 4 hard-cooked eggs, chopped
> 1-1/2 cups finely chopped celery
> 8 green onions, sliced

Place sweet potatoes in a large saucepan and cover with water. Cover and boil gently until the potatoes can easily be pierced with the tip of a sharp knife, about 30-45 minutes. Drain. When potatoes are cool, peel and dice. In a large bowl, combine mayonnaise, mustard and salt. Stir in eggs, celery and onions. Add potatoes; stir gently to mix. Cover and refrigerate for 2-4 hours. **Yield:** 8-10 servings.

SPANISH STRING BEANS

Vera Heyl, Wilmington, Delaware

I found this recipe years ago and have made it often. It's so simple to prepare.

- 1-1/2 pounds green beans, cut into 2-inch pieces
- 1 medium onion, chopped
- 1 medium green pepper, chopped
- 2 tablespoons butter *or* margarine
- 1 can (14-1/2 ounces) stewed tomatoes
- 2 teaspoons sugar
- 1/2 teaspoon salt
- 1 bay leaf
- 2 whole cloves

Place beans in a saucepan and cover with water; cook for 8-10 minutes or until crisp-tender. Meanwhile, in a skillet, saute onion and green pepper in butter until tender. Stir in tomatoes, sugar, salt, bay leaf and cloves; simmer for 10 minutes. Drain beans; add to tomato mixture. Cover and cook for 5 minutes or until heated through. Discard bay leaf and cloves. **Yield:** 8-10 servings.

ASPARAGUS VINAIGRETTE SALAD

Mary Bengtson-Almquist, Petersburg, Illinois

(Pictured below)

My mom has a large asparagus bed, so I'm kept well-supplied with asparagus for this salad.

- 1-1/4 pounds fresh asparagus, cut into 2-inch pieces
- 1 jar (4 ounces) diced pimientos, drained

- 1/3 cup sliced green onions
- 1/2 cup olive *or* vegetable oil
- 1/4 cup cider *or* white wine vinegar
- 1 teaspoon Dijon mustard
- 1 teaspoon Worcershire sauce
- 1/2 teaspoon dried basil
- 1/2 teaspoon salt
- 1/4 teaspoon pepper
- 1/4 teaspoon dried thyme

In a saucepan, cook the asparagus in a small amount of water for 5 minutes or until crisp-tender. Rinse with cold water; drain well. Place in a bowl; add pimientos and onions. In a small bowl, whisk oil, vinegar, mustard, Worcestershire sauce, basil, salt, pepper and thyme; pour over asparagus mixture and toss to coat. Cover and refrigerate for at least 2 hours. Serve with a slotted spoon. **Yield:** 4-6 servings.

SPANISH SLAW

Mary Ann Valdez, San Antonio, Texas

Colorful and tangy, this coleslaw adds some zip to an ordinary meal. Try it and see if it doesn't perk up your next meal.

- 3 cups shredded cabbage
- 1/4 cup chopped green pepper
- 1/3 cup vinegar
- 3 tablespoons vegetable oil
- 4 teaspoons sugar
- 1 tablespoon diced pimientos
- 1 teaspoon grated onion
- 1 teaspoon celery salt
- 1/2 teaspoon ground mustard
- 1/4 teaspoon salt
- 1/4 teaspoon pepper

In a bowl, combine cabbage and green pepper. In a jar with tight-fitting lid, combine remaining ingredients; shake well. Pour over cabbage mixture just before serving; toss to coat. Serve with a slotted spoon. **Yield:** 6 servings.

STRAWBERRY TOSSED SALAD

Patricia McNamara, Kansas City, Missouri

One reason I particularly like this recipe is that it's so versatile. I've served the salad with poultry, ham and pork all throughout the year and even used it to add color to the table at Christmas.

- 1/2 cup vegetable oil
- 1/3 cup sugar
- 1/4 cup cider *or* red wine vinegar

1 garlic clove, minced
1/4 teaspoon salt
1/4 teaspoon paprika
Pinch white pepper
8 cups torn romaine
4 cups torn Bibb *or* Boston lettuce
2-1/2 cups sliced fresh strawberries
1 cup (4 ounces) shredded Monterey Jack cheese
1/2 cup chopped walnuts, toasted

Combine the first seven ingredients in a jar with tight-fitting lid; shake well. Just before serving, toss the salad greens, strawberries, cheese and walnuts in a large salad bowl. Drizzle with dressing and toss. **Yield:** 6-8 servings.

***

CREAMY GARLIC FRENCH DRESSING

Diana Parkinson, Darlington, Wisconsin

This French dressing whips up in no time and tastes better than any bottled dressing. Why don't you see if your family likes it as much as mine does?

1 cup plain yogurt
1/4 cup ketchup
4 teaspoons honey
2 teaspoons Dijon mustard
2 garlic cloves, minced
1/2 teaspoon pepper
Mixed salad greens

In a blender or food processor, combine the first six ingredients. Cover and process until smooth. Pour into a jar or bowl; chill for 20 minutes before serving. Serve over salad greens. Store in the refrigerator. **Yield:** 1-1/3 cups.

***

RUBY GELATIN SALAD

Joann Murray, Columbus, Ohio

(Pictured above right)

I remember when I was a child that my older siblings and I didn't care for cranberry sauce. So every Thanksgiving, Mom would fix this gelatin salad just for us, and we would devour it.

☑ Uses less fat, sugar or salt. Includes Nutritional Analysis and Diabetic Exchanges.

1 package (3 ounces) cherry gelatin
1 cup boiling water
1 cup orange juice
1 cup diced peeled apple
1 cup chopped celery
1/2 cup chopped walnuts

In a bowl, dissolve gelatin in water. Add orange juice; refrigerate until partially set. Stir in apple, celery and walnuts. Refrigerate until firm. **Yield:** 8 servings. **Nutritional Analysis:** One 1/2-cup serving (prepared with sugar-free gelatin) equals 72 calories, 13 mg sodium, 0 cholesterol, 7 gm carbohydrate, 2 gm protein, 5 gm fat. **Diabetic Exchanges:** 1 fat, 1/2 fruit.

***

PEPPER RICOTTA PRIMAVERA

Janet Boulger, Botwood, Newfoundland

Not only is this nicely seasoned pasta and vegetable blend good, it's good for you.

☑ Uses less fat, sugar or salt. Includes Nutritional Analysis and Diabetic Exchanges.

1 cup light ricotta cheese
1/2 cup skim milk
1 garlic clove, minced
1/2 teaspoon crushed red pepper flakes
4 teaspoons olive *or* vegetable oil
1 *each* medium green, sweet red and yellow pepper, julienned
1 medium zucchini, sliced
1 cup frozen peas
1/4 teaspoon dried oregano
1/4 teaspoon dried basil
6 ounces fettuccine, cooked and drained

In a small bowl, whisk ricotta cheese and milk; set aside. In a large skillet, saute garlic and pepper flakes in oil for 1 minute. Add peppers, zucchini, peas, oregano and basil. Cook and stir over medium heat until vegetables are crisp-tender, about 5 minutes. Place fettuccine in a large bowl; add vegetables and cheese mixture. Toss to coat; serve immediately. **Yield:** 6 servings. **Nutritional Analysis:** One 1-cup serving equals 209 calories, 142 mg sodium, 13 mg cholesterol, 27 gm carbohydrate, 10 gm protein, 7 gm fat. **Diabetic Exchanges:** 2 starch, 1 fat, 1/2 meat.

THE BREAD BASKET *won't be brimming for long when it contains some of this chapter's scrumptious quick breads, rolls, coffee cakes, yeast breads and muffins.*

BAKED GOODIES. Clockwise from top left: Swedish Doughnuts (p. 81), Cherry Danish (p. 83), Pineapple Cheese Braid (p. 81) and Almond Streusel Rolls (p. 82).

Breads & Rolls

PINEAPPLE CHEESE BRAID

Shirley Kensinger
Roaring Spring, Pennsylvania

(Pictured at left)

Folks are always pleasantly surprised by this bread's pineapple filling. When in a hurry, I'll use canned pie filling.

>   2 packages (1/4 ounce *each*) active dry
>   yeast
>   1 cup warm water (110° to 115°)
>   1/2 cup butter *or* margarine, softened
>   5 tablespoons sugar
>   2 eggs
>   1/4 teaspoon salt
> 4-1/4 to 4-1/2 cups all-purpose flour
> PINEAPPLE FILLING:
>   1 can (8 ounces) crushed pineapple,
>   undrained
>   1/2 cup sugar
>   3 tablespoons cornstarch
> CREAM CHEESE FILLING:
>   2 packages (8 ounces *each*) cream cheese,
>   softened
>   1/3 cup sugar
>   1 tablespoon lemon juice
>   1/2 teaspoon vanilla extract
> ICING (optional):
>   1 cup confectioners' sugar
>   2 to 3 tablespoons milk

In a mixing bowl, dissolve yeast in water; let stand for 5 minutes. Add butter, sugar, eggs, salt and 2 cups flour; beat on low speed for 3 minutes. Add enough remaining flour to form a soft dough. Turn onto a floured surface; knead until smooth and elastic, about 6-8 minutes. Place in a greased bowl, turning once to grease top. Cover and let rise in a warm place until doubled, about 45 minutes. Meanwhile, combine pineapple filling ingredients in a saucepan. Bring to a boil; reduce heat. Cook and stir until thickened. Cool. Combine cream cheese filling ingredients; mix well. Divide dough in half. On a floured surface, roll each portion into a 15-in. x 9-in. rectangle. Place on greased baking sheets. Spread the cream cheese filling lengthwise down center third of each rectangle. Spread the pineapple filling on top. On each long side, cut 1-in.-wide strips 3 in. into center. Starting at one end, fold alternating strips at an angle across filling. Seal ends. Cover and let rise for 20 minutes. Bake at 350° for 25-30 minutes or until golden brown. Cool. If desired, combine icing ingredients and drizzle over braids. **Yield:** 2 loaves.

SWEDISH DOUGHNUTS

Lisa Bates, Dunham, Quebec

(Pictured at left)

One day, my father got a hankering for doughnuts and asked me to make him some. I ended up trying these. Dad—and everyone else—loved the results. They come out so golden and plump.

>   2 eggs
>   1 cup sugar
>   2 cups cold mashed potatoes (mashed
>   with milk and butter)
>   3/4 cup buttermilk
>   2 tablespoons butter *or* margarine,
>   melted
>   1 teaspoon vanilla *or* almond extract
> 4-1/2 cups all-purpose flour
>   4 teaspoons baking powder
>   1 teaspoon baking soda
>   1 teaspoon salt
>   2 teaspoons ground nutmeg
>   1/8 teaspoon ground ginger
> Oil for deep-fat frying
> Additional sugar, optional

In a mixing bowl, beat eggs and sugar. Add the potatoes, buttermilk, butter and vanilla; mix well. Combine the flour, baking powder, baking soda, salt, nutmeg and ginger; add to egg mixture and mix well. Cover and refrigerate for 1-2 hours. On a floured surface, roll dough to 1/2-in. thickness. Cut with a 2-1/2-in. doughnut cutter. In an electric skillet or deep-fat fryer, heat oil to 375°. Fry doughnuts, a few at a time, for 2 minutes on each side or until browned. Drain on paper towels. Roll in sugar if desired. **Yield:** about 2-1/2 dozen.

Almond Rolls Rate a '10'

COUNTRY COOK Perlene Hoekema is accustomed to having her kitchen creations carefully considered by a panel of judges. In fact, it happens all the time at her home in Lynden, Washington.

"I'll try out a new recipe every few weeks," Perlene relates. "My family of taste-testers then will rate it on a scale of 1 to 10. Almond Streusel Rolls received an enthusiastic 10 here!

"Actually," she notes, "this recipe was a collaboration between our grown daughter, Janis, and me. She developed the rolls, then I came up with the idea for the filling and streusel topping.

"Like their mother, my two young grandchildren even like to get involved when baking is involved. They help out when the dough needs extra kneading," she smiles.

"In our farming region, a morning coffee break, afternoon tea break and bedtime snack are givens. These rolls are perfect for any of those occasions. Plus, they go well at a brunch."

Perlene adds that she makes the rolls for Sunday family breakfasts and for giving as gifts as well. "I've used them as a different dessert also," she reports. "Often, the rolls don't even get time to cool before the pan is empty!

"With our Dutch heritage, making pastry comes naturally to me. I use a lot of almond paste. Generally, I order a 7-pound supply at a time."

Why not try her prize-winning pastry at your place? You're sure to score big points with all of the "judges" around your table, too!

ALMOND STREUSEL ROLLS

(Pictured on page 80)

2 packages (1/4 ounce *each*) active dry yeast
3/4 cup warm water (110° to 115°)
3/4 cup warm milk (110° to 115°)
1/4 cup butter *or* margarine, softened
1/2 cup sugar
2 eggs
1 teaspoon salt
5-1/4 to 5-1/2 cups all-purpose flour

FILLING:
1/2 cup almond paste
1/4 cup butter *or* margarine, softened
1/2 cup packed brown sugar
1/4 teaspoon almond extract

TOPPING:
3 tablespoons sugar
1 tablespoon all-purpose flour
1 tablespoon butter *or* margarine

ICING:
1-1/2 cups confectioners' sugar
1 to 2 tablespoons milk
1/4 teaspoon almond extract

In a mixing bowl, dissolve yeast in water; let stand 5 minutes. Add milk, butter, sugar, eggs and salt; mix well. Add 2 cups of flour; beat until smooth. Stir in enough of the remaining flour to form a soft dough. Turn onto a floured surface; knead until smooth and elastic, about 6-8 minutes. Place in a greased bowl, turning once to grease top. Cover and let rise in a warm place until doubled, about 1 hour. Punch dough down; roll out to a 15-in. x 10-in. rectangle. In a mixing bowl, beat filling ingredients until smooth. Spread over dough. Roll up jelly-roll style, starting with a short side; seal seams. Cut into 12 slices. Place in a greased 13-in. x 9-in. x 2-in. baking pan. Cover and let rise in a warm place until doubled, about 30 minutes. Combine topping ingredients; sprinkle over rolls. Bake at 350° for 35-40 minutes or until golden brown. Cool on a wire rack. Combine icing ingredients; drizzle over rolls. **Yield:** 1 dozen.

ALMOND Streusel Rolls call for almond paste. If you can't find it at your local grocery store, try this handy recipe from the Almond Board of California.

ALMOND PASTE

1-1/2 cups (8 ounces) whole blanched almonds
1-1/2 cups sifted confectioners' sugar
1 egg white
1 teaspoon almond extract
1/4 teaspoon salt

In a food processor, grind half of the almonds until very fine. Remove and repeat with the remaining almonds. Total ground nuts will yield 1-3/4 cups. Put all of the nuts and the confectioners' sugar, egg white, almond extract and salt in the food processor. Cover and process until a paste forms. Gather together and refrigerate in a tightly sealed plastic bag. **Yield:** 1-1/3 cups (13 ounces).

STRAWBERRY SPREAD

Ruth Hodges, Harrisonville, Missouri

A friend gave me the simple recipe for this tasty spread years ago, and I've been using it on a variety of breads ever since.

    1 package (8 ounces) cream cheese,
      softened
    2 tablespoons confectioners' sugar
    3 fresh strawberries, mashed

In a mixing bowl, beat cream cheese and confectioners' sugar until smooth. Add strawberries; mix well. Serve on bagels, English muffins or toast. **Yield:** about 1 cup.

CHERRY DANISH

Christie Cochran, Canyon, Texas

(Pictured on page 80)

I won an award when I first made these delicious danish for a 4-H competition years ago. They're still a family favorite today.

    1 package (1/4 ounce) active dry yeast
    1/4 cup warm water (110° to 115°)
    1 cup warm milk (110° to 115°)
    3/4 cup shortening, *divided*
    1/3 cup sugar
    3 eggs, *divided*
    1 teaspoon salt
    1/4 teaspoon ground mace
    1/4 teaspoon lemon extract
    1/4 teaspoon vanilla extract
    4 to 4-1/2 cups all-purpose flour
    1 can (21 ounces) cherry pie filling
GLAZE:
    1-1/2 cups confectioners' sugar
    2 to 3 tablespoons milk
    1/2 teaspoon vanilla extract
    1/3 cup chopped almonds

In a mixing bowl, dissolve yeast in water. Add milk, 1/4 cup shortening, sugar, 2 eggs, salt, mace, extracts and 2 cups of flour; beat until smooth. Add enough remaining flour to form a soft dough. Turn onto a floured surface; knead until smooth and elastic, about 6-8 minutes. Place in a greased bowl, turning once to grease top. Cover and let rise in a warm place until doubled, about 1 hour. Punch dough down. On a large floured surface, roll dough out to a 24-in. x 16-in. rectangle. Dot half of the dough with 1/4 cup of shortening; fold dough lengthwise. Fold the dough three times lengthwise, then two times widthwise, each time dotting with some of the remaining shortening.

Place dough in a greased bowl; cover and let rise 20 minutes. On a floured surface, roll dough into a 16-in. x 15-in. rectangle. Cut into 8-in. x 3/4-in. strips; coil into a spiral shape, tucking end underneath the coil. Place in two greased 15-in. x 10-in. x 1-in. baking pans. Cover and let rise in a warm place until doubled, about 1 hour. Beat remaining egg. Make a depression in the center of each roll; brush with egg. Fill with 1 tablespoon of pie filling. Bake at 375° for 15-18 minutes or until golden brown. Cool on a wire rack. Combine the first three glaze ingredients; drizzle over rolls. Sprinkle with almonds. **Yield:** 40 rolls.

MAPLE PANCAKES

Mary Colbath, Concord, New Hampshire

(Pictured below)

Our family looks forward to tapping the maple trees in March...and then enjoying the pure maple syrup year-round. This is just one of the recipes I like to make that has maple syrup as an ingredient.

    1 cup all-purpose flour
    1-1/2 teaspoons baking powder
    1/2 teaspoon salt
    1 egg
    1 cup milk
    2 tablespoons vegetable oil
    1 tablespoon maple syrup

In a bowl, combine flour, baking powder and salt. In another bowl, combine egg, milk, oil and syrup; stir into dry ingredients just until blended. Pour batter by 1/4 cupfuls onto a lightly greased hot griddle; turn when bubbles form on top of pancakes. Cook until second side is golden brown (pancakes will be thin). **Yield:** 6-7 pancakes.

APRICOT CRANBERRY BREAD

Diane Roth, Milwaukee, Wisconsin

(Pictured below)

I was making cranberry bread one day and wanted to try something a little different. I found a jar of apricot jam in the refrigerator and decided to spoon the jam into the center of the bread. It looked lumpy, so I took a knife and cut the jam into the bread. The end result was delicious.

        2 cups all-purpose flour
        1 cup sugar
        1 to 2 teaspoons grated orange peel
1-1/2 teaspoons baking powder
    1/2 teaspoon baking soda
    1/2 teaspoon salt
        1 egg
    3/4 cup water
    1/4 cup vegetable oil
        1 cup fresh *or* frozen halved cranberries
    1/4 cup apricot preserves

In a large bowl, combine flour, sugar, orange peel, baking powder, baking soda and salt. In a small bowl, beat egg, water and oil; stir into dry ingredients just until moistened. Fold in the cranberries. Pour into a greased and floured 9-in. x 5-in. x 3-in. loaf pan. Cut apricots in the preserves into small pieces; spoon preserves over batter. Cut

through batter with a knife to swirl. Bake at 350° for 65-70 minutes or until a toothpick inserted near the center comes out clean. Cool for 10 minutes; remove from pan to a wire rack. **Yield:** 1 loaf.

FRENCH TOAST WITH ORANGE SYRUP

Jesse and Anne Foust, Bluefield, West Virginia

Thick slices of French toast combine with a citrusy syrup for a delicious brunch treat that can't be beat! This dish is easy enough to serve anytime.

        3 eggs
        1 cup milk
        2 tablespoons sugar
    1/4 teaspoon salt
    1/8 teaspoon ground cinnamon
    1/8 teaspoon ground nutmeg
        8 slices day-old French bread
            (1 inch thick)
ORANGE SYRUP:
    1/2 cup orange juice
    1/3 cup corn syrup
    1/4 cup sugar
        4 teaspoons butter *or* margarine
        1 teaspoon grated orange peel
    1/2 teaspoon orange extract

In a bowl, beat eggs; add milk, sugar, salt, cinnamon and nutmeg. Soak the slices of bread for 30 seconds on each side. Cook on a hot greased griddle until golden brown on both sides and cooked through. In a saucepan, combine orange juice, corn syrup, sugar, butter and orange peel. Bring to a boil; boil, stirring constantly, for 2 minutes. Remove from the heat; stir in extract. Pour over French toast or serve on the side. **Yield:** 4-6 servings.

LOW-FAT COFFEE CAKE

Coleen Roberts, Seffner, Florida

I served this to friends without telling them it was low-fat and nobody ever guessed. They all thought it was delicious!

✓ Uses less fat, sugar or salt. Includes Nutritional Analysis and Diabetic Exchanges.

1-1/2 cups all-purpose flour
    3/4 cup sugar
        2 teaspoons baking powder
    1/2 teaspoon salt
        2 egg whites
    1/4 cup unsweetened applesauce
    1/2 cup skim milk

TOPPING:
- 1/3 cup packed brown sugar
- 1/4 cup sugar
- 2 teaspoons ground cinnamon

In a medium bowl, combine flour, sugar, baking powder and salt. In another bowl, beat egg whites, applesauce and milk. Add to dry ingredients. Pour into a 9-in. square baking pan that has been coated with nonstick cooking spray. Combine topping ingredients; sprinkle over batter. Bake at 375° for 25 minutes or until a toothpick inserted near the center comes out clean. Serve warm. **Yield:** 9 servings. **Nutritional Analysis:** One serving equals 206 calories, 261 mg sodium, trace cholesterol, 48 gm carbohydrate, 3 gm protein, trace fat. **Diabetic Exchanges:** 2 starch, 1 fruit.

▰▰▰▰▰▰▰▰▰▰▰▰

GOLDEN RAISIN WHEAT BREAD

Nilah Schenck, Beloit, Wisconsin

Since I'm single, I freeze extra loaves in freezer bags when I bake this moist bread. Then the night before I'm about to run out of bread, I take a loaf out and thaw it at room temperature. It was only after I retired that I became interested in cooking and baking. Now, when relatives and I get together at Christmastime, I'm the one who's asked to bring the bread.

- 3/4 cup golden raisins
- 1/2 cup boiling water
- 3 cups whole wheat flour
- 2 packages (1/4 ounce *each*) active dry yeast
- 1 tablespoon salt
- 1 teaspoon baking soda
- 1 carton (16 ounces) plain yogurt
- 1 cup water
- 1/3 cup honey
- 5 tablespoons butter *or* margarine
- 4-1/2 to 5 cups all-purpose flour

In a bowl, combine raisins and water; let stand for 10 minutes. Drain well; set aside. In a mixing bowl, combine whole wheat flour, yeast, salt and baking soda. In a saucepan, heat yogurt, water, honey and butter to 120°-130°. Add to flour mixture and mix well. Add raisins and enough all-purpose flour to form a soft dough. Turn onto a floured surface; knead until smooth and elastic, about 6-8 minutes. Place in a greased bowl, turning once to grease top. Cover and let rise in a warm place until doubled, about 1 hour. Punch dough down; divide into thirds. Shape into loaves. Place in three greased 9-in. x 5-in. x 3-in. loaf pans. Cover and let rise until doubled, about 30 minutes. Bake at 350° for 35-40 minutes or until golden brown. Cool on wire racks. **Yield:** 3 loaves.

▰▰▰▰▰▰▰▰▰▰▰▰

BEAUTIFUL BROWN ROLLS

Anna Anderson, Atwater, Minnesota

(Pictured above)

I love to make bread and have baked many, many dozens of these rolls over the years. I've given the recipe to numerous friends, and they all agree these light-textured rolls are outstanding.

- 2 cups boiling water
- 1 cup quick-cooking oats
- 2 packages (1/4 ounce *each*) active dry yeast
- 1/4 cup warm water (110° to 115°)
- 2 eggs, beaten
- 1/2 cup molasses
- 1/2 cup vegetable oil
- 1/3 cup sugar
- 1/2 teaspoon salt
- 5-3/4 to 6-1/4 cups all-purpose flour
- Melted butter *or* margarine

In a large mixing bowl, combine boiling water and oats; cool to lukewarm (110° to 115°). Meanwhile, dissolve yeast in warm water; stir into oat mixture. Add the eggs, molasses, oil, sugar and salt. Add enough flour to form a soft dough. Turn onto a floured surface; knead until smooth and elastic, about 6-8 minutes. Place in a greased bowl, turning once to grease top. Cover and let rise in a warm place until doubled, about 1 hour. Punch dough down. Divide into 36 pieces and shape into rolls. Place on greased baking sheets. Cover and let rise until doubled, about 30 minutes. Bake at 375° for 20-25 minutes. Brush with butter. Cool on wire racks. **Yield:** 3 dozen.

down on greased baking sheets. Bake at 350° for 16-20 minutes or until lightly browned. Immediately remove to wire racks to cool. For icing, combine sugar, milk and vanilla until smooth; drizzle over the twists. Sprinkle with pecans. **Yield:** 64 twists. **Editor's Note:** The yeast does not need to be dissolved in liquid, and no rising time is necessary before baking.

STRAWBERRY BREAKFAST SAUCE

Marie Harrell, Donna, Texas

My mother used peaches to make this sauce, but my family prefers fresh strawberries. It's wonderful warm over waffles or pancakes.

- 1 cup sugar
- 1/4 cup cornstarch
- 1/2 cup orange juice
- 6 cups sliced fresh strawberries
- 8 to 10 drops red food coloring, optional

In a saucepan, combine the sugar and cornstarch. Stir in orange juice; bring to a boil over medium heat. Add strawberries; return to a boil. Cook and stir for 2 minutes. Add food coloring if desired. Serve warm over waffles or pancakes. **Yield:** 3-1/2 cups.

WHEAT-OATMEAL HONEY BREAD

Ellie Conlon, Proctor, West Virginia

My husband, Steve, and I stay busy as bees harvesting honey from our 500 hives. The bees supply our ThistleDew Farm market with 80,000 pounds of honey! I won first prize at West Virginia's Honey Festival a few years ago with this recipe.

- 2 cups whole wheat flour
- 5 to 5-1/2 cups all-purpose flour, *divided*
- 1 cup quick-cooking oats
- 2 packages (1/4 ounce *each*) active dry yeast
- 1 teaspoon salt
- 1 cup warm water (120° to 130°)
- 1 cup warm sour milk* (120° to 130°)
- 1/2 cup honey
- 1/3 cup butter *or* margarine, melted
- 2 eggs, beaten

TOPPING:
- 1 egg white
- 1 tablespoon water
- 1/4 cup quick-cooking oats

In a mixing bowl, combine whole wheat flour, 2 cups of all-purpose flour, oats, yeast and salt. Stir in water, milk, honey and butter; beat until

AUSTRIAN APPLE TWISTS

Kathy Bless, Fayetteville, Pennsylvania

(Pictured above)

This recipe has been one of my favorites for years. I like to make these sweet treats for special occasions because everyone enjoys them.

- 1 package (1/4 ounce) active dry yeast
- 3 cups all-purpose flour
- 1 cup butter *or* margarine, softened
- 3 egg yolks, beaten
- 1 cup (8 ounces) sour cream
- 1/2 cup sugar
- 1/2 cup finely chopped pecans
- 3/4 teaspoon ground cinnamon
- 1 medium tart apple, peeled, cored and finely chopped

ICING:
- 1 cup confectioners' sugar
- 4 teaspoons milk
- 1/4 teaspoon vanilla extract

Finely chopped pecans

In a mixing bowl, combine the yeast and flour; add butter and mix well. Add egg yolks and sour cream; mix well. Shape into four balls. Place in separate resealable plastic bags or wrap in plastic wrap; refrigerate overnight. In a small bowl, combine sugar, pecans and cinnamon; set aside. On a floured surface, roll each ball of dough into a 9-in. circle. Sprinkle with sugar mixture and apple. Cut each circle into 16 wedges; roll up from wide edge and pinch to seal. Place with point side smooth. Beat in eggs. Add enough remaining all-purpose flour to form a soft dough. Turn onto a floured surface; knead until smooth and elastic, about 8 minutes. Place in a greased bowl, turning once to grease top. Cover and let rise in a warm place until doubled, about 1 hour. Punch the dough down. Shape into two loaves; place in greased 9-in. x 5-in. x 3-in. loaf pans. Cover and let rise until doubled, about 45 minutes. Beat egg white and water; brush over loaves. Sprinkle with oats. Bake at 375° for 40-45 minutes or until golden brown. Remove from pans to cool on wire racks. **Yield:** 2 loaves. ***Editor's Note:** To sour milk, place 1 tablespoon vinegar in a measuring cup; add milk to equal 1 cup.

BRAIDED CARDAMOM RINGS

Jo Learman, Caro, Michigan

(Pictured below)

Most Christmases, I'll take one of my rings to my husband's family and one to my family. Of course, I make sure to keep enough at home, too. They look so festive with the colorful cherries.

 1 package (1/4 ounce) active dry yeast
 1/4 cup warm water (110° to 115°)
 2-1/2 cups warm milk (110° to 115°)
 3/4 cup butter *or* margarine, softened
 1 egg, beaten

 1 cup sugar
 1-1/2 teaspoons ground cardamom
 1/2 teaspoon salt
 8-3/4 to 9-1/4 cups all-purpose flour
LEMON ICING:
 2 cups confectioners' sugar
 3 to 4 tablespoons milk
 1/4 teaspoon lemon extract
**Red and green candied cherries, halved,
 optional**

In a mixing bowl, dissolve yeast in water. Add milk, butter, egg, sugar, cardamom and salt; mix well. Add 6 cups of flour; beat until smooth. Stir in enough of the remaining flour to form a soft dough. Turn onto a floured surface; knead until smooth and elastic, about 6-8 minutes. Place in a greased bowl, turning once to grease top. Cover and let rise in a warm place until doubled, about 1-1/2 to 2 hours. Punch dough down and divide in half. Divide each half into three portions. Shape each portion into a 24-in.-long rope. Place three ropes on a greased baking sheet; braid. Form into a ring; pinch edges tightly together. Repeat with remaining dough. Cover and let rise until doubled, about 40 minutes. Bake at 350° for 30-35 minutes or until golden brown. Cool on wire racks. For icing, combine sugar, milk and extract; spoon over rings, allowing icing to drizzle down the sides. Decorate with cherries if desired. **Yield:** 2 coffee cakes. **Editor's Note:** Rings may be iced and served warm if desired.

Speedy Sweet Breads

THE EMPHASIS is on "convenience" with these streamlined recipes. Because each of them relies on a convenience mix or dough, all require less than 30 minutes of preparation before baking.

MAPLE APPLE BREAD

June Smith, Byron Center, Michigan

(Pictured below)

This decorative bread gives crescent rolls a creative new twist.

      1/4 cup packed brown sugar
        2 tablespoons all-purpose flour
        1 teaspoon ground cinnamon
        1 egg, beaten
        1 teaspoon maple flavoring
      1/2 cup chopped peeled tart apple
      1/4 cup chopped walnuts
        2 packages (8 ounces *each*) refrigerated
          crescent rolls
GLAZE:
      1/2 cup confectioners' sugar
        1 tablespoon milk
      1/2 teaspoon vanilla extract

In a bowl, combine brown sugar, flour, cinnamon, egg and maple flavoring; mix well. Add apple and nuts; stir to coat. Unroll crescent roll dough and separate into eight rectangles; seal the seams and perforations. Spread each rectangle with apple mixture. Roll up, starting with a short side. Place lengthwise in a greased 8-in. x 4-in. x 2-in. loaf pan, making two layers of four rolls. Bake at 350° for 20 minutes. Cover with foil and bake 30 minutes longer or until golden brown, uncovering the last 5 minutes. Cool for 10 minutes; remove from pan to a wire rack to cool completely. Combine glaze ingredients; drizzle over bread. **Yield:** 1 loaf.

BANANA STICKY BUNS

Debbie Hibbert, Kenton, Delaware

My love of cooking comes from my grandmother, who always took time to show me how to prepare recipes from scratch.

36 pecan halves
1/2 cup butter *or* margarine, softened
1/3 cup packed brown sugar
DOUGH:
2 cups biscuit/baking mix
2/3 cup mashed ripe banana
2 tablespoons butter *or* margarine, melted
1/4 cup packed brown sugar

Place three pecan halves each in 12 ungreased muffin cups. Evenly divide butter over pecans and sprinkle with brown sugar. Bake at 375° for 5 minutes or until butter and sugar are melted. Meanwhile, combine biscuit mix and banana to form a soft dough. On a lightly floured surface, knead dough 5 times. Roll into a 15-in. x 9-in. rectangle. Spread with butter; sprinkle with brown sugar. Roll up, jelly-roll style, starting with a long side; seal the seams. Slice into 12 rolls; place cut side down in muffin cups. Bake at 375° for 12-14 minutes or until golden. Cool 1 minute; invert onto a serving platter. Serve warm. **Yield:** 1 dozen.

CINNAMON CREAM CHEESE SQUARES

Gay Snyder, Deerfield, Ohio

I like to make these cream cheese squares for a quick breakfast treat or easy dessert. Even my young daughter can help out.

2 tubes (8 ounces *each*) refrigerated crescent rolls
2 packages (8 ounces *each*) cream cheese, softened
1-1/2 cups sugar, *divided*

1 teaspoon vanilla extract
1/4 cup butter *or* margarine, melted
1 teaspoon ground cinnamon

Unroll one tube of crescent roll dough and place in a lightly greased 13-in. x 9-in. x 2-in. baking pan. Seal seams and perforations; set aside. In a mixing bowl, beat cream cheese, 1 cup of sugar and vanilla until smooth. Spread over dough. Unroll remaining tube of dough and place over cream cheese mixture, stretching to fit. Brush butter evenly over top; sprinkle with cinnamon and remaining sugar. Bake at 350° for 30 minutes or until done. Cool; cut into squares. **Yield:** about 3 dozen.

CARAMEL BUBBLE RING

Laura Clifton, Wenatchee, Washington

Lots of caramel and ice cream topping make this quick pull-apart bread oh so gooey and delicious. It truly is a finger-lickin' good baked good.

3/4 cup sugar
4 teaspoons ground cinnamon
1/2 cup caramel ice cream topping
2 tablespoons maple syrup
1/3 cup chopped pecans
2 tubes (11 ounces *each*) refrigerated breadsticks
1/3 cup butter *or* margarine, melted

Combine the sugar and cinnamon; set aside. Combine caramel topping and maple syrup; set aside. Sprinkle half the pecans in a greased 10-in. fluted tube pan. Drizzle with a third of the caramel mixture. Open the tubes of breadstick dough (do not unroll). Cut each into eight slices; dip in butter, then roll in cinnamon-sugar. Place half in the pan; sprinkle with remaining pecans. Drizzle with half of the caramel mixture. Top with remaining dough. Drizzle with remaining caramel mixture. Bake at 350° for 20-25 minutes or until golden brown. Cool for 2 minutes. Invert onto a serving platter; serve warm. **Yield:** 12-16 servings.

FRENCH ONION BREAD

Dorothy Jorgensen, Fort Dodge, Iowa

(Pictured above)

I make this bread every week, and my family never tires of it. I've shared it with friends and have received many compliments.

>   2 packages (1/4 ounce *each*) active dry
>   yeast
>   1 cup warm water (110° to 115°)
> 5-1/4 to 5-3/4 cups all-purpose flour, *divided*
>   4 tablespoons sugar, *divided*
>   3/4 teaspoon salt
> 1-1/4 cups hot water (120° to 130°)
>   1 envelope onion soup mix
>   3 tablespoons shortening

In a mixing bowl, dissolve yeast in warm water. Add 1/2 cup flour, 2 tablespoons sugar and salt; beat until smooth, about 1 minute. Cover and let rise in a warm place for 20 minutes. In a small bowl, combine hot water, soup mix, shortening and remaining sugar. Cool to 115°. Add to yeast mixture with 2 cups flour; mix for 1-2 minutes. Stir in enough remaining flour to form a soft dough. Turn onto a floured surface; knead until smooth and elastic, about 6-8 minutes. Place in a greased bowl, turning once to grease top. Cover and let rise in a warm place until doubled, about 1 hour. Punch the dough down; divide into thirds. Shape into loaves; place in three greased 8-in. x 4-in. x 2-in. loaf pans. Cover and let rise until doubled, about 30 minutes. Bake at 375° for 30 minutes or until golden brown. Remove from pans to cool on wire racks. **Yield:** 3 loaves.

CRANBERRY PUMPKIN BREAD

Blanche Whytsell, Arnoldsburg, West Virginia

The result of pairing canned pumpkin and cranberry sauce in a quick bread is moist and tasty. The orange glaze drizzled over the loaf adds a colorful finishing touch and a slight citrus flavor.

> 3-1/2 cups all-purpose flour
> 1-1/2 cups sugar
>   2 teaspoons pumpkin pie spice
>   1 teaspoon baking soda
>   1 teaspoon baking powder
>   3/4 teaspoon salt
>   1 can (16 ounces) whole-berry cranberry
>   sauce
>   1 can (15 ounces) solid-pack pumpkin
>   3/4 cup chopped pecans
>   2/3 cup vegetable oil
>   4 eggs
> GLAZE:
>   1 cup confectioners' sugar

1/4 cup orange juice concentrate
1/8 teaspoon ground allspice

In a large bowl, combine flour, sugar, pie spice, baking soda, baking powder and salt. In another bowl, combine the cranberry sauce, pumpkin, pecans, oil and eggs; stir into dry ingredients and mix well. Pour into two greased 9-in. x 5-in. x 3-in. loaf pans. Bake at 350° for 65 minutes or until a toothpick inserted in the center comes out clean. Cool for 10 minutes; remove from pans to a wire rack to cool completely. Combine glaze ingredients; drizzle over loaves. **Yield:** 2 loaves.

.•.•.•.•.•.•.•.•.•.•.

STRAWBERRY BUTTER

Kim Hammond, Watsonville, California

There are several farms in our community where families can pick their own strawberries. We usually pick a bucketful and sample some on the way home. But we always save enough for this butter.

1 package (8 ounces) cream cheese, softened
1/2 cup butter (no substitutes), softened
1 cup confectioners' sugar
1 teaspoon vanilla extract
1 cup fresh strawberries, pureed

In a mixing bowl, beat cream cheese and butter until smooth. Gradually add sugar and vanilla; mix well. Stir in strawberries. Cover tightly and refrigerate for several hours or overnight. May be stored in the refrigerator up to 1 week. Serve with English muffins, toast, waffles or pancakes. **Yield:** 2 cups.

.•.•.•.•.•.•.•.•.•.•.

MAPLE STICKY BUNS

Priscilla Rossi, East Barre, Vermont

(Pictured at right)

My family has a small sugaring operation in our backyard. This recipe makes good use of the maple syrup we make. It's a family tradition to serve these sticky buns on Thanksgiving every year.

2 packages (1/4 ounce *each*) active dry yeast
2 cups warm water (110° to 115°)
1/4 cup shortening
1/2 cup sugar
1 egg
2 teaspoons salt
6 to 6-1/2 cups all-purpose flour
6 tablespoons butter *or* margarine, softened

3/4 cup packed brown sugar
1 tablespoon ground cinnamon
3/4 cup chopped walnuts
1-1/2 cups maple syrup
Additional brown sugar

In a mixing bowl, dissolve yeast in water. Add shortening, sugar, egg, salt and enough flour to form a soft dough. Cover and refrigerate for 24 hours. Punch dough down. Turn onto a floured surface; knead until smooth and elastic, about 6-8 minutes, adding more flour if needed. Divide into thirds. Roll each portion into a 16-in. x 10-in. rectangle. On each rectangle, spread 2 tablespoons butter and sprinkle with 1/4 cup brown sugar, 1 teaspoon cinnamon and 1/4 cup walnuts. Pour syrup into three greased 9-in. round baking pans*. Sprinkle with brown sugar. Tightly roll up each rectangle, jelly-roll style, starting with the short side. Slice each roll into 10 pieces; place over syrup. Cover and let rise until doubled, about 30 minutes. Bake at 350° for 25-30 minutes or until golden brown. Cool in pans for 5 minutes; invert onto a wire rack. **Yield:** 2-1/2 dozen. ***Editor's Note:** 11-in. x 7-in. x 2-in. baking pans may be substituted for the 9-in. round pans.

PEACHY POPPY SEED MUFFINS

Judi Oudekerk, St. Michael, Minnesota

(Pictured below)

I discovered this recipe several years ago and have made it many times since. You might be surprised that the "secret ingredient" is peach baby food—it makes these tasty muffins moist. My family just loves them.

- 1/2 cup plus 2 tablespoons butter *or* margarine, softened
- 1 cup sugar
- 2 eggs
- 1/2 teaspoon vanilla extract
- 1-1/4 cups all-purpose flour
- 2 tablespoons poppy seeds
- 1 teaspoon baking soda
- 1/4 teaspoon salt
- 1 jar (6 ounces) peach baby food

In a mixing bowl, cream butter and sugar. Add eggs and vanilla; mix well. Combine the flour, poppy seeds, baking soda and salt; add to creamed mixture alternately with baby food. Fill paper-lined muffin cups two-thirds full. Bake at 350° for 20-25 minutes or until muffins test done. **Yield:** 1 dozen.

WHOLESOME QUICK BREAD

Rebecca Harris, Raytown, Missouri

I make all my breads healthy and low in fat. My family and friends are pleased with this good and good-for-you bread.

✓ Uses less fat, sugar or salt. Includes Nutritional Analysis and Diabetic Exchanges.

- 1 cup mashed ripe bananas
- 3/4 cup sugar
- 1/3 cup unsweetened applesauce
- Egg substitute equivalent to 2 eggs
- 1 teaspoon vanilla extract
- 2 cups whole wheat flour
- 1/4 cup quick-cooking oats
- 1 teaspoon baking powder
- 1 teaspoon baking soda
- 1 teaspoon ground cinnamon
- 1/4 teaspoon ground nutmeg
- 3/4 cup buttermilk

TOPPING:
- 1/3 cup chopped pecans
- 2 tablespoons brown sugar
- 2 tablespoons quick-cooking oats
- 1/2 teaspoon ground cinnamon
- 1/4 teaspoon ground nutmeg

Breads & Rolls

In a mixing bowl, combine the bananas, sugar and applesauce. Add egg substitute and vanilla; mix well. Combine the flour, oats, baking powder, baking soda, cinnamon and nutmeg; add to banana mixture alternately with buttermilk. Pour into two 8-in. x 4-in. x 2-in. loaf pans that have been coated with nonstick cooking spray. Combine topping ingredients; sprinkle over top. Bake at 350° for 55-60 minutes or until a toothpick inserted in the center comes out clean. Cool in pans for 10 minutes before removing to a wire rack to cool completely. **Yield:** 2 loaves (16 slices each). **Nutritional Analysis:** One slice equals 73 calories, 69 mg sodium, trace cholesterol, 14 gm carbohydrate, 2 gm protein, 1 gm fat. **Diabetic Exchanges:** 1 starch.

SWEDISH RYE BREAD

Mary Ann Ross, Crown Point, Indiana

This recipe came from my mother, and it's long been a family favorite. You can make a meal of it with soup and a salad.

> 1 package (1/4 ounce) active dry yeast
> 1-3/4 cups warm water (110° to 115°), *divided*
> 1/4 cup packed brown sugar
> 1/4 cup molasses
> 2 tablespoons shortening
> 2 teaspoons salt
> 2-1/2 cups rye flour
> 3-3/4 to 4-1/4 cups all-purpose flour
> 2 tablespoons butter *or* margarine, melted

In a mixing bowl, dissolve yeast in 1/4 cup water. Add sugar, molasses, shortening, salt and remaining water; stir well. Add rye flour; beat until smooth. Add enough all-purpose flour to form a soft dough. Turn onto a floured surface; knead until smooth and elastic, about 6-8 minutes. Place in a greased bowl, turning once to grease top. Cover and let rise in a warm place until doubled, about 1-1/2 hours. Punch dough down. Shape into four round loaves. Place on greased baking sheets. Cover and let rise until doubled, about 45-60 minutes. Bake at 350° for 30-35 minutes or until golden brown. Brush with butter. **Yield:** 4 loaves.

CINNAMON-ORANGE SWIRL BREAD

Nancy Means, Moline, Illinois

(Pictured above right)

I've been making this recipe for more than 15 years and have modified it through the years. I won second place at our state fair in 1990 with this scrumptious recipe. I didn't mind taking second, because my best friend finished first!

> 1/2 cup butter-flavored shortening
> 1-1/4 cups sugar, *divided*
> 2 eggs
> 3/4 cup sour cream
> 1 teaspoon vanilla extract
> 2 cups all-purpose flour
> 1-1/2 teaspoons baking powder
> 1 teaspoon baking soda
> 1/2 teaspoon salt
> 2 teaspoons ground cinnamon
> 2 teaspoons grated orange peel

In a mixing bowl, cream shortening and 1 cup sugar. Add eggs, sour cream and vanilla; mix well. Combine flour, baking powder, baking soda and salt; stir into creamed mixture just until moistened. Pour half the batter into a greased 9-in. x 5-in. x 3-in. loaf pan. Combine cinnamon, orange peel and remaining sugar; set 1 tablespoon aside for the topping. Sprinkle remaining sugar mixture over batter. Carefully top with batter. Cut through batter with a knife to swirl. Sprinkle with reserved sugar mixture. Bake at 350° for 55-60 minutes or until a toothpick inserted near the center comes out clean. Cool for 10 minutes; remove from pan to a wire rack to cool completely. **Yield:** 1 loaf.

Add Sizzle to Soup with Lighthearted Loaves!

IF YOUR FAMILY is bored with the same old soup-and-sandwich routine, surprise them—by fixing carefree fun right along with the food.

How? Shape and bake bread loaves into personable party pigs for a country gathering. Or serve chowder in deliciously edible bread bowls.

It's easy to do! All the clever creations that you see here were formed from frozen bread (or roll) dough using recipes the folks at Rhodes shared. Be sure you read through their tips below, though, before starting on your "sculpting":

● For easiest shaping, dough should be thawed but still cold. It should, however, reach room temperature before baking.

● Dough is ready to be baked when you poke a finger in it and the indentation stays. If the dough springs right back out, it needs to rise a little longer (try not to let dough over-rise).

● Subtle features (such as the pig's tail) sometimes will vanish since dough expands as it rises and bakes. Because of that, make each one as distinct as you can.

● After 5 minutes of baking, take a peek at your dough sculpture. If you notice that a mouth is closing or that a piece (an ear or tail, for instance) has to be repositioned, carefully remove your creation from the oven and reshape it. Then continue to bake.

● To leave a beautiful glazed finish on your breads, brush the entire surface with a beaten egg before baking (as directed in the recipes at right). One beaten egg will cover more than one bread sculpture. Be sure to lift up and brush under the edge of your dough creation, in addition to on the top and on the sides, since the dough will rise even more as it bakes.

PERK UP parties with Porky's Sandwiches and a Crusty Pig Loaf. And don't forget Vegetable Chowder in edible Bread Bowls (shown below, clockwise from bottom left).

CRUSTY PIG LOAF

1 loaf (1 pound) frozen bread dough,
   thawed
1 raisin
1 egg, beaten

Roll dough into a 10-in. x 7-in. rectangle with
rounded corners. Cut off one corner (see Fig. 1).
Pinch the nose to cre-
ate a flared snout. Place
on a greased baking
sheet. Divide the cor-
ner piece of dough into
two large pieces and
one small piece the size
of a quarter. Roll one
large piece into a 2-
1/2-in. x 2-in. rectan-
gle; cut in half diagonally
to make two triangles for
ears. Referring to photo
below left, attach short
side of each triangle to
head, one on top of dough

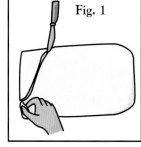
Fig. 1

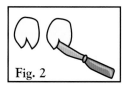
Fig. 2

and one underneath, folding over the tips. Shape
the other large piece of dough into four teardrops.
Slice hooves (see Fig. 2); position under body. For
tail, roll small piece of dough into a 4-in. rope.
Curl and position on pig. Add raisin for eye; cut
the mouth. Cover with plastic wrap that has been
sprayed with nonstick cooking spray. Let rise in a
warm place until doubled, about 30 minutes.
Brush with egg. Bake at 350° for 20 minutes or until golden brown. **Yield:** 1 loaf.

PORKY'S SANDWICHES

8 frozen Texas Rolls (2 ounces *each*),
   thawed
4 raisins
1 egg, beaten
Sandwich fillings of your choice

For each sandwich, press two rolls together and
flatten into a 5-in. circle for the head. Place on a
greased baking sheet. Form two rolls into 4-in. x
3-in. rectangles; cut in half diagonally to make
two triangles. Referring to photo, press short side
of triangles into top of head and fold over for ears.
Cut remaining rolls into four pieces; form two
pieces into teardrops. Cut and shape to form
hooves (see Fig. 2 above); position under head.
Roll third piece into a 6-in. rope for the tail; place

between ears. Form last piece into a flat circle for
the snout. Cut out nostrils with a drinking straw
and position on face. Add raisins for eyes. Cover
with plastic wrap that has been sprayed with nonstick cooking spray. Let rise in a warm place until
doubled, about 30 minutes. Widen nostrils again.
Brush with egg. Bake at 350° for 20 minutes or until golden brown. Cool. Slice horizontally; fill
with sandwich ingredients. **Yield:** 2 sandwiches.

BREAD BOWLS

1 loaf (1 pound) frozen bread dough,
   thawed
1 egg, beaten

Cut loaf into three equal portions; form each into
a ball. Place 4 in. apart on a greased baking sheet.
Cover with plastic wrap that has been sprayed with
nonstick cooking spray. Let rise in a warm place
until doubled, about 2-3 hours. Brush with egg.
Bake at 350° for 25 minutes or until golden brown.
Cool. Cut the top fourth off each loaf; carefully
hollow out top and bottom, leaving a 1/2-in. shell.
(Discard bread from inside or save to make croutons or bread crumbs.) Fill with soup, dip or salsa. Replace top if desired. **Yield:** 3 medium bowls.

VEGETABLE CHOWDER

3 cups diced peeled potatoes
2-1/2 cups broccoli florets
1 cup chopped onion
1 cup grated carrots
2 celery ribs, diced
4 teaspoons chicken bouillon granules
3 cups water
3/4 cup butter *or* margarine
3/4 cup all-purpose flour
4 cups milk
1 teaspoon salt
1/4 teaspoon pepper
1 cup cubed fully cooked ham
1 cup (4 ounces) shredded cheddar cheese

In a soup kettle, combine the potatoes, broccoli,
onion, carrots, celery, bouillon and water; simmer
for 20 minutes or until vegetables are tender. In
a saucepan, melt butter; stir in flour. Cook and stir
over medium heat for 2 minutes. Whisk in milk,
salt and pepper. Bring to a boil; boil and stir for 2
minutes. Add to vegetable mixture with the ham;
simmer 10 minutes. Stir in cheese just until melted. **Yield:** 12 servings (3 quarts).

OATMEAL PANCAKES

Gladys Forseth, Williston, North Dakota

(Pictured below)

These pancakes were served for a fund-raiser at our church many years ago. We fed about 140 people and had a lot of fun. The buttermilk syrup is a nice change from maple syrup.

    1 cup whole wheat flour
    1 cup old-fashioned oats
    1/4 cup wheat germ
    1/4 cup instant nonfat dry milk powder
    1 tablespoon brown sugar
    1 teaspoon baking soda
    2 eggs
    2 cups buttermilk
    1/4 cup vegetable oil
BUTTERMILK SYRUP:
    1 cup sugar
    1/4 cup butter *or* margarine
    1 tablespoon light corn syrup
    3/4 cup buttermilk
    1 teaspoon vanilla extract

In a large bowl, combine dry ingredients. In another bowl, beat eggs, buttermilk and oil; mix well. Stir into dry ingredients just until blended. Pour batter by 1/4 cupfuls onto a lightly greased hot griddle; turn when bubbles form on top of pancakes. Cook until second side is golden. Meanwhile, for syrup, combine sugar, butter and corn syrup in a saucepan. Bring to a boil over medium heat; boil and stir for 5 minutes or until golden brown. Remove from the heat; stir in buttermilk and vanilla. Let stand 5 minutes. Stir; serve with pancakes. **Yield:** 16 pancakes (about 1-1/2 cups syrup).

CITRUS STREUSEL QUICK BREAD

Debra White, Williamson, West Virginia

(Pictured on page 99)

As a minister's wife, I do a lot of baking and cooking for church. Often, I'll find myself copying down recipes to share. This one's generally in demand.

    1 package (18-1/4 ounces) lemon *or*
      orange cake mix, *divided*
    2 tablespoons brown sugar
    1 teaspoon ground cinnamon
    1 tablespoon cold butter *or* margarine
    1/2 cup chopped pecans
    1 package (3.4 ounces) instant vanilla
      pudding mix
    4 eggs
    1 cup (8 ounces) sour cream
    1/3 cup vegetable oil
GLAZE:
    1 cup confectioners' sugar
    2 to 3 tablespoons milk

In a small bowl, combine 2 tablespoons cake mix, brown sugar and cinnamon; cut in butter until crumbly. Stir in pecans; set aside. In a mixing bowl, combine the pudding mix, eggs, sour cream, oil and remaining cake mix; beat on medium speed for 2 minutes. Pour into two greased 8-in. x 4-in. x 2-in. loaf pans. Sprinkle with pecan mixture. Bake at 350° for 45-50 minutes or until a toothpick inserted near the center comes out clean. Cool in pans for 10 minutes before removing to wire racks. Combine glaze ingredients; drizzle over warm bread. **Yield:** 2 loaves.

WALNUT COFFEE CAKE

Beatrice Richard, Posen, Michigan

(Pictured on page 99)

This has been in the family some time. I am now a great-grandmother myself, and it's one of the recipes that my mother used to make long ago.

    1 package (8 ounces) cream cheese,
      softened
    1/2 cup butter *or* margarine, softened
    1-1/4 cups sugar
    2 eggs
    1 teaspoon vanilla extract
    1/4 cup milk
    1-3/4 cups all-purpose flour
    1 teaspoon baking powder
    1 teaspoon ground cinnamon
    1/2 teaspoon baking soda
    1 cup chopped walnuts

TOPPING:

1/2 cup all-purpose flour
1/2 cup packed brown sugar
1/2 teaspoon ground cinnamon
1/4 cup cold butter *or* margarine
1/2 cup finely chopped walnuts

In a mixing bowl, beat cream cheese, butter and sugar until smooth. Add eggs and vanilla; beat until light and fluffy. Blend in milk. Combine flour, baking powder, cinnamon and baking soda. Add to the creamed mixture; beat on low just until mixed. Stir in walnuts. Pour into a greased 13-in. x 9-in. x 2-in. baking pan. For the topping, combine flour, sugar and cinnamon; cut in butter until coarse crumbs form. Stir in walnuts. Sprinkle over coffee cake. Bake at 350° for 40 minutes or until a toothpick inserted near the center comes out clean. Serve warm. **Yield:** 12-15 servings.

***

MARTHA WASHINGTON'S FAN

Susan Peck, Springfield, Missouri

(Pictured on page 98)

Easter morning would not be the same at our house without this bread. The impressive loaves also make nice Christmas gifts.

6 to 7 cups all-purpose flour, *divided*
1/2 cup sugar
2 tablespoons instant nonfat dry milk powder
2 packages (1/4 ounce *each*) active dry yeast
1-1/4 teaspoons salt
2/3 cup butter *or* margarine, softened
1-1/4 cups warm water (120° to 130°)
3 eggs

FILLING:

1-1/2 cups flaked coconut
1 cup chopped pecans
1/2 cup packed brown sugar
6 tablespoons butter *or* margarine, melted, *divided*

ICING:

1 cup confectioners' sugar
2 to 3 tablespoons milk

In a mixing bowl, combine 2 cups flour, sugar, milk powder, yeast and salt. Add butter and water; beat on low for 2 minutes. Add eggs; beat on high for 2 minutes. Add enough remaining flour to form a soft dough. Turn onto a floured surface; knead until smooth and elastic, about 6-8 minutes. Place in a greased bowl, turning once to grease top. Cover and let rise in a warm place until doubled, about 1 hour. Combine coconut, pecans and brown sugar in a bowl. Blend in 3 ta-

blespoons butter; set aside. Punch dough down; divide into thirds. Roll one portion into a 20-in. x 6-in. rectangle, with a short side facing you. Brush top two-thirds of dough with 1 tablespoon of remaining butter; sprinkle buttered portion with one-third of filling. Starting at plain short side, fold dough over half of filling; fold over again. Seal edges and end. Place on a greased baking sheet with folded edge facing away from you. With scissors, cut into eight strips to within 1 in. from folded edge. Separate strips slightly; twist to allow filling to show. Pinch ends into points. Repeat with remaining dough and filling. Cover and let rise until doubled, about 45 minutes. Bake at 350° for 20-25 minutes. Remove to wire racks to cool. Combine icing ingredients; drizzle over fans. **Yield:** 3 loaves.

***

APRICOT CHEESE CRESCENTS

Ruth Gilhousen, Knoxdale, Pennsylvania

(Pictured on page 99)

Traditionally, I bake these treats for Christmas. A cross between sweet breads and cookies, they're also something I've been asked to make for weddings.

2 cups all-purpose flour
1/2 teaspoon salt
1 cup cold butter *or* margarine
1 cup (8 ounces) small-curd cottage cheese

FILLING:

1 package (6 ounces) dried apricots
1/2 cup water
1/2 cup sugar

TOPPING:

3/4 cup finely chopped almonds
1/2 cup sugar
1 egg white, lightly beaten

In a large bowl, combine flour and salt; cut in butter until crumbly. Add cottage cheese; mix well. Shape into 1-in. balls. Cover and refrigerate several hours or overnight. For the filling, combine apricots and water in a saucepan. Cover and simmer for 20 minutes. Cool for 10 minutes. Pour into a blender; cover and process on high speed until smooth. Transfer to a bowl; stir in sugar. Cover and chill. For topping, combine almonds and sugar; set aside. On a floured surface, roll the balls into 2-1/2-in. circles. Spoon about 1 teaspoon of filling onto each. Fold dough over filling and pinch edges to seal. Place on greased baking sheets. Brush tops with egg white; sprinkle with almond mixture. Bake at 375° for 12-15 minutes or until lightly browned. **Yield:** 4-1/2 dozen.

HOW SWEET they are! These yummy yeast breads, quick breads and fried creations will make any special occasion extra-special.

RISING TO THE OCCASION. Clockwise from top right: Banana Yeast Bread (p. 101), Walnut Coffee Cake (p. 96), Citrus Streusel Quick Bread (p. 96), Apricot Cheese Crescents (p. 97), Funnel Cakes (p. 100), Cinnamon Crisps (p. 100), Martha Washington's Fan (p. 97) and Cocoa Ripple Squares (p. 100).

COCOA RIPPLE SQUARES

Phyllis Rank, Wapato, Washington

(Pictured on page 98)

When my four children were growing up, this marbled cake was a frequent birthday treat. Now, my grandchildren request it. I also serve it at card parties.

> 1/2 cup shortening
> 1 cup sugar, *divided*
> 2 eggs
> 1-1/2 cups all-purpose flour
> 2 teaspoons baking powder
> 3/4 teaspoon salt
> 2/3 cup milk
> 2 tablespoons baking cocoa
> 2/3 cup chopped walnuts, *divided*
> 3 tablespoons butter *or* margarine

In a mixing bowl, cream shortening and 3/4 cup sugar. Add eggs; beat until light and fluffy. Combine the flour, baking powder and salt; add to creamed mixture alternately with milk, beating well after each addition. Set aside. Combine cocoa, 1/3 cup walnuts and remaining sugar. Spoon a third of the batter into a greased 9-in. square baking pan. Sprinkle with half of the cocoa mixture. Dot with half of the butter. Repeat layers; top with remaining batter. Sprinkle with remaining walnuts. Bake at 350° for 35-40 minutes or until a toothpick inserted near the center comes out clean. Serve warm. **Yield:** 9 servings.

FUNNEL CAKES

Mary Faith Yoder, Unity, Wisconsin

(Pictured on page 98)

These are much simpler to make than doughnuts but taste just as good. They have been a favorite of ours since we came across them living in the Ozarks.

> 2 eggs
> 1 cup milk
> 1 cup water
> 1/2 teaspoon vanilla extract
> 3 cups all-purpose flour
> 1/4 cup sugar
> 1 tablespoon baking powder
> 1/4 teaspoon salt
> Oil for deep-fat frying
> Confectioners' sugar

In a mixing bowl, beat eggs. Add milk, water and vanilla; mix well. Combine flour, sugar, baking powder and salt; beat into egg mixture until smooth. In an electric skillet or deep-fat fryer, heat oil to 375°. Cover the bottom of a funnel spout with your finger; ladle 1/2 cup of batter into the funnel. Holding the funnel several inches above the skillet, release your finger and move the funnel in a spiral motion until all the batter is released (scraping with a rubber spatula if needed). Fry for 2 minutes on each side or until golden brown. Drain on paper towels. Dust with confectioners' sugar and serve warm. **Yield:** 8 cakes. **Editor's Note:** The batter can be poured from a liquid measuring cup instead of a funnel.

CINNAMON CRISPS

Sarah Bueckert, Austin, Manitoba

(Pictured on page 98)

I first tried this recipe when I still lived at home. My dad especially loved them.

> 4 cups all-purpose flour, *divided*
> 1 package (1/4 ounce) active dry yeast
> 1-1/4 cups warm milk (120° to 130°)
> 1/4 cup shortening
> 1/4 cup sugar
> 1 teaspoon salt
> 1 egg
> **FILLING:**
> 1/2 cup packed brown sugar
> 1/2 cup sugar
> 1/4 cup butter *or* margarine, melted
> 1 teaspoon ground cinnamon
> **TOPPING:**
> 1 cup sugar
> 1 teaspoon ground cinnamon
> 1/2 cup chopped pecans
> 1/4 cup butter *or* margarine, melted

In a mixing bowl, combine 2 cups flour and yeast. Combine milk, shortening, sugar and salt; add to flour mixture and beat for 1 minute. Add egg; beat on low speed for 1 minute. Beat on medium for 3 minutes. Add enough remaining flour to form a soft dough. Turn onto a floured surface; knead until smooth and elastic, about 6-8 minutes. Place in a greased bowl, turning once to grease top. Cover and let rise in a warm place until doubled, about 1 hour. Meanwhile, combine filling ingredients; set aside. For topping, combine sugar, cinnamon and pecans; set aside. Punch dough down; divide in half. On a floured surface, roll one portion into a 12-in. square. Spread with half of the filling. Roll up tightly and pinch to seal. Cut into 1-in. slices and place on greased baking sheets (four slices per sheet). Cover with waxed paper; flatten slices with palm of hand into 3-in. circles. Repeat with remaining dough and filling. Cover and let rise until doubled, about 30 minutes. Cover with waxed paper and flatten or roll to 5-in. di-

ameter. Brush with butter; sprinkle with topping. Cover with waxed paper; roll or flatten again. Bake at 400° for 10-12 minutes or until browned. **Yield:** 2 dozen.

BANANA YEAST BREAD

Maralee Meyer, Milford, Nebraska

(Pictured on page 99)

Though our two grown children never liked bananas, they've always enjoyed this bread. It's been a standby since my grandmother shared the recipe before I was married.

  3/4 cup milk
  1/2 cup butter *or* margarine
  1/2 cup sugar
5-1/4 to 6 cups all-purpose flour
    2 packages (1/4 ounce *each*) active dry
      yeast
    1 teaspoon salt
    3 eggs, *divided*
    3 medium ripe bananas, mashed
    1 teaspoon water

In a saucepan, cook and stir milk, butter and sugar over medium heat until butter is melted; cool to 120°-130°. In a mixing bowl, combine 2 cups of flour, yeast, salt, 2 eggs, bananas and milk mixture; beat on low speed until combined. Beat on medium for 3 minutes. Stir in enough of the remaining flour to form a firm dough. Turn onto a floured surface; knead until smooth and elastic, about 4-6 minutes. Place in a greased bowl, turning once to grease top. Cover and let rise in a

warm place until doubled, about 45 minutes. Divide dough in half; shape each into a round loaf. Place on a greased baking sheet; cut slits in tops. Cover and let rise until doubled, about 45 minutes. Beat remaining egg with water; brush over the loaves. Bake at 375° for 30-35 minutes or until golden brown. **Yield:** 2 loaves.

APPLE PUMPKIN MUFFINS

Beth Knapp, Littleton, New Hampshire

(Pictured above)

The combination of apples and pumpkin makes this recipe a perfect treat for cool autumn days. The muffins are great for breakfast or dessert.

2-1/2 cups all-purpose flour
    2 cups sugar
    1 teaspoon baking soda
    1 teaspoon ground cinnamon
  1/2 teaspoon ground ginger
  1/2 teaspoon salt
  1/4 teaspoon ground nutmeg
    2 eggs
    1 cup cooked *or* canned pumpkin
  1/2 cup vegetable oil
    2 cups finely chopped peeled tart apples

In a large bowl, combine the first seven ingredients. In a small bowl, combine eggs, pumpkin and oil; stir into dry ingredients just until moistened. Fold in apples. Fill greased or paper-lined muffin cups two-thirds full. Bake at 350° for 30-35 minutes or until muffins test done. Cool for 10 minutes before removing from pan. **Yield:** 1-1/2 dozen.

til smooth and elastic, about 6-8 minutes. Place in a greased bowl, turning once to grease top. Cover and let rise in a warm place until doubled, about 1 hour. Meanwhile, for filling, combine the chocolate chips, milk and sugar in a saucepan; cook and stir over low heat until smooth. Stir in cinnamon; set aside. For topping, combine the flour, sugar and cinnamon in a bowl; cut in butter until mixture resembles coarse crumbs. Set aside. Punch the dough down; roll into a 20-in. x 10-in. rectangle. Spread with filling. Roll up, jelly-roll style, starting with a long side; seal seam. Place in a well-greased 10-in. fluted tube pan, with seam facing the inside of the pan. Sprinkle with topping. Cover and let rise in a warm place until doubled, about 30 minutes. Bake at 350° for 45-50 minutes or until golden brown. Let stand for 10 minutes before inverting onto a wire rack to cool. **Yield:** 12-16 servings.

.•.•.•.•.•.•.•.•.•.•.

ASPARAGUS YEAST ROLLS

Margaret Peterson, Forest City, Iowa

(Pictured on the front cover)

I came across this recipe in a magazine. It sounded so good and easy, plus I like recipes with unusual ingredients. Whenever I serve the lovely moist rolls, folks can't believe they're eating asparagus!

  1 package (1/4 ounce) active dry yeast
  1 cup plus 2 tablespoons warm water (110° to 115°), *divided*
  1 tablespoon mashed potato flakes
  1/2 cup butter *or* margarine, softened
  1/4 cup sugar
  2 eggs
1-1/2 teaspoons salt
5-1/4 to 5-3/4 cups all-purpose flour
  1 cup finely chopped fresh asparagus, cooked and drained

In a mixing bowl, dissolve yeast in 2 tablespoons water; let stand for 5 minutes. Combine potato flakes and remaining water; add to yeast mixture. Add butter, sugar, eggs, salt and 2 cups flour; beat until smooth. Add the asparagus and enough of the remaining flour to form a soft dough. Turn onto a floured surface; knead until smooth and elastic, about 6-8 minutes. Place in a greased bowl, turning once to grease top. Cover and refrigerate for 2 hours or overnight. Form dough into 2-in. balls and place in well-greased muffin cups. Cover and let rise in a warm place until doubled, about 45 minutes. Bake at 400° for 14-16 minutes or until golden brown. Cool for 5 minutes. Carefully run a knife around the outside of each roll before removing from pan. Serve warm. **Yield:** 2 dozen.

.•.•.•.•.•.•.•.•.•.•.

CHOCOLATE COFFEE CAKE

Deborah Keller, Goose Creek, South Carolina

(Pictured above)

My grandmother used to make this coffee cake every year during the holidays. Now I serve it to my family every Christmas morning.

  1 package (1/4 ounce) active dry yeast
  1 cup warm water (110° to 115°)
  3 tablespoons butter *or* margarine, softened
  3 tablespoons sugar
  1 egg, beaten
  1 teaspoon salt
  2 tablespoons instant nonfat dry milk powder
  3 to 3-1/2 cups all-purpose flour
FILLING:
  1 cup (6 ounces) semisweet chocolate chips
  1/3 cup evaporated milk
  2 tablespoons sugar
  1/2 teaspoon ground cinnamon
TOPPING:
  1/4 cup all-purpose flour
  1/4 cup sugar
  1 teaspoon ground cinnamon
  1/4 cup cold butter *or* margarine

In a mixing bowl, dissolve yeast in water; let stand for 5 minutes. Add butter, sugar, egg, salt and milk powder; mix well. Add 2 cups flour; beat until smooth. Stir in enough remaining flour to form a soft dough. Turn onto a floured surface; knead un-

Spicy Cranberry Jam

Janet Rowney, Stone Lake, Wisconsin

Living in the middle of cranberry country, I use the fruit in my cooking quite often. We love the tart taste. The honey-sweetened spread tops muffins and holiday roasts flavorfully.

✓ **Uses less fat, sugar or salt. Includes Nutritional Analysis and Diabetic Exchanges.**

    8 cups fresh *or* frozen cranberries (about
      2 pounds)
    1 cup water
    1 cup cider vinegar
    3 cups honey
  1-1/2 teaspoons ground cinnamon
    1/2 teaspoon ground allspice

In a large kettle, combine the cranberries, water and vinegar; bring to a boil. Reduce heat; simmer, uncovered, for 15 minutes or until cranberries soften, stirring occasionally. Press through a sieve or food mill; discard skins. Return to kettle. Stir in honey, cinnamon and allspice; bring to a boil. Reduce heat to medium; cook and stir until thickened, about 8 minutes. Remove from the heat; skim off foam. Pour hot mixture into hot jars, leaving 1/4-in. headspace. Adjust caps. Process for 10 minutes in a boiling-water bath. **Yield:** about 7 half-pints.

Nutmeg Loaf

Dorothy Knapp, Mt. Morris, New York

This is a newly acquired recipe that I've already made countless times. Nutmeg adds a palate-pleasing taste.

✓ **Uses less fat, sugar or salt. Includes Nutritional Analysis and Diabetic Exchanges.**

    1/2 cup margarine, softened
    3/4 cup sugar
      1 egg
      2 cups all-purpose flour
  1-1/4 teaspoons ground nutmeg
      1 teaspoon baking powder
    1/2 teaspoon baking soda
      1 cup buttermilk

In a mixing bowl, cream margarine and sugar. Add egg; mix well. Combine the flour, nutmeg, baking powder and baking soda; add to creamed mixture alternately with buttermilk. Pour into a 9-in. x 5-in. x 3-in. loaf pan that has been coated with nonstick cooking spray. Bake at 350° for 45-50 minutes or until a toothpick inserted near the center comes out clean. Cool in pan 10 minutes before removing to a wire rack to cool complete-

ly. **Yield:** 1 loaf (16 slices). **Nutritional Analysis:** One slice equals 156 calories, 157 mg sodium, 14 mg cholesterol, 22 gm carbohydrate, 3 gm protein, 6 gm fat. **Diabetic Exchanges:** 1-1/2 starch, 1 fat.

Strawberries 'n' Cream Bread

Suzanne Randall, Dexter, Maine

(Pictured below)

Once strawberry-picking time arrives here each summer, my husband and I look forward to this bread. Since only fresh strawberries will do, I have been thinking of trying a different kind of berry…so we can enjoy it more often.

    1/2 cup butter *or* margarine, softened
    3/4 cup sugar
      2 eggs
    1/2 cup sour cream
      1 teaspoon vanilla extract
  1-3/4 cups all-purpose flour
    1/2 teaspoon baking powder
    1/2 teaspoon baking soda
    1/2 teaspoon salt
    1/4 teaspoon ground cinnamon
    3/4 cup chopped fresh strawberries
    3/4 cup chopped walnuts, toasted, *divided*

In a mixing bowl, cream butter and sugar until fluffy. Beat in eggs, one at a time. Add sour cream and vanilla; mix well. Combine the flour, baking powder, baking soda, salt and cinnamon; stir into creamed mixture just until moistened. Fold in strawberries and 1/2 cup nuts. Pour into a greased 8-in. x 4-in. x 2-in. loaf pan. Sprinkle with remaining nuts. Bake at 350° for 65-70 minutes or until a toothpick inserted near the center comes out clean. Cool for 10 minutes; remove from pan to a wire rack to cool completely. **Yield:** 1 loaf.

*WHAT BETTER way to treat family
and friends than with platters piled high with
fresh-from-the-oven cookies and slices of cake?*

SWEET-TO-EAT. Top to bottom: Cherry Chocolate
Marble Cake (p. 106), Fruitcake Bars (p. 105)
and Prize-Winning Jelly Roll (p. 105).

Cakes & Cookies

FRUITCAKE BARS

Terry Mercede, Danbury, Connecticut

(Pictured at left)

This recipe has been a family favorite for years. People who declare they won't eat fruitcake love them!

> 3/4 cup butter *or* margarine, softened
> 1-3/4 cups packed brown sugar
> 3 eggs
> 1 tablespoon vanilla extract
> 1-1/2 cups all-purpose flour
> 3 cups coarsely chopped walnuts
> 1-1/2 cups coarsely chopped candied pineapple
> 1-3/4 cups red and green candied cherries, halved
> 2 cups pitted dates, halved

In a mixing bowl, cream butter and brown sugar. Add eggs, one at time, beating well after each addition. Stir in vanilla. Add flour and walnuts; mix well. Spread evenly into a greased and floured 15-in. x 10-in. x 1-in. baking pan. Sprinkle with pineapple, cherries and dates; press lightly into dough. Bake at 325° for 45-50 minutes or until lightly browned. Cool before cutting. **Yield:** 8 dozen.

PRIZE-WINNING JELLY ROLL

Linda Andersen, Karlstad, Minnesota

(Pictured at left and on the front cover)

Twice I've won first place at our county fair with this recipe. I enjoy cooking and trying new recipes.

> 1-1/4 cups cake flour
> 1-1/2 cups sugar, *divided*
> 1/2 teaspoon baking powder
> 6 eggs, *separated*
> 1 teaspoon cream of tartar
> 1/2 teaspoon salt
> 1/4 cup water
> 1 teaspoon vanilla extract
> 1 teaspoon lemon extract
> Confectioners' sugar
> 1 jar (12 ounces) strawberry, raspberry *or* currant jelly

In a bowl, combine cake flour, 1 cup sugar and baking powder; set aside. In a mixing bowl, beat the egg whites, cream of tartar and salt until soft peaks form. Add remaining sugar, 1 tablespoon at a time, beating well after each addition. Beat until stiff peaks form; set aside. In another mixing bowl, combine the egg yolks, water and extracts; mix well. Add dry ingredients; beat on medium for 1 minute. Gently fold in egg white mixture. Line a greased 15-in. x 10-in. x 1-in. baking pan with waxed paper; spread batter into pan. Bake at 350° for 15-18 minutes or until cake springs back when lightly touched. Turn onto a linen towel dusted with confectioners' sugar; remove waxed paper. Roll cake up, starting with a short side; cool. Unroll cake; spread evenly with jelly. Roll up; dust with confectioners' sugar. **Yield:** 8-10 servings.

LEMON SNOWBALLS

Audrey Thibodeau, Fountain Hills, Arizona

These crunchy little cookies are great for a light dessert. The bright taste of lemon makes them a winner!

> 1/2 cup butter (no substitutes), softened
> 2/3 cup sugar
> 1 egg
> 1/4 cup lemon juice
> 1 tablespoon grated lemon peel
> 1-3/4 cups all-purpose flour
> 1/4 teaspoon baking soda
> 1/4 teaspoon cream of tartar
> 1/4 teaspoon salt
> 1/2 cup finely chopped almonds
> Confectioners' sugar

In a mixing bowl, cream butter, sugar and egg until well blended. Add lemon juice and peel. Combine flour, baking soda, cream of tartar and salt; stir into creamed mixture. Add almonds. Cover and refrigerate the dough for at least 1 hour or overnight. Roll into 1-in. balls. Place on ungreased baking sheets. Bake at 350° for 10-12 minutes or until bottoms are lightly browned (cookies will not brown on top). Remove immediately to wire racks; cool for 5 minutes, then roll in confectioners' sugar. **Yield:** about 3 dozen.

mint if desired. Refrigerate or serve immediately. **Yield:** 16 servings. ***Editor's Note:*** If using fresh roses, be sure they have not been chemically treated. Also, thoroughly rinse and dry them before using. When using any kind of garden flowers in your cooking, be sure what you're picking is safe.

▪▪▪▪▪▪▪▪▪▪▪▪▪
CHERRY CHOCOLATE MARBLE CAKE

Sandra Campbell, Chase Mills, New York

(Pictured on page 104)

I got this recipe from one of my husband's co-workers. It's now a favorite of our family and friends.

> 1 cup butter *or* margarine, softened
> 2 cups sugar
> 3 eggs
> 6 tablespoons maraschino cherry juice
> 6 tablespoons water
> 1 teaspoon almond extract
> 3-3/4 cups all-purpose flour
> 2-1/4 teaspoons baking soda
> 3/4 teaspoon salt
> 1-1/2 cups (12 ounces) sour cream
> 3/4 cup chopped maraschino cherries, drained
> 3/4 cup chopped walnuts, toasted
> 3 squares (1 ounce *each*) unsweetened chocolate, melted

Confectioners' sugar, optional

In a mixing bowl, cream butter and sugar. Add the eggs, one at a time, beating well after each addition. Add the cherry juice, water and extract; mix well. Combine flour, baking soda and salt; add to creamed mixture alternately with sour cream. Mix just until combined. Divide batter in half. To one portion, add cherries and walnuts; mix well. To the second portion, add chocolate; mix well. Spoon half of the cherry mixture into a greased and floured 10-in. fluted tube pan. Cover with half of the chocolate mixture. Repeat layers. Bake at 350° for 1 hour and 15 minutes or until a toothpick inserted near the center comes out clean. Cool for 15 minutes; remove from pan to a wire rack to cool completely. Dust with confectioners' sugar if desired. **Yield:** 10-12 servings.

▪▪▪▪▪▪▪▪▪▪▪▪▪
BABY CHICK COOKIES

Phyllis Madonna, Cleveland, New York

(Pictured at far right)

When you serve these cookies, you won't hear a peep from guests—they'll be too busy gobbling up the sweet treats! I serve them to friends and family all the time.

1-3/4 cups all-purpose flour

▪▪▪▪▪▪▪▪▪▪▪▪▪
ANNIVERSARY ANGEL FOOD

Sarah Curci, San Jose, California

(Pictured above)

For my daughter's first birthday, I baked this cake— and I've been doing so every year since. Over 50 years later, she still looks forward to her special treat.

> 1 cup cake flour
> 1-1/2 cups sugar, *divided*
> 1-1/2 cups egg whites (10 to 12 large eggs)
> 1 teaspoon cream of tartar
> 1 teaspoon vanilla extract
> 1/2 teaspoon salt
> 2 cups whipping cream, whipped
> 6 tablespoons confectioners' sugar
> 1 teaspoon ground cinnamon
> 1/2 to 1 teaspoon ground ginger

Fresh *or* silk roses* and mint, optional

Sift flour and 3/4 cup sugar four times; set aside. In a mixing bowl, beat egg whites, cream of tartar, vanilla and salt on high speed until soft peaks form but mixture is still moist and glossy. Add remaining sugar, 2 tablespoons at a time, beating well after each addition. Sift flour mixture, a fourth at a time, over egg white mixture; fold gently, using about 15 strokes for each addition. Pour into an ungreased 10-in. tube pan. Bake at 325° for 40-45 minutes or until lightly browned and cracks feel dry. Immediately invert cake pan; cool completely. Remove to a serving plate. Combine cream, sugar, cinnamon and ginger; frost top and sides of cake. Decorate with roses and

1/2 cup plus 1 tablespoon butter *or*
  margarine, softened
1/3 cup sugar
3 egg yolks
12 drops yellow food coloring
TOPPING:
3 egg whites
Pinch salt
3/4 cup sugar
1 teaspoon ground cinnamon
1 teaspoon lemon juice
1-3/4 cups finely ground almonds
2 ounces white candy coating*
2 drops yellow food coloring
1 drop red food coloring

In a mixing bowl, combine flour, butter, sugar, egg yolks and food coloring. Beat on medium speed for 2 minutes. Knead mixture 3-4 times to form a ball. On a floured surface, roll out to 1/8-in. thickness. Cut with a chick-shaped cookie cutter. Place 1 in. apart on greased baking sheets. In another mixing bowl, beat egg whites and salt until soft peaks form. Gradually beat in sugar until stiff peaks form. Fold in the cinnamon, lemon juice and almonds. Place 2 teaspoons of topping on each chick, spreading to cover all but the beak and feet. Bake at 375° for 12-14 minutes or until lightly browned. Cool completely on wire racks. In a microwave or double boiler, melt candy coating. Stir in yellow and red food coloring to make orange; spread on beak and feet of each chick. **Yield:** 4 dozen (2-inch cookies). ***Editor's Note:** Dark, white or milk candy coating is found in the baking section of most grocery stores. It is sometimes labeled "almond bark" and is often sold in bulk packages of 1 to 1-1/2 pounds.

🔲🔲🔲🔲🔲🔲🔲🔲

Frosted Carrot Bars

Rita Pearl, Norwalk, Iowa

(Pictured at right)

Rich in flavor, these luscious bars are extra moist thanks to a secret ingredient—baby food!

2 cups sugar
1 cup vegetable oil
4 eggs
2 jars (6 ounces *each*) carrot baby food
2 cups all-purpose flour
2 teaspoons baking powder
2 teaspoons ground cinnamon
1 teaspoon baking soda
1 teaspoon salt
FROSTING:
1 package (8 ounces) cream cheese,
  softened

1/4 cup butter *or* margarine, softened
1 teaspoon vanilla extract
4 cups confectioners' sugar
Yellow, red and green liquid food coloring

In a mixing bowl, beat sugar, oil, eggs and carrots. Combine flour, baking powder, cinnamon, baking soda and salt; add to carrot mixture and mix well. Pour into a greased 15-in. x 10-in. x 1-in. baking pan. Bake at 350° for 20-25 minutes or until a toothpick inserted near the center comes out clean. Cool. In a mixing bowl, beat cream cheese, butter and vanilla. Blend in sugar until smooth. Place 1/4 cup of frosting in a small bowl; stir in yellow and red food coloring to make orange. Set aside. Place 3 tablespoons frosting in a small bowl; stir in green food coloring. Spread white frosting on cake. Cut a small hole in the corner of a pastry or plastic bag; fill with orange frosting. Mark off 20 squares on the cake; pipe a small carrot in the center of each square. Place green frosting in another bag; cut a small hole in the corner. Pipe greens on top of each carrot. **Yield:** 20 servings.

DELIVER your own goodies at Easter with springtime sweets like Baby Chick Cookies and Frosted Carrot Bars (shown below, top to bottom).

PECAN POUND CAKE

Fleta West, Hayes, Virginia

This cake always turns out great. It's wonderful with a steaming cup of coffee on a chilly winter day.

1-1/2 cups butter (no substitutes), softened
3-3/4 cups confectioners' sugar
  1 tablespoon vanilla extract
  6 eggs
2-1/2 cups all-purpose flour
  1/2 teaspoon salt
  1 cup flaked coconut
  2/3 cup chopped pecans, toasted

In a mixing bowl, cream butter and sugar; beat in vanilla until smooth. Add eggs, one at a time, beating well after each addition. Combine flour and salt; stir into creamed mixture just until combined. Add coconut and pecans. Pour into a greased and floured 10-in. tube pan; spread evenly. Bake at 325° for 60-65 minutes or until cake tests done. Cool in pan for 10 minutes; remove to a wire rack to cool completely. **Yield:** 12-16 servings.

HOLIDAY PEPPERNUTS

Chandra Koehn, Rich Hill, Missouri

(Pictured below)

We have many pecan trees in this part of the country, so I like to make recipes with the nuts. I usually make these cookies during the holidays.

  1 cup butter (no substitutes), softened
  4 cups packed brown sugar
  4 eggs
  1/4 teaspoon anise extract
  6 cups all-purpose flour
  1 tablespoon baking soda
  1 teaspoon cream of tartar

  1/2 teaspoon *each* ground allspice,
    cinnamon, cloves and ginger
  3 cups finely chopped pecans

In a mixing bowl, cream butter and brown sugar. Add eggs, one at a time, beating well after each addition. Add extract. Combine dry ingredients; gradually add to the creamed mixture. Add pecans; mix well. Shape dough into four 15-in. rolls; wrap in plastic wrap. Refrigerate overnight. Cut rolls into 1/4-in.-thick slices. Place 1 in. apart on ungreased baking sheets. Bake at 350° for 7-8 minutes or until golden brown. **Yield:** 20 dozen.

SESAME SEED COOKIES

Maxine Trively, Highlands, North Carolina

These are very special cookies served often in the South. They're perfect with tea or coffee. My whole family loves them.

1-1/4 cups butter (no substitutes), softened
  2 cups packed brown sugar
  1 egg
  1 teaspoon vanilla extract
  1 cup all-purpose flour
  1/2 teaspoon baking powder
  1/4 teaspoon salt
  1 cup sesame seeds, toasted

In a mixing bowl, cream butter and brown sugar; add egg and vanilla. Combine remaining ingredients; add to the creamed mixture. Drop by teaspoonfuls 2 in. apart onto greased baking sheets. Bake at 350° for 7-9 minutes or until golden brown. Cool on pan for 30 seconds before removing to a wire rack to cool completely. **Yield:** about 9 dozen.

TOFFEE NUT SQUARES

Anna Marie Cobb, Pearland, Texas

My mother passed along this yummy recipe. Her soft but chewy bars—packed with brown sugar, coconut and nuts—will be a hit at any party.

  1/2 cup butter *or* margarine, softened
  1/2 cup packed brown sugar
  1 cup all-purpose flour
  1/4 cup whipping cream
FILLING:
  1 cup packed brown sugar
  2 eggs
  1 teaspoon vanilla extract
  2 tablespoons all-purpose flour
  1 teaspoon baking powder
  1/4 teaspoon salt

Corn Puts the 'Pop' in Popular Cake

FLUFFY WHITE STUFF is the secret ingredient in Roberta Uhl's favorite holiday cake—but it's not the kind that falls from the sky in winter.

"This fun cake's made of popcorn," Roberta relates from her Summerville, Oregon country home. "It's sweetened with gumdrops and miniature marshmallows, so kids love it!

"When I was growing up, I used to spend Thanksgiving with an aunt and uncle. My aunt always put a plate of this cake by the back door. We youngsters grabbed a piece on our way out."

At right, Roberta shares her sticky-finger treat so you, too, can give your family a nice sweet surprise any time of year.

POPCORN CANDY CAKE

(Pictured at right)

1 package (16 ounces) miniature marshmallows
3/4 cup vegetable oil
1/2 cup butter *or* margarine
5 quarts popped popcorn
1 package (24 ounces) spiced gumdrops
1 cup salted peanuts

In a large saucepan, melt marshmallows, oil and butter until smooth. In a large bowl, combine popcorn, gumdrops and peanuts. Add marshmallow mixture and mix well. Press into a greased 10-in. tube pan*. Cover and refrigerate for 5 hours or overnight. Dip pan in hot water for 5-10 seconds to unmold. Slice cake with an electric or serrated knife. **Yield:** 16-18 servings. *Editor's Note: A one-piece tube pan is recommended.

1 cup flaked coconut
1 cup chopped nuts

In a mixing bowl, cream the butter and brown sugar. Stir in flour. Add cream, 1 tablespoon at a time, until a soft dough forms. Press into an ungreased 9-in. square baking pan. Bake at 350° for 15 minutes. Meanwhile, in a mixing bowl, combine brown sugar, eggs and vanilla; mix well. Add flour, baking powder and salt. Stir in the coconut and nuts. Spread over crust. Bake for 25-30 minutes or until a toothpick inserted near the center comes out clean. Cool before cutting. **Yield:** about 1-1/2 dozen.

STRAWBERRY JELLY ROLL

Jeanette Fuehring, Concordia, Missouri
This pretty jelly roll makes a wonderful dessert for summer or any time of year. It gets a head start with a convenient angel food cake mix.

✓ Uses less fat, sugar or salt. Includes Nutritional Analysis and Diabetic Exchanges.

1 package (16 ounces) angel food cake mix
1 quart fresh strawberries, sliced
1/4 cup sugar
4 cups nonfat whipped topping

Mix cake according to package directions. Spread batter into a greased and waxed paper-lined 15-in. x 10-in. x 1-in. baking pan. Bake at 375° for 15-17 minutes or until center of cake springs back when lightly touched. Turn onto a linen towel dusted with confectioners' sugar. Peel off waxed paper; roll up, jelly roll-style, starting with a short side. Cool on a wire rack. Combine strawberries and sugar; set aside. To serve, drain strawberries. Unroll cake; spread with half of the topping. Cover with the berries. Roll up again. Place on a serving plate, seam side down. Spread with remaining topping. Refrigerate for 30 minutes before serving. **Yield:** 10 servings. **Nutritional Analysis:** One serving equals 244 calories, 348 mg sodium, 0 cholesterol, 55 gm carbohydrate, 4 gm protein, trace fat. **Diabetic Exchanges:** 2 starch, 1-1/2 fruit.

▰▰▰▰▰▰▰▰▰▰▰▰
🎀 TUNNEL OF BERRIES CAKE

Shirley Noe, Lebanon Junction, Kentucky

(Pictured above)

This cake goes a long way. While it's not overly sweet or heavy, its rich taste makes just one piece satisfying. If your family doesn't care for strawberries, substitute peaches.

>   6 eggs, *separated*
>   3/4 cup water
>   1/2 cup vegetable oil
> 1-1/2 teaspoons vanilla extract, *divided*
> 2-1/4 cups cake flour
>   2 cups sugar, *divided*
>   1 tablespoon baking powder
>   1 teaspoon ground cinnamon
>   3/4 teaspoon salt
>   1/4 teaspoon cream of tartar
>   4 cups fresh whole strawberries, *divided*
> 2-1/2 cups whipping cream

In a small bowl, combine the egg yolks, water, oil and 1 teaspoon of vanilla; set aside. In a mixing bowl, combine flour, 1 cup sugar, baking powder, cinnamon and salt. Gradually add egg yolk mixture, beating just until smooth. In another mixing bowl, beat egg whites until foamy. Add cream of tartar; beat until soft peaks form. Fold into batter. Pour into an ungreased 10-in. tube pan. Cut through batter with a knife. Bake at 325° for 60-70 minutes or until top springs back when lightly touched and cracks feel dry. Immediately invert cake; cool completely. Remove from pan. Slice off the top 1/2 in. of the cake; set aside. With a knife, cut a tunnel about 1-1/2 in. deep in top of cake, leaving a 3/4-in. shell. Remove cake from tunnel and save for another use. Chop half of the strawberries; set aside. In a mixing bowl, beat whipping cream until soft peaks form. Gradually add the remaining sugar and vanilla, beating until stiff peaks form. Combine 1-1/2 cups cream mixture and chopped berries; fill the tunnel. Replace cake top. Frost cake with the remaining cream mixture. Refrigerate. Just before serving, cut the remaining strawberries in half and use to garnish the cake. **Yield:** 12 servings.

▰▰▰▰▰▰▰▰▰▰▰▰
FROSTED MAPLE COOKIES

Connie Borden, Marblehead, Massachusetts

Many people here in New England enjoy the flavor of maple in their recipes, and I love this adaptation of an old favorite.

>   1/2 cup shortening
> 1-1/2 cups packed brown sugar
>   2 eggs
>   1 cup (8 ounces) sour cream

1 tablespoon maple flavoring
2-3/4 cups all-purpose flour
1 teaspoon salt
1/2 teaspoon baking soda
1 cup chopped nuts
FROSTING:
   1/2 cup butter (no substitutes)
   2 cups confectioners' sugar
   2 teaspoons maple flavoring
   2 to 3 tablespoons hot water

In a mixing bowl, cream shortening and brown sugar. Add eggs, one at a time, beating well after each addition. Stir in sour cream and maple flavoring. Combine flour, salt and baking soda; add to the creamed mixture and mix well. Stir in nuts. Cover and refrigerate for 1 hour. Drop dough by rounded tablespoonfuls 2 in. apart onto greased baking sheets. Bake at 375° for 8-10 minutes or until edges are lightly browned. Cool on wire racks. For frosting, in a small saucepan, heat butter over low heat until golden brown. Remove from the heat; blend in confectioners' sugar, maple flavoring and enough water to achieve spreading consistency. Frost cookies. **Yield:** 4 dozen (2-1/2-inch cookies).

HOOSIER CRUMB CAKE

Linda Coleman, Eaton, Ohio

My husband and I live about 15 miles east of Indiana. I received this recipe years ago from a friend, but I'm not sure of its origins. Because of its name, I'm guessing it had its beginnings in the "Hoosier State".

   1/2 cup butter *or* margarine, softened
   2 cups packed brown sugar
   2 cups all-purpose flour
   1 egg, beaten
   1 cup buttermilk *or* sour milk*
   1 teaspoon vanilla extract
   1 teaspoon baking soda
   1/2 teaspoon salt
Whipped cream and fresh mint, optional

In a mixing bowl, cream butter and brown sugar. Add flour; mix until blended. Set aside 1/2 cup for topping. To the remaining mixture, add egg, buttermilk, vanilla, baking soda and salt; stir just until blended. Pour into a greased 13-in. x 9-in. x 2-in. baking pan. Sprinkle with the reserved flour mixture. Bake at 375° for 30-35 minutes or until a toothpick inserted near the center comes out clean. Cool on a wire rack. Garnish with whipped cream and mint if desired. **Yield:** 12-16 servings. ***Editor's Note:** To sour milk, place 1 tablespoon white vinegar in a measuring cup; add milk to measure 1 cup.

CRANBERRY DATE BARS

Mrs. Richard Grams
La Crosse, Wisconsin

(Pictured below)

I enjoy making this when the cranberry season arrives. It's very easy to put together, which is perfect for busy moms like me.

   1 package (12 ounces) fresh *or* frozen cranberries
   1 package (8 ounces) chopped dates
   1 teaspoon vanilla extract
   2 cups all-purpose flour
   2 cups quick-cooking oats
1-1/2 cups packed brown sugar
   1/2 teaspoon baking soda
   1/4 teaspoon salt
   1 cup butter *or* margarine, melted
ORANGE GLAZE:
   2 cups confectioners' sugar
   2 to 3 tablespoons orange juice
   1/2 teaspoon vanilla extract

In a saucepan, combine cranberries and dates. Cover and cook over low heat for 15 minutes or until berries pop, stirring often. Remove from the heat and stir in vanilla; set aside. In a bowl, combine flour, oats, sugar, baking soda and salt. Stir in butter until crumbly. Press half into an ungreased 13-in. x 9-in. x 2-in. baking pan. Bake at 350° for 8 minutes. Spoon cranberry mixture over the crust; spread gently. Sprinkle with remaining crumb mixture; pat down gently. Bake at 350° for 20-25 minutes or until golden brown. Cool. Combine glaze ingredients; drizzle over bars. **Yield:** 4 dozen.

MOCHA SHORTBREAD

Carolyn Van Boening, Blue Springs, Nebraska

Everyone seems to love the mocha flavor of these crispy wedges. For an added touch of sweetness, serve with ice cream and fruit or chocolate sauce.

1-1/4 cups all-purpose flour
1/3 cup sugar
2 tablespoons baking cocoa
1 teaspoon instant coffee granules, finely crushed
1/2 cup butter (no substitutes)

In a bowl, combine flour, sugar, cocoa and coffee. Cut in butter until mixture resembles fine crumbs. Form into a ball and knead for 2 minutes. On an ungreased baking sheet, pat dough into a 7-1/2-in. circle. Cut circle into 16 wedges (do not separate). Pierce each wedge several times with a fork. Bake at 325° for 25-30 minutes. Remove from oven; recut wedges. Cool for 5 minutes; remove from pan to a wire rack to cool completely. **Yield:** 16 servings.

BLACK WALNUT BUTTER COOKIES

Patsy Bell Hobson, Liberty, Missouri

(Pictured below)

This part of the "Show Me State" has an abundance of black walnuts, so these cookies certainly represent my region of the country. I created this recipe after a lot of experimentation…my family thinks they're a hit!

3/4 cup butter (no substitutes), softened
1 cup all-purpose flour

1/2 cup cornstarch
1/2 cup confectioners' sugar
1/2 cup chopped black walnuts *or* walnuts
Additional confectioners' sugar

In a mixing bowl, cream butter. Combine flour, cornstarch and sugar; add to butter and mix well. Stir in walnuts. Roll into 3/4-in. balls and place 1 in. apart on greased baking sheets. Bake at 300° for 20-25 minutes or until set. Cool on wire racks. Dust with confectioners' sugar. **Yield:** 6 dozen.

SWEET POTATO CAKE

Wanda Rolen, Sevierville, Tennessee

Just like my mom, I love to cook. I bake a lot for church dinners and homecomings, and many people have told me how much they like this cake.

1 cup vegetable oil
2 cups sugar
4 eggs
1-1/2 cups finely shredded uncooked sweet potato (about 1 medium)
1/4 cup hot water
1 teaspoon vanilla extract
2-1/2 cups self-rising flour*
1 teaspoon ground cinnamon
1 cup sliced almonds
FROSTING:
1/2 cup butter *or* margarine
1 cup packed brown sugar
1 cup evaporated milk
3 egg yolks, beaten
1-1/2 cups flaked coconut
1 cup sliced almonds
1 teaspoon vanilla extract

In a mixing bowl, beat oil and sugar. Add eggs, one at a time, beating well after each addition. Add sweet potato, water and vanilla; mix well. Combine flour and cinnamon; add to potato mixture. Stir in almonds. Pour into a greased 13-in. x 9-in. x 2-in. baking pan. Bake at 350° for 40-45 minutes or until cake tests done. For frosting, melt butter in a saucepan; whisk in brown sugar, milk and egg yolks until smooth. Bring to a boil over medium heat; boil gently for 2 minutes. Remove from the heat; stir in coconut, almonds and vanilla. Spread over warm cake. Cool on a wire rack. **Yield:** 12-15 servings. ***Editor's Note:** As a substitute for *each* cup of self-rising flour, place 1-1/2 teaspoons baking powder and 1/2 teaspoon salt in a measuring cup; add all-purpose flour to equal 1 cup. For 1/2 cup of self-rising flour, place 3/4 teaspoon baking powder and 1/4 teaspoon salt in a measuring cup; add all-purpose flour to equal 1/2 cup.

MERRY CHERRY BARS

Joan Wood, Shelton, Washington

These festive bars are an especially nice treat during the holidays.

- 1 cup all-purpose flour
- 3 tablespoons confectioners' sugar
- 1/2 cup cold butter *or* margarine
- 1 cup sugar
- 1/4 cup all-purpose flour
- 1/2 teaspoon baking powder
- 1/4 teaspoon salt
- 2 eggs, beaten
- 1 teaspoon vanilla extract
- 3/4 cup chopped nuts
- 1/2 cup flaked coconut
- 1/2 cup maraschino cherries, quartered

In a bowl, combine flour and confectioners' sugar; cut in butter until the mixture resembles coarse crumbs. Pat into a greased 11-in. x 7-in. x 2-in. baking pan. Bake at 375° for 10 minutes or until edges are lightly browned. Cool. In a bowl, combine sugar, flour, baking powder and salt. Add eggs and vanilla; mix well. Fold in nuts, coconut and cherries; spread over crust. Bake at 375° for 17-22 minutes or until lightly browned. Cool before cutting. **Yield:** 1-1/2 dozen.

LIGHT CHRISTMAS CAKE

Sandy Wood, Hiawassee, Georgia

Folks are pleasantly surprised to see the red and green layers when I cut them a slice of this light and festive cake.

✓ Uses less fat, sugar or salt. Includes Nutritional Analysis and Diabetic Exchanges.

- 1 package (.3 ounce) sugar-free raspberry gelatin
- 2-1/2 cups unsweetened applesauce, *divided*
- 1 package (.3 ounce) sugar-free lime gelatin
- 21 whole graham crackers (4-3/4 inches x 2-1/2 inches), *divided*
- 1 carton (8 ounces) light frozen whipped topping, thawed

In a bowl, combine raspberry gelatin powder and 1-1/4 cups of applesauce; mix well. In another bowl, combine lime gelatin powder and remaining applesauce; mix well. Place three graham crackers side by side on a plate. Cover with a third of raspberry-flavored applesauce. Top with three more crackers and a third of lime-flavored applesauce. Repeat layers twice; top with remaining crackers. Frost the top and sides with whipped topping. Refrigerate overnight. Cut into 1/2-in. slices. **Yield:**

16 servings. **Nutritional Analysis:** One slice equals 95 calories, 97 mg sodium, 0 cholesterol, 15 gm carbohydrate, 1 gm protein, 3 gm fat. **Diabetic Exchanges:** 1/2 starch, 1/2 fruit, 1/2 fat.

BLUEBERRY PUDDING CAKE

Jan Bamford, Sedgwick, Maine

(Pictured above)

My family loves blueberries, so I'm always looking for new ways to use them. This recipe is popular.

- 2 cups fresh *or* frozen blueberries
- 1 teaspoon ground cinnamon
- 1 teaspoon lemon juice
- 1 cup all-purpose flour
- 3/4 cup sugar
- 1 teaspoon baking powder
- 1/2 cup milk
- 3 tablespoons butter *or* margarine, melted

TOPPING:
- 3/4 cup sugar
- 1 tablespoon cornstarch
- 1 cup boiling water

Toss the blueberries with cinnamon and lemon juice; place in a greased 8-in. square baking dish. In a bowl, combine flour, sugar and baking powder; stir in milk and butter. Spoon over berries. Combine sugar and cornstarch; sprinkle over batter. Slowly pour boiling water over all. Bake at 350° for 45-50 minutes or until the cake tests done. **Yield:** 9 servings.

Homemade Cookies for the Holidays

HERE'S a tasty selection of cookies to fill your holiday serving trays and gift tins.

PINK PEPPERMINT COOKIES

Renee Schwebach, Dumont, Minnesota

The combination of cool peppermint and chocolate makes these treats irresistible.

> 1 cup butter (no substitutes), softened, *divided*
> 1/2 cup sugar
> 1 egg
> 10 to 12 drops red food coloring
> 3/4 teaspoon peppermint extract
> 2 cups all-purpose flour, *divided*
> 1/2 teaspoon baking soda
> 1/4 teaspoon cream of tartar
> 1/4 teaspoon salt
> 1 tablespoon chocolate syrup

In a mixing bowl, cream 3/4 cup butter and the sugar. Beat in egg, food coloring and peppermint extract. Combine 1-3/4 cups flour, baking soda, cream of tartar and salt; add to creamed mixture. Shape into a ball. Cover and chill for 1-2 hours. Meanwhile, in a bowl, combine chocolate syrup and remaining butter and flour; stir until well blended. Spoon into a pastry bag with a small round tip. Shape dough into 3/4-in. balls. Place on ungreased baking sheets; flatten into 1-1/2-in. circles. Pipe chocolate mixture on top of cookies in simple holiday designs. Bake at 375° for 5-7 minutes. Cool on wire racks. **Yield:** 4 dozen.

CASHEW SANDWICH COOKIES

Melissa Boder, Salem, Virginia

If your family and friends enjoy rich-tasting confections, these treats are bound to be a hit!

> 1 cup butter (no substitutes), softened
> 3/4 cup sugar
> 2 egg yolks
> 1/2 cup sour cream
> 1 teaspoon vanilla extract
> 1 teaspoon lemon juice
> 3 cups all-purpose flour

FILLING:

> 2 cups (12 ounces) semisweet chocolate chips
> 1/2 cup butter (no substitutes)
> 1 can (10 ounces) salted cashews, finely chopped

In a mixing bowl, cream butter and sugar. Add egg yolks, sour cream, vanilla and lemon juice; mix well. Add flour; mix well. Cover and chill for at least 2 hours or until easy to handle. On a floured surface, roll out dough to 1/8-in. thickness. Cut with a 2-in. round cookie cutter. Place 1 in. apart on ungreased baking sheets. Bake at 350° for 11-13 minutes or until edges are lightly browned. Cool on wire racks. For filling, melt chocolate chips and butter in a small saucepan. Remove from the heat; stir in cashews. Spread on the bottom of half of the cookies; top each with another cookie. Dust tops with confectioners' sugar. **Yield:** about 4 dozen.

SPICED CHERRY BELLS

Peggy Graving, Butte, Montana

I always bake up a batch of these cookies for the dessert buffet I host on Christmas Eve.

> 1 cup butter (no substitutes), softened
> 1-1/4 cups packed brown sugar
> 1/4 cup dark corn syrup
> 1 egg
> 1 tablespoon whipping cream
> 3-1/4 cups all-purpose flour
> 1 teaspoon ground ginger
> 1/2 teaspoon instant coffee granules
> 1/2 teaspoon baking soda
> 1/2 teaspoon salt

FILLING:

> 1/3 cup packed brown sugar
> 3 tablespoons maraschino cherry juice
> 1 tablespoon butter (no substitutes), softened
> 1-1/2 cups finely chopped pecans
> 14 maraschino cherries, quartered

In a mixing bowl, cream butter and brown sugar. Beat in corn syrup, egg and cream. Combine dry ingredients; gradually add to the creamed mixture and mix well. Cover and refrigerate dough for 2-4 hours or overnight. On a lightly floured surface, roll out dough to 1/8-in. thickness. Cut with a 2-1/2-in. cookie cutter. Place 2 in. apart on ungreased baking sheets. In a bowl, combine the first three filling ingredients; mix well. Stir in pecans. Place 1/2 teaspoon of filling in the center of each cookie. Shape into a cone by folding edges of dough to meet over filling; pinch edges together. Place a piece of cherry at open end of each bell for clapper. Bake at 350° for 12-15 minutes or until golden brown. Immediately remove to wire racks to cool. **Yield:** about 4-1/2 dozen.

CUTOUT SUGAR COOKIES

Sherry Taylor, Metropolis, Illinois

Decorating cookies with icing and candies is a Christmastime tradition for many families, including mine.

> 1 cup butter (no substitutes), softened
> 1-1/2 cups confectioners' sugar
> 1 egg
> 1 teaspoon vanilla extract
> 1/2 teaspoon almond extract
> 2-1/2 cups all-purpose flour
> 1 teaspoon baking soda
> 1 teaspoon cream of tartar

ICING:

> 1/2 cup butter (no substitutes), softened
> 1/2 cup shortening
> 1-1/2 teaspoons vanilla extract
> 1/4 teaspoon salt
> 5-1/2 cups confectioners' sugar
> 4 to 5 tablespoons milk

Food coloring

In a mixing bowl, cream butter and sugar. Add egg and extracts. Combine flour, baking soda and cream of tartar; gradually add to creamed mixture and mix well. Cover and chill for 2-3 hours or until easy to handle. On a floured surface, roll out dough to 1/4-in. thickness. Cut into desired shapes. Place 1 in. apart on greased baking sheets. Bake at 375° for 6-8 minutes or until the edges begin to brown. Remove to wire racks to cool completely. For icing, cream the butter and shortening in a mixing bowl. Add vanilla and salt. Gradually add the sugar, 1 cup at a time, beating well after each addition. Add milk; beat until light and fluffy. Tint icing with desired colors of food coloring; decorate the cookies. **Yield:** about 2-1/2 dozen (3-inch cookies).

BUTTERSWEETS

LeeAnn McCue, West Springfield, Massachusetts

(Pictured above)

With cream cheese, cherries and a sweet topping, these cookies are a family favorite we enjoy at Christmas—and year-round!

> 1 tube (18 ounces) refrigerated chocolate chip cookie dough
> 1 package (3 ounces) cream cheese, softened
> 3/4 cup confectioners' sugar
> 1/4 cup chopped maraschino cherries
> 1 drop red food coloring, optional
> 1/2 cup semisweet chocolate chips
> 2 tablespoons butter (no substitutes)

With a sharp knife, cut cookie dough into eight equal slices. Cut each slice into quarters; roll into balls. Place 2 in. apart on ungreased baking sheets. Bake at 375° for 10 minutes or until golden brown. Immediately make a deep impression in the center of each cookie using the back of a small melon baller or small spoon. Cool for 5 minutes; remove to wire racks to cool completely. Meanwhile, in a mixing bowl, cream the cream cheese and sugar. Pat cherries dry with paper towels. Stir cherries and food coloring if desired into creamed mixture. Place a teaspoonful of filling into the center of each cookie. In a heavy saucepan over low heat, melt chocolate chips and butter, stirring occasionally. Drizzle over cookies. Store in the refrigerator. **Yield:** 32 cookies.

ASPARAGUS BUNDT CAKE

Debbie Purdue, New London, Wisconsin

(Pictured below)

I served this unusual dessert at a ladies' luncheon at church several years ago…and everyone had to have a taste of "that green cake".

>   3 cups all-purpose flour
>   2 cups sugar
>   2 teaspoons baking soda
>   1 teaspoon ground cinnamon
>   1/2 teaspoon salt
> 1-1/2 cups vegetable oil
>   3 eggs, beaten
>   2 cups grated fresh asparagus (about 1 pound), drained
>   1 can (8 ounces) crushed pineapple, undrained
>   1 to 2 tablespoons grated orange peel
>   2 teaspoons vanilla extract
> 1-1/2 cups chopped pecans

ICING:
>   1 package (3 ounces) cream cheese, softened
> 2-3/4 cups confectioners' sugar
>   2 teaspoons grated orange peel
>   1 teaspoon vanilla extract
>   3 to 4 tablespoons milk

In a large bowl, combine the first five ingredients. Add oil, eggs, asparagus, pineapple, orange peel and vanilla; mix well. Fold in pecans. Pour into a greased and floured 10-in. fluted tube pan. Bake at 350° for 1 hour or until a toothpick inserted near the center comes out clean. Cool for 10 minutes; remove from pan to a wire rack to cool completely. For icing, beat cream cheese and sugar in a small mixing bowl until smooth. Add orange peel, vanilla and enough milk until icing reaches desired consistency. Spoon over cake, allowing icing to drip down sides. **Yield:** 16-20 servings.

SURPRISE SUGAR STARS

Joyce Berry, Sandpoint, Idaho

Come holiday time, I roll out dozens of these buttery cookies. The basic sugar cookie recipe is my mother's, and I came up with the sweet "surprise" inside.

>   1 cup butter (no substitutes), softened
> 1-1/4 cups sugar
>   2 eggs
>   1 teaspoon vanilla extract
>   4 cups all-purpose flour
>   2 teaspoons baking powder
>   2 teaspoons ground nutmeg
>   1 teaspoon baking soda
>   1/2 teaspoon salt
>   2/3 cup buttermilk
>   1 can (21 ounces) cherry pie filling

ICING:
>   2 cups confectioners' sugar
>   2 to 3 tablespoons milk
>   1/2 teaspoon almond extract

Colored sugar, optional

In a mixing bowl, cream butter and sugar. Add the eggs, one at a time, beating well after each addition. Stir in vanilla. Combine the dry ingredients; add to the creamed mixture alternately with buttermilk. Refrigerate for 2-3 hours or until easy to handle. On a floured surface, roll out dough to 1/4-in. thickness. Cut with 2-in. star cookie cutter or the cutter of your choice. Place half of the stars on ungreased baking sheets. Spoon 1-1/2 teaspoonfuls of pie filling into the center of each. Top with remaining stars. Pinch edges to seal; cut a small slit in top of each cookie. Bake at 350° for 12-15 minutes or until lightly browned. Cool on wire racks. For icing, combine confectioners' sugar, milk and extract in a bowl; whisk until smooth. Spread over cookies. Sprinkle with colored sugar if desired. **Yield:** 4 dozen.

CANDIED FRUIT COOKIES

Florence Monson, Denver, Colorado

These no-fuss drop cookies are both nutty and fruity, so they're always a hit at holiday time.

>   1/2 cup butter *or* margarine, softened
>   3/4 cup sugar
>   1 egg
> 1-1/4 cups all-purpose flour

1/2 teaspoon baking soda
1/2 teaspoon salt
1/2 teaspoon ground cinnamon
2-1/2 cups pitted dates, chopped
1/2 cup *each* chopped candied cherries and
   pineapple
3/4 cup coarsely chopped Brazil nuts,
   toasted
3/4 cup chopped almonds, toasted

In a mixing bowl, cream butter and sugar. Add egg; mix well. Combine flour, baking soda, salt and cinnamon; gradually add to the creamed mixture and mix well. Fold in fruits and nuts. Drop by teaspoonfuls 2 in. apart onto greased baking sheets. Bake at 375° for 8-10 minutes or until lightly browned. Cool on wire racks. **Yield:** 7 dozen.

FROSTED CRANBERRY DROP COOKIES

Shirley Kidd, New London, Minnesota

I started making these treats after tasting a batch my friend whipped up and have been baking them since.

1/2 cup butter (no substitutes), softened
1 cup sugar
3/4 cup packed brown sugar
1/4 cup milk
1 egg
2 tablespoons orange juice
3 cups all-purpose flour
1 teaspoon baking powder
1/2 teaspoon salt
1/4 teaspoon baking soda
2-1/2 cups chopped fresh *or* frozen
   cranberries
1 cup chopped walnuts
FROSTING:
1/3 cup butter (no substitutes)
2 cups confectioners' sugar
1-1/2 teaspoons vanilla extract
2 to 4 tablespoons hot water

In a mixing bowl, cream butter and sugars. Add milk, egg and orange juice; mix well. Combine flour, baking powder, salt and baking soda; add to creamed mixture and mix well. Stir in cranberries and nuts. Drop by tablespoonfuls 2 in. apart onto greased baking sheets. Bake at 350° for 12-15 minutes or until golden brown. Cool on wire racks. For frosting, heat butter in a saucepan over low heat until golden brown, about 5 minutes. Cool for 2 minutes; transfer to a small mixing bowl. Add sugar and vanilla. Beat in water, 1 tablespoon at a time, until frosting reaches desired consistency. Frost cookies. **Yield:** about 5 dozen.

CHRISTMAS SANDWICH CREMES

Janice Poechman, Walkerton, Ontario

(Pictured above)

These melt-in-your-mouth sandwich cookies have a scrumptious filling. I helped my sister make these in high school when she needed a project in her home economics class. She got an A+!

1 cup butter (no substitutes), softened
1/3 cup whipping cream
2 cups all-purpose flour
Sugar
FILLING:
1/2 cup butter (no substitutes), softened
1-1/2 cups confectioners' sugar
2 teaspoons vanilla extract
Food coloring

In a mixing bowl, combine butter, cream and flour; mix well. Cover and refrigerate for 2 hours or until dough is easy to handle. Divide into thirds; let one portion stand at room temperature for 15 minutes (keep remaining dough refrigerated until ready to roll out). On a floured surface, roll out dough to 1/8-in. thickness. Cut with a 1-1/2-in. round cookie cutter. Place cutouts in a shallow dish filled with sugar; turn to coat. Place on ungreased baking sheets. Prick with a fork several times. Bake at 375° for 7-9 minutes or until set. Cool on wire racks. For filling, in a mixing bowl, cream butter and sugar. Add vanilla. Tint with food coloring. Spread about 1 teaspoon of filling over half of the cookies; top with remaining cookies. **Yield:** 4 dozen.

BRING *any meal to a fabulous finish with these pleasing fruit and cream pies, puddings, candies and more.*

ELEGANT ENDINGS. Clockwise from top left: Strawberry Ice Cream (p. 121), Lemon Ladyfinger Dessert (p. 121) and Bittersweet Chocolate Cheesecake (p. 122).

Pies & Desserts

STRAWBERRY ICE CREAM

Leone Mayne, Frostproof, Florida

(Pictured at left)

I've made this ice cream often, and it comes out smooth and creamy every time.

     2 eggs
     2 cups milk
 1-1/4 cups sugar
     1 cup miniature marshmallows
     2 cups pureed unsweetened strawberries
     1 cup half-and-half cream
   1/2 cup whipping cream
     1 teaspoon vanilla extract

In a heavy saucepan, combine eggs and milk; stir in sugar. Cook and stir over medium-low heat until mixture is thick enough to coat a metal spoon and a thermometer reads at least 160°, about 14 minutes. Remove from the heat; stir in the marshmallows until melted. Set saucepan in ice and stir the mixture for 5-10 minutes or until cool. Stir in the remaining ingredients. Cover and refrigerate overnight. When ready to freeze, pour into the cylinder of an ice cream freezer and freeze according to manufacturer's directions. **Yield:** about 2 quarts.

LEMON LADYFINGER DESSERT

Katherine Buch, Waterford, New Jersey

(Pictured at left)

This pretty dessert is a delicious and light finale to any luncheon or dinner.

     1 package (3 ounces) lemon gelatin
     1 cup confectioners' sugar
     2 cups boiling water
     2 cups whipping cream
   1/2 teaspoon almond extract
     1 teaspoon grated lemon peel
     1 package (3 ounces) ladyfingers
 Lemon peel strips, optional

In a mixing bowl, dissolve gelatin and sugar in water; stir until completely dissolved. Refrigerate until syrupy, about 45 minutes. Add cream and extract; beat until it mounds slightly, about 10 minutes. Fold in lemon peel. Split ladyfingers and arrange upright around the edge of a 2-1/2-qt. serving bowl (about 8-in. diameter). Set aside any unused ladyfingers for garnish or another use. Pour cream mixture into bowl. Garnish with remaining ladyfingers and lemon peel strips if desired. Cover and refrigerate for 2-3 hours. **Yield:** 8-10 servings.

FRESH STRAWBERRY PIE

Florence Robinson, Lenox, Iowa

Whether I've served this pie at family meals or club luncheons, I have never met a person who didn't enjoy it. It is easy to prepare, tasty and very pretty.

   3/4 cup all-purpose flour
   1/2 cup quick-cooking oats
   1/2 cup chopped pecans
     2 tablespoons sugar
   1/8 teaspoon salt
   1/2 cup butter *or* margarine, melted
 FILLING:
   3/4 cup sugar
     2 tablespoons cornstarch
     1 cup water
     2 tablespoons light corn syrup
     2 tablespoons strawberry gelatin powder
     1 quart fresh strawberries
 Whipped cream, optional

In a bowl, combine the flour, oats, pecans, sugar and salt; stir in the butter until blended. Press onto the bottom and up the sides of a 9-in. pie plate. Bake at 400° for 12-15 minutes or until lightly browned. Cool on a wire rack. Meanwhile, combine sugar and cornstarch in a saucepan. Gradually add water and corn syrup; bring to a boil over medium heat. Cook and stir for 2 minutes. Remove from the heat; stir in gelatin until dissolved. Cool to room temperature. Arrange berries in the crust. Carefully pour gelatin mixture over berries. Refrigerate for 2 hours or until set. Serve with whipped cream if desired. **Yield:** 6-8 servings.

 ## HORN OF PLENTY PIE

Liz Fernald, Mashpee, Massachusetts

(Pictured above)

I've been making this pie for over 25 years, especially during the holidays. Since we live on Cape Cod, we have plenty of access to abandoned cranberry bogs.

✓ Uses less fat, sugar or salt. Includes Nutritional Analysis and Diabetic Exchanges.

1-1/2 cups sugar
1/3 cup water
3 cups fresh *or* frozen cranberries
1/2 cup raisins
1/2 cup chopped walnuts
1/2 cup chopped peeled tart apple
1 tablespoon butter *or* margarine
Pinch salt
1 unpricked pastry shell (9 inches), baked
MERINGUE:
3 egg whites
6 tablespoons brown sugar

In a large saucepan, bring sugar and water to a boil. Add cranberries, raisins, walnuts and apple; cover and simmer for 15 minutes, stirring occasionally. Stir in butter and salt. Spoon into pie shell. In a mixing bowl, beat egg whites until stiff peaks form; gradually beat in sugar. Pour over hot filling, sealing to edges of pastry. Bake at 325° for 20 minutes or until golden brown. Cool completely. Store in the refrigerator. **Yield:** 6-8 servings.

FLUFFY STRAWBERRY DESSERT

Linette Arnold, Simsbury, Connecticut

I've been a cake decorator for years but really enjoy taking it easy with a fabulous dessert like this one. It's very light and refreshing.

2 packages (10 ounces *each*) frozen sweetened strawberries, thawed
2-1/2 cups miniature marshmallows
1 cup chopped pecans
1 cup whipping cream
1 teaspoon vanilla extract

In a bowl, combine the strawberries, marshmallows and pecans. In a mixing bowl, beat cream and vanilla until stiff peaks form; fold into strawberry mixture. Spoon into dessert dishes. **Yield:** 8-10 servings.

BITTERSWEET CHOCOLATE CHEESECAKE

Amelia Gregory, Omemee, Ontario

(Pictured on page 120)

I'm a great-grandmother, and my whole family enjoys this dessert. I received this recipe from my niece. It's very chocolaty.

1 cup chocolate wafer crumbs
1/2 cup finely chopped toasted hazelnuts

1/3 cup butter *or* margarine, melted
3 packages (8 ounces *each*) cream cheese, softened
1 cup sugar
12 squares (1 ounce *each*) bittersweet baking chocolate*, melted and cooled
3 eggs
1 cup (8 ounces) sour cream
1-1/2 teaspoons vanilla extract
1/2 teaspoon almond extract
Pinch salt
GLAZE:
4 squares (1 ounce *each*) bittersweet baking chocolate*
1/4 cup whipping cream
1 teaspoon vanilla extract
Whipped cream and toasted chopped hazelnuts, optional

In a bowl, combine crumbs, hazelnuts and butter; press onto the bottom of an ungreased 9-in. springform pan. In a mixing bowl, beat cream cheese and sugar until smooth. Add chocolate; beat in eggs, one at a time. Stir in sour cream, extracts and salt; pour over the crust. Bake at 350° for 60-65 minutes or until the center is nearly set. Cool to room temperature. For glaze, melt chocolate and cream in a microwave or double boiler; stir until smooth. Add vanilla. Carefully run a knife between the cake and the sides of the pan; remove sides of pan. Spread glaze over top. Refrigerate overnight. Garnish with whipped cream and hazelnuts if desired. **Yield:** 16 servings.
*Editor's Note: Semisweet baking chocolate may be substituted for the bittersweet chocolate.

SPRING AND FALL PIE

Laura Collins, Rapid City, South Dakota

Every spring, I have a good crop of rhubarb in my garden, and one of my favorite ways to use it is in this pie. I adapted this version from a recipe I received from our county Extension service.

1-1/2 cups sugar
3 tablespoons all-purpose flour
1-1/2 cups diced fresh *or* frozen rhubarb, thawed and drained
1-1/2 cups fresh *or* frozen cranberries, halved
1-1/2 cups chopped peeled tart apples
Pastry for double-crust pie (9 inches)

In a large bowl, combine sugar and flour; stir in rhubarb, cranberries and apples. Line a 9-in. pie plate with the bottom pastry; add filling. Cover with a lattice crust; seal and flute edges. Bake at 450° for 10 minutes. Reduce heat to 350°; bake 40 minutes longer or until filling is bubbly. Cover

edges with foil to prevent overbrowning if necessary. **Yield:** 6-8 servings.

OAT-FASHIONED STRAWBERRY DESSERT

Linda Forrest, Belleville, Ontario

(Pictured below)

Thanks to this dessert, our house is a popular place in summertime. I make it for family get-togethers, picnics and potlucks, too. It's a treat on a breakfast or brunch buffet also. We like it best with whipped cream or a scoop of vanilla ice cream on top.

4 cups sliced fresh strawberries
1-1/4 cups whole wheat flour
1-1/4 cups quick-cooking oats
2/3 cup packed brown sugar
1/4 teaspoon baking soda
1/8 teaspoon salt
2/3 cup cold butter *or* margarine
2 tablespoons sugar
1/4 to 1/2 teaspoon ground cinnamon

Drain strawberries on paper towels; set aside. In a large bowl, combine flour, oats, brown sugar, baking soda and salt. Cut in butter until mixture resembles coarse crumbs. Reserve 1-1/2 cups for topping. Pat remaining crumb mixture into a greased 9-in. square baking pan. In a bowl, combine sugar and cinnamon; stir in strawberries. Spoon over the prepared crust. Sprinkle with the reserved crumb mixture. Bake at 350° for 35-40 minutes or until golden brown. Serve warm. **Yield:** 9 servings.

STRAWBERRY SHORTCAKE CUPS

Althea Heers, Jewell, Iowa

(Pictured below)

Back when store-bought shortcake was an unheard-of thing, my grandmother passed this recipe down to my mother. Mother later shared it with me...and I've since given it to my daughter.

> 1 quart fresh strawberries
> 4 tablespoons sugar, *divided*
> 1-1/2 cups all-purpose flour
> 1 tablespoon baking powder
> 1/2 teaspoon salt
> 1/4 cup cold butter *or* margarine
> 1 egg
> 1/2 cup milk
> Whipped cream

Mash or slice the strawberries; place in a bowl. Add 2 tablespoons sugar and set aside. In another bowl, combine flour, baking powder, salt and remaining sugar; cut in butter until crumbly. In a small bowl, beat egg and milk; stir into flour mixture just until moistened. Fill eight greased muffin cups two-thirds full. Bake at 425° for 12 minutes or until golden. Remove from the pan to cool on a wire rack. Just before serving, split shortcakes in half horizontally. Spoon berries and whipped cream between layers and over the top. **Yield:** 8 servings.

BUTTERMILK RAISIN PIE

John Ferren, Paris, Tennessee

Buttermilk is as common in the South as iced tea. This old-fashioned pie is just another fine way to cook with it. It's one of my favorites.

> 1-1/2 cups sugar
> 6 tablespoons cornstarch
> 1/4 teaspoon salt
> 3 egg yolks
> 3 cups buttermilk
> 3/4 cup raisins
> 3 tablespoons lemon juice
> 1 tablespoon butter *or* margarine
> 1 teaspoon vanilla extract
> 1 pastry shell (9 inches), baked
> **MERINGUE:**
> 3 egg whites
> 1/4 teaspoon cream of tartar
> 6 tablespoons sugar

In a saucepan, combine sugar, cornstarch and salt. Beat egg yolks and buttermilk; stir into the sugar mixture until smooth. Add raisins and lemon juice; cook and stir over medium heat until mixture comes to a gentle boil. Cook and stir 2 minutes longer. Remove from the heat; stir in butter and vanilla. Pour into pie shell. For meringue, beat egg whites and cream of tartar in a mixing bowl until soft peaks form. Gradually add sugar, beating until stiff peaks form. Spread over hot filling and seal to the edges. Bake at 350° for 12-15 minutes or until lightly browned. Store in the refrigerator. **Yield:** 6-8 servings.

STRAWBERRY YOGURT DESSERT

Ronda Hale, Minneapolis, Minnesota

This is the first recipe I always make after picking the season's first strawberries. My family loves its light, sweet taste.

> 1 can (14 ounces) sweetened condensed milk
> 1 cup (8 ounces) strawberry yogurt
> 2 tablespoons lemon juice
> 1 carton (8 ounces) frozen whipped topping, thawed
> 4 cups sliced fresh strawberries

In a large bowl, combine milk, yogurt and lemon juice; fold in whipped topping and berries. Chill until serving. **Yield:** 8-10 servings.

A Basket of Berry Secrets

• For shortcake or scones, I make a rich hot fudge strawberry filling with 1 cup warmed hot fudge topping and 1 cup sliced strawberries.
—*Mrs. Joe Miller Jr.*
Sugarcreek, Ohio

• The ladies of our church have an annual strawberry festival. One year, I baked several loaves of my favorite strawberry bread and paired them with a strawberry butter made from mashed berries, butter and confectioners' sugar. It was a big seller. —*Anna Higbee*
Absecon, New Jersey

• It's best to pick strawberries when they are firm and red. However, berries that are a little green will ripen if you leave them on the kitchen counter for a day.
—*Peggy Sue Ulrey*
Virginia Beach, Virginia

• When I make a glazed strawberry pie, I arrange the whole strawberries pointed ends up before spooning glaze over them. —*Kimberley Pleiman*
Newberry, Florida

• To make a pretty dessert perfect for guests, slice whole fresh berries in half, leaving the stem on. Spread softened fruit-flavored cream cheese between the halves and press the strawberries together, allowing some cream cheese to peek out. Then gently roll the cream cheese in finely chopped nuts.
—*Germaine Burm*
Wallaceburg, Ontario

• Using a pastry blender for mashing strawberries is much quicker than using a fork. —*Beverly Grubrich*
Novinger, Missouri

• To remove the stem and hull from fresh strawberries, I use a tomato corer. —*Julie Raines, Calhoun, Georgia*

• Since strawberries are fragile, use small shallow containers when picking to avoid crushing them.
—*Janice Pond*
Ludlow, New Brunswick

• When I want to quickly cut fresh strawberries into perfectly even slices, I use an egg slicer. —*Marsha Rutland*
Ovalo, Texas

• We use mashed or sliced berries sprinkled with sugar for shortcake. If the berries stand 20-30 minutes, they form their own juice. —*Frances Okroi*
Little Falls, Minnesota

• My children love my strawberry quick bread with a pretty spread that I make from cream cheese and strawberry syrup. I just drain and save the syrup from the frozen strawberries I use in the bread recipe.
—*Angie Wilson*
Montrose, Colorado

• At our pick-your-own strawberry farm, we remind customers not to forget to look under the leaves—that's where the best berries often hide!
The best way to pick strawberries is to pinch and twist the stems, leaving the hulls intact. —*Lois Cuff*
Hortonville, Wisconsin

• Berries will keep for up to a week if they are refrigerated unwashed and unstemmed in a loosely covered container. —*Mary Ann Brannen*
Lexington, South Carolina

Doubly Delicious Dipped Berries

NOTHING is sweeter than a ripe strawberry plucked direct from the patch. Well, *almost* nothing.

"I dip plump red berries in chocolate and vanilla chips," strawberry lover Marlene Wiczek from Little Falls, Minnesota notes.

Marlene passes along her recipe so you can serve the pretty striped strawberries if you like. They'll be the red, white and ooh center of attention at your place, too.

DIPPED STRAWBERRIES

1 quart medium fresh strawberries (with stems)

1-2/3 cups (10 ounces) vanilla baking chips

2 tablespoons shortening, *divided*

1 cup (6 ounces) semisweet chocolate chips

Wash strawberries and gently pat until completely dry. In a microwave or double boiler, melt vanilla chips and 1 tablespoon shortening. Dip each strawberry until two-thirds of the berry is coated, allowing the excess to drip off. Place on a waxed paper-lined tray or baking sheet; refrigerate for 30 minutes or until set. Melt chocolate chips and remaining shortening. Dip each strawberry until one-third is coated. Return to tray; refrigerate for 30 minutes or until set. **Yield:** 2-1/2 to 3 dozen.

GRANDMA'S LEMON PIE

Gwen Johnson, Medford, Oregon

This recipe comes from my Grandma Mapel, a true country woman from Iowa. Growing up to me meant going to Grandma's house on the farm and eating the best food ever. Her lemon pie is tops!

1-1/4 cups sugar
6 tablespoons cornstarch
2 cups water
3 egg yolks
3 tablespoons butter *or* margarine
1/3 cup lemon juice
2 teaspoons vinegar
1-1/2 teaspoons lemon extract
1 pastry shell (9 inches), baked
MERINGUE:
1/2 cup plus 2 tablespoons water
1 tablespoon cornstarch
3 egg whites
6 tablespoons sugar
1 teaspoon vanilla extract
Pinch salt

In a saucepan, combine sugar and cornstarch. Gradually add water. Cook and stir over medium-high heat until thickened and bubbly. Reduce heat to low; cook and stir for 2 minutes. Remove from the heat. Stir 1 cup of hot filling into egg yolks. Return all to pan and bring to a gentle boil. Cook for 2 minutes, stirring constantly. Remove from the heat. Stir in butter. Gently stir in lemon juice, vinegar and extract. Pour hot filling into pastry shell. For meringue, combine water and cornstarch in a saucepan until smooth. Cook and stir until thickened and clear, about 2 minutes. Cool completely. Meanwhile, beat egg whites in a mixing bowl until foamy. Gradually beat in sugar until stiff peaks form. Beat in vanilla and salt. Gradually add cornstarch mixture, beating well on high. Immediately spread over warm filling, sealing edges to pastry. Bake at 350° for 10-12 minutes or until the meringue is golden brown. Cool. Store in the refrigerator. **Yield:** 6-8 servings.

STRAWBERRY SWIRLS

Paula Steele, Obion, Tennessee

My mother-in-law's apple cobbler was the inspiration for my variation. It's our special spring treat—and it's amazing how many family members and friends "pop over" during strawberry season! Actually, though, any time is the right time to enjoy it.

- 2 cups sugar
- 2 cups water
- 1/2 cup butter *or* margarine, melted
- 1/2 cup shortening
- 1-1/2 cups self-rising flour*
- 1/2 cup milk
- 2 cups finely chopped fresh strawberries, drained

Whipped cream, optional

In a saucepan, combine sugar and water; cook and stir over medium heat until sugar is dissolved. Remove from the heat; allow to cool. Pour butter into a 13-in. x 9-in. x 2-in. baking dish; set aside. In a bowl, cut shortening into flour until mixture resembles coarse crumbs. Stir in milk until moistened. Turn onto a lightly floured surface; knead until smooth, about 8-10 times. Roll into a 12-in. x 8-in. rectangle; sprinkle with the strawberries. Roll up, jelly-roll style, starting with a long side; seal the seam. Cut into 12 slices. Place with cut side down over butter. Carefully pour syrup around rolls. Bake at 350° for 40-45 minutes or until golden brown and edges are bubbly. Serve warm with whipped cream if desired. **Yield:** 12 servings. *Editor's Note: As a substitute for the 1-1/2 cups of self-rising flour called for in this recipe, place 1-1/2 teaspoons baking powder and 1/2 teaspoon salt in a 1-cup measuring cup; add enough all-purpose flour to equal 1 cup. Then place 3/4 teaspoon baking powder and 1/4 teaspoon salt in a 1/2-cup measuring cup; add all-purpose flour to equal 1/2 cup.

Sweet Butter Tarts

Charlene Turnbull, Wainwright, Alberta

A friend of mine first introduced me to this easy recipe. I usually make six or eight batches at Christmas time.

Pastry for three single-crust pies
- 1/4 cup butter *or* margarine, softened
- 1 cup packed brown sugar
- 1 egg
- 2 tablespoons milk
- 1 teaspoon vanilla extract
- 1/4 teaspoon maple flavoring
- 1/2 cup raisins

Roll out pastry on a lightly floured surface; cut into twelve 4-in. circles. Press onto the bottom and up the sides of greased muffin cups. In a small mixing bowl, cream the butter and brown sugar. Add egg, milk, vanilla and maple flavoring. Stir in raisins. Fill each cup half full. Bake at

375° for 25 minutes or until crust is golden brown. **Yield:** 1 dozen.

Black-Bottom Ice Cream Pie

Mrs. Malvin Mauney Jr., Cordova, Tennessee

(Pictured below)

Since we live in an area where dairy farming flourishes, an ice cream pie seemed like a natural dish to create. It's an easy dessert to prepare anytime.

- 1-1/2 cups crushed gingersnaps (about 24 cookies)
- 1/4 cup confectioners' sugar
- 1/3 cup butter *or* margarine, melted
- 1 cup chocolate ice cream, softened
- 1 cup (6 ounces) semisweet chocolate chips
- 1/2 cup whipping cream
- 1/2 teaspoon vanilla extract
- 1 quart vanilla ice cream, softened

Combine the first three ingredients; press onto the bottom and up the sides of an ungreased 9-in. pie plate. Refrigerate for at least 30 minutes. Spoon chocolate ice cream into crust; freeze until firm, about 1 hour. Meanwhile, in a heavy saucepan, melt chocolate chips with cream over low heat, stirring constantly. Remove from the heat; add extract. Cool. Spread half of the chocolate sauce over chocolate ice cream; freeze until set, about 1 hour. Spoon vanilla ice cream over chocolate sauce; freeze until firm, about 1 hour. Spread remaining chocolate sauce evenly over pie; freeze for 4-6 hours or overnight. Remove from the freezer 5-10 minutes before serving. **Yield:** 6-8 servings. **Editor's Note:** This dessert takes time to make since each layer must be set before the next layer is added.

STRAWBERRY DESSERT SAUCE

B.G. Saelhof, Edmonton, Alberta

Topping off plain ice cream, cheesecake or pound cake is a dream with this fruity sauce. There's no cooking involved—you just mix the ingredients and serve.

1 pint fresh strawberries, hulled
3 tablespoons confectioners' sugar
2 tablespoons orange juice

Place strawberries in a food processor; cover and process until pureed. Add sugar and orange juice; mix well. Serve over ice cream or cheesecake. Store in the refrigerator. **Yield:** 1-1/2 cups.

BLACKBERRY DUMPLINGS

Maria Stuhlemmer, London, Ontario

(Pictured below)

I received this recipe from a native Indian lady. We've exchanged many tips and recipes over the years, and this dessert has become a favorite.

3 pints fresh *or* frozen blackberries*
1 cup sugar
3/4 cup water
1 tablespoon butter *or* margarine
DUMPLINGS:
1 cup all-purpose flour
5 teaspoons baking powder
5 teaspoons sugar
1/2 teaspoon salt
1 egg

1/3 cup milk
Cream *or* whipped cream, optional

In a 6-qt. kettle, combine blackberries, sugar, water and butter; bring to a boil. For dumplings, combine flour, baking powder, sugar and salt. In a bowl, beat egg and milk; stir in dry ingredients until a soft dough forms. Drop by tablespoonfuls onto boiling berry mixture. Reduce heat; cover and simmer for 15-20 minutes or until dumplings test done (do not lift the cover while simmering). Serve warm with cream if desired. **Yield:** 8 servings. ***Editor's Note:** Raspberries may be substituted for the blackberries.

CREAMY PASTEL MINTS

Janice Brady, Seattle, Washington

For a refreshing addition to your party fare, be sure to fix these easy-as-can-be candies. I use the mints for all sorts of occasions, including showers and birthdays.

1 package (3 ounces) cream cheese,
softened
3/8 teaspoon peppermint extract
1 drop red food coloring
1 drop blue food coloring
1 drop yellow food coloring
3 cups confectioners' sugar

Divide cream cheese into thirds; place in three small bowls. Stir 1/8 teaspoon mint flavoring and 1 drop of food coloring into each bowl. Gradually stir 1/2 cup sugar into each portion. Knead remaining sugar into each color until smooth. Roll out to 1/4-in. thickness. (No sugar or flour is necessary on the rolling surface.) Use 1-in. cookie cutters to cut out various shapes. Store tightly covered in the refrigerator. **Yield:** about 5 dozen.

ICY SUMMER TREATS

Darlene Markel, Sublimity, Oregon

This frozen snack, made from fruity gelatin and powdered soft drink mix, can be whipped up in no time. Our kids loved them when they were little. Now grown, they still request the treats when they visit.

1 cup sugar
1 package (3 ounces) cherry gelatin
1 package (.13 ounce) unsweetened
cherry soft drink mix
2 cups boiling water
2 cups cold water
10 disposable plastic cups (5 ounces)
Heavy-duty aluminum foil
10 Popsicle sticks

In a bowl, combine sugar, gelatin and soft drink mix in boiling water until dissolved. Add cold water. Pour into cups. Cover each cup with foil; insert sticks through foil (foil will hold sticks upright). Place in a 13-in. x 9-in. x 2-in. pan; freeze. To serve, remove foil and plastic cups. **Yield:** 10 servings. **Editor's Note:** Any flavor gelatin and soft drink mix may be used.

▰▰▰▰▰▰▰▰▰▰▰▰▰

SODA FOUNTAIN PIE

Marsha Hanson, Ponsford, Minnesota

(Pictured above)

The first time I made this pie was during winter, using frozen berries. It was a hit even then. For a change of pace, make it with an Oreo cookie crust.

1-1/2 cups crushed sugar cones (about 12)
1/2 cup butter *or* margarine, melted
1/4 cup sugar
3-1/2 cups fresh strawberries, *divided*
1 quart vanilla ice cream, softened
1/3 cup malted milk powder
1-1/2 cups fudge ice cream topping, softened
Additional strawberries, optional

Combine crushed sugar cones, butter and sugar. Press onto the bottom and up the sides of an ungreased 10-in. pie plate. Freeze. Place 3 cups of strawberries in a blender or food processor; cover and puree. Chop the remaining strawberries. Place pureed and chopped strawberries in a large bowl. Add ice cream and malted milk powder; stir

to blend. Pour into prepared crust. Cover and freeze overnight. Spread fudge topping over the pie to within 1 in. of edge; freeze for at least 2 hours. Remove from the freezer 20 minutes before serving. Garnish with additional berries if desired. **Yield:** 8-10 servings.

▰▰▰▰▰▰▰▰▰▰▰▰▰

STRAWBERRY MOUSSE

Julie Gesicki, Tracyton, Washington

I enjoy making this light and refreshing dessert for my husband and two young boys. They eat it up as fast as I can make it!

✓ Uses less fat, sugar or salt. Includes Nutritional Analysis and Diabetic Exchanges.

1 package (.3 ounce) sugar-free strawberry gelatin
1/2 cup boiling water
1 pint fresh strawberries, halved
1 cup (8 ounces) nonfat sour cream
1 cup fat-free vanilla ice cream
2 cups light whipped topping

Dissolve gelatin in water; place in a blender. Add strawberries; cover and puree until smooth. Add sour cream and ice cream; puree until smooth. Fold in whipped topping. Pour into a serving dish or individual dessert dishes. Cover and refrigerate for at least 2 hours. **Yield:** 10 servings. **Nutritional Analysis:** One 1/2-cup serving equals 86 calories, 45 mg sodium, 2 mg cholesterol, 14 gm carbohydrate, 3 gm protein, 2 gm fat. **Diabetic Exchanges:** 1 fruit, 1/2 fat.

ways make plenty of this delicious toffee to serve at Christmas and give as gifts.

1-3/4 cups finely chopped hazelnuts
1-1/2 cups sugar
1/2 cup water
1/3 cup light corn syrup
1 cup butter (no substitutes)
1/4 teaspoon salt
1/4 teaspoon baking soda
1/4 teaspoon orange extract
1 cup (6 ounces) semisweet chocolate chips

Place hazelnuts in a greased 15-in. x 10-in. x 1-in. baking pan. Bake at 300° for 15 minutes or until toasted; set aside. In a large heavy saucepan, combine sugar, water and corn syrup; bring to a boil over medium heat. Cover and boil for 2 minutes. Stir in butter; cook over medium heat, stirring occasionally, until mixture reaches 300° (hard-crack stage) on a candy thermometer. Remove from the heat; quickly stir in salt, baking soda, orange extract and 1-1/4 cups toasted hazelnuts. Pour onto a greased baking sheet and spread to 1/4-in. thickness. Let stand at room temperature until cool, about 1 hour. In a microwave or double boiler, melt chocolate chips; spread over toffee. Sprinkle with the remaining hazelnuts. Let stand for 1 hour. Break into bite-size pieces. **Yield:** 2 pounds.

PUDDING TEDDY BEARS

Sherry Bonner, Winnsboro, Louisiana

Figure some extra fun into this pleasingly creamy pudding—fill small graham cracker crusts with the treat, then fashion cute cub faces from cookies and candy. They'll be a hit with kids of any age!

1/2 cup sugar
1/4 cup baking cocoa
1/4 cup all-purpose flour
Dash salt
2 cups milk
2 eggs, beaten
1 tablespoon butter *or* margarine
1 teaspoon vanilla extract
8 individual graham cracker crusts
1 strip red shoestring licorice
1/2 cup flaked coconut, toasted
16 vanilla wafers
16 M&M's
8 red-hot candies

In a saucepan, combine sugar, cocoa, flour and salt. Gradually stir in milk until smooth. Add eggs; bring to a gentle boil, stirring constantly. Cook and stir over low heat for 2 minutes or until thickened. Remove from the heat; stir in butter and

STRAWBERRY MELON FIZZ

Teresa Messick, Montgomery, Alabama

(Pictured above)

Experimenting in the kitchen's fun for me. That's how I came up with this—I adapted it from two different recipes I got from friends.

2 cups sugar
1 cup water
5 fresh mint sprigs
1 quart fresh strawberries, halved
2 cups cubed honeydew
1-3/4 cups cubed cantaloupe
Ginger ale *or* sparkling white grape juice

In a saucepan, combine the sugar, water and mint; bring to a boil. Boil and stir until a candy thermometer reads 240° (soft-ball stage). Remove from the heat; allow to cool. Discard mint. Combine the strawberries and melon. Just before serving, fill tall glasses with fruit and drizzle with 1 tablespoon syrup. Add ginger ale to each. **Yield:** 8-10 servings.

HAZELNUT TOFFEE

Earlene Ertelt, Woodburn, Oregon

The Willamette Valley produces a lot of hazelnuts, so this recipe is truly representative of our area. I al-

vanilla. Spoon into crusts; refrigerate. Cut licorice into eight 1-in. pieces and eight 1/2-in. pieces; set aside. Just before serving, sprinkle coconut over pudding. Insert two vanilla wafers in each for ears. Add M&M's for eyes and a red-hot for nose. Bend 1-in. pieces of licorice into a semicircle; place 1/2 in. below nose for mouth. Connect nose and mouth with 1/2 in. pieces of licorice. **Yield:** 8 servings.

MAPLE RAISIN PUDDING

JoAnne Holmes, Ayers Cliff, Quebec

Quebec supplies 80% of the world's maple syrup, due to its large maple forests and ideal weather. My husband, Stanley, and I are veteran sugar makers who still do many things the old-fashioned way. For 6 weeks each spring, we tend to 8,000 tree taps in addition to the milk "spigots" on the 50 cows at our dairy farm.

   2 tablespoons butter *or* margarine,
      softened
 1/4 cup sugar
   2 eggs
1-1/2 cups all-purpose flour
   1 tablespoon baking powder
 1/2 teaspoon salt
 1/2 cup raisins
   1 cup milk
1-1/2 cups pure maple syrup
Whipping cream *or* ice cream, optional

In a mixing bowl, cream butter and sugar. Add the eggs, one at a time, beating well after each addition. Combine flour, baking powder, salt and raisins; add alternately with milk to creamed mixture. In a small saucepan, bring syrup to a boil; pour into a greased 1-1/2-qt. baking dish. Pour batter over hot syrup; do not stir. Bake, uncovered, at 375° for 30-35 minutes. Serve hot with cream or ice cream if desired. **Yield:** 6-8 servings.

MACAROON APPLE PIE

Frances Musser
Newmanstown, Pennsylvania

(Pictured at right)

I found this recipe in a rural newspaper years ago. It's become one of my favorite recipes. I like to serve it warm with vanilla ice cream.

1-1/2 cups all-purpose flour
 1/2 teaspoon salt
 1/2 cup shortening

   2 to 3 tablespoons cold water
FILLING:
   4 cups sliced peeled tart apples
 1/2 cup sugar
 1/4 teaspoon ground cinnamon
TOPPING:
 1/2 cup all-purpose flour
 1/2 cup sugar
 1/2 teaspoon baking powder
 1/4 teaspoon salt
   1 egg
   2 tablespoons butter *or* margarine, melted
 1/2 teaspoon vanilla extract
 1/4 cup flaked coconut

In a bowl, combine flour and salt; cut in shortening until crumbly. Gradually add cold water, tossing with a fork until a ball forms. Roll out pastry to fit a 9-in. pie plate; flute edges. Toss apples with sugar and cinnamon; pour into crust. Bake at 375° for 20 minutes. Meanwhile, combine the first four topping ingredients in a bowl. Stir in egg, butter and vanilla until smooth. Add coconut. Spoon over hot apples, carefully spreading to cover. Bake 30 minutes longer or until apples are tender. **Yield:** 6-8 servings.

Meals in Minutes

Give new meaning to the term "fast food" with six complete meals that can be made in half an hour or less.

Timely Teacher's Meal Makes The Grade

TIME FLIES when you have four young children. At least, that's the way it seems to Carolene Esayenko from Calgary, Alberta. "Unless it's my imagination," she grins, "our clock jumps from 8 a.m. to 4 p.m. in just a matter of minutes!"

Because of that, Carolene—who's a home-school teacher—relies on meals like this that take 30 minutes or less.

"My husband, Darren, loves it," she reports. "William, Amy-Lynn and Melissa enjoy it as well. And I'm sure that when he's a little older, our youngest, Matthew, will, too."

Instead of chicken breasts, Carolene suggests trying cut-up chicken or even browned turkey in her main dish. "It's also interesting," she notes, "to try different types of pasta or to substitute rice for the spaghetti.

"In summer," Carolene says, "I'll mix fresh tomato slices and vegetables from our garden in with the salad. I also experiment with different kinds of lettuce than romaine."

As to the dessert, "It leaves plenty of room for imagination," Carolene assures. "Chocolate sauce can replace the caramel…you can substitute your favorite nut topping…or you can create a mini sundae by serving the bananas along with scoops of ice cream."

CHICKEN SPAGHETTI SUPPER

6 boneless skinless chicken breast halves
  (1-1/2 pounds)
3 tablespoons vegetable oil, *divided*
1/2 cup julienned green pepper
1/2 cup sliced onion
2 garlic cloves, minced
1 can (14-1/2 ounces) Italian diced
  tomatoes, undrained
1 can (8 ounces) tomato sauce
1 jar (4-1/2 ounces) sliced mushrooms,
  drained
1 teaspoon Italian seasoning
1 teaspoon salt
1/2 teaspoon dried oregano
1/4 teaspoon pepper
4 to 6 cups cooked spaghetti

Cut chicken into 1/2-in. strips. In a large skillet, heat 2 tablespoons of oil; stir-fry chicken until no longer pink, about 6-8 minutes. Remove and keep warm; drain drippings. Add remaining oil to skillet; saute green pepper, onion and garlic until tender. Add tomatoes, tomato sauce, mushrooms and seasonings; bring to a boil. Return chicken to the pan and heat through. Serve over spaghetti. **Yield:** 4-6 servings.

SIMPLE CAESAR SALAD

6 cups torn romaine
1/2 cup Caesar croutons
2 bacon strips, cooked and crumbled
1/4 cup grated *or* shredded Parmesan cheese
1/3 cup Caesar salad dressing

In a large bowl, combine romaine, croutons, bacon and cheese. Add dressing; toss to coat. **Yield:** 4-6 servings.

CARAMEL BANANA DESSERT

4 medium firm bananas, sliced
4 to 6 tablespoons caramel ice cream
  topping
4 to 6 tablespoons chopped pecans
Whipped topping, optional

Place the bananas in individual serving dishes. Top with caramel topping and pecans. Garnish with whipped topping if desired. **Yield:** 4-6 servings.

Speedy Supper Saves Time For Family

FOR Leann Jasper of Newmarket, Ontario, family time's worth planning for. And no one complains when the planning includes this speedy meal that has become a standby in her kitchen.

"My husband, John, and I have two children—Alisha and Levi," she says. "After a day of school and work, we like to take walks around the nearby nature preserve or maybe go skating together.

"That kind of family time is much more enjoyable than waiting for supper to be ready."

Leann serves this satisfying supper once or twice a month. "The hamburger entree came from my mother, who is a real down-to-earth country cook," she reports. "Because it calls for a can of soup, there's no fussing. The filling can also double as a flavorful baked potato topping.

"The pea salad is also a recipe from Mom. I like that there's not much chopping involved. Plus, what needs cutting can be done ahead.

"Vary the type of nuts to suit your family's taste," Leann suggests. "Or mix in your favorite fresh-from-the-garden chopped vegetables.

"The basis of the cake was in a local church cookbook. Using purchased sponge cakes eliminates the baking step. And the instant pudding topping sets up in no time at all."

Leann's cake can easily be adapted to a fancy one. "Just cut it into serving-size pieces," she advises. "Then you can spoon them into clear glass dishes to simulate a trifle.

"For taste variety, use banana pudding—or another favorite flavor—in place of the vanilla on occasion."

SLOPPY JOE BURGERS

1 pound ground beef
2 tablespoons all-purpose flour
1 can (10-1/2 ounces) condensed French onion soup, undiluted
1/4 teaspoon Worcestershire sauce
6 hamburger buns, split and toasted

In a skillet, brown the beef; drain. Stir in flour, soup and Worcestershire sauce. Bring to a boil over medium heat; boil and stir for 2 minutes. Serve on buns. **Yield:** 6 servings.

CRUNCHY PEA SALAD

1 package (16 ounces) frozen peas, thawed
1 cup chopped cauliflower
1 cup diced celery
1 cup slivered almonds
1/4 cup sliced green onions
1 cup ranch salad dressing
1/2 cup sour cream
1/2 teaspoon dill weed
1/4 teaspoon salt
1/8 teaspoon pepper
Lettuce leaves, optional

In a large bowl, combine the peas, cauliflower, celery, almonds, onions, salad dressing, sour cream, dill weed, salt and pepper. Cover and chill until serving. Serve on lettuce if desired. **Yield:** 6-8 servings.

CREAMY PINEAPPLE CAKE

5 individual cream-filled sponge cakes, split in half lengthwise *or* 7 slices pound cake (about 3/4 inch thick)
1 can (20 ounces) crushed pineapple, drained
1-1/2 cups cold milk
1 package (3.4 ounces) instant vanilla pudding mix
2 cups whipped topping, *divided*
1/2 cup chopped walnuts

Place cake in an ungreased 11-in. x 7-in. x 2-in. dish. Top with pineapple; cover and set aside. In a bowl, beat milk and pudding mix until smooth. Fold in 1/2 cup whipped topping; pour over pineapple. Spread remaining whipped topping over pudding. Sprinkle with nuts. Chill until serving. **Yield:** 6-8 servings.

LESS SLOPPY JOES

Want to serve your family sloppy joes in a way that's not quite so sloppy?

Purchase unsliced buns instead of precut hamburger buns. Cut off the top quarter of each bun and hollow out the bottom portion. Spoon in the sloppy joe filling and replace the top. Eat with a knife and fork.

Pleasing Pork Chop Dinner Made Pronto

SUPPERTIME can sort of sneak up on Kenna Robinson of Sault Ste. Marie, Ontario.

The day care she runs at home ends just about in time for her to pick up her daughter, Whitney, and son, Grant, then chauffeur them to their after-school activities.

On top of that, her husband Jeff's job can have him out hunting a water main break at almost any time of day. So Kenna relies on fast fare, including this timely menu which can be made in under 30 minutes.

"I came up with the main dish simply by substituting pork for veal," she reports. The pork chops can be served with the sauce only or over a bed of egg noodles or spaghetti. "You can also adapt the recipe for boneless skinless chicken breasts," Kenna suggests.

"My salad started as a Caesar—but I ran out of ingredients! It tastes good with nearly any kind of dressing," Kenna says. "If you'd like, feel free to substitute other kinds of chopped vegetables and salad accents...along with a mixture of leaf lettuce.

"The mother of my shortcake recipe was necessity. I needed a quick way to use the bounty of wild berries that we picked on a family camping trip one summer.

"Occasionally, I'll replace the angel food called for in the dessert with whatever leftover cake I happen to have on hand. Sometimes, I've even used brownies. That chocolaty version tastes similar to Black Forest cake.

"This made-in-minutes meal can make a special lunch as well. I prepare it at least twice a month. Not only is it a big family favorite, I've also served it to company—then passed the recipes to other on-the-run moms."

▪▪▪▪▪▪▪▪▪▪▪▪▪▪
PORK PARMESAN

1/2 cup dry bread crumbs
1/4 cup grated Parmesan cheese
1/4 teaspoon salt
1/8 teaspoon pepper
1/8 teaspoon paprika
 1 egg

6 boneless pork loin chops (3/8 inch thick)
2 tablespoons vegetable oil
1/2 cup tomato sauce
6 slices mozzarella cheese

In a shallow bowl, combine the bread crumbs, Parmesan cheese, salt, pepper and paprika. In another bowl, beat egg. Dip each pork chop in egg, then coat with crumb mixture. In a skillet, cook pork chops in oil over medium heat for 6 minutes on each side or until juices run clear. Top each chop with tomato sauce and cheese; cover and simmer for 1 minute or until cheese is melted. **Yield:** 6 servings. **Editor's Note:** To prepare this recipe in a microwave, place breaded pork chops on a microwave-safe plate. (Omit oil.) Microwave on high for 4 minutes. Rotate plate and microwave 4 minutes longer or until juices run clear. Top each chop with tomato sauce and cheese; microwave for 1-2 minutes or until cheese is melted. This recipe was tested using a 700-watt microwave.

▪▪▪▪▪▪▪▪▪▪▪▪▪▪
FAMILY FAVORITE SALAD

1/4 cup vegetable oil
 1 garlic clove, minced
1/4 teaspoon salt
1/8 teaspoon pepper
 1 medium bunch romaine, torn
1/2 cup chopped cucumber
1/2 cup sliced celery
 2 tablespoons grated Parmesan cheese
 1 cup seasoned croutons

In a jar with a tight-fitting lid, combine oil, garlic, salt and pepper; shake well. In a large bowl, combine romaine, cucumber, celery, cheese and croutons. Just before serving, add dressing and toss to coat. **Yield:** 6 servings. **Editor's Note:** This salad dressing does not contain vinegar.

▪▪▪▪▪▪▪▪▪▪▪▪▪▪
SHORTCAKE SUPREME

2-1/4 cups fresh *or* frozen blueberries *and/or* raspberries, thawed
 2 to 3 tablespoons sugar
 1 envelope whipped topping mix
12 thin slices angel food cake

In a bowl, combine berries and sugar; set aside. Prepare the whipped topping mix according to package directions. To serve, top angel food cake slices with berries and whipped topping. **Yield:** 6 servings.

Summer Menu Sets the Table For Good Eating

SETTING the table takes a good deal of Nanci Keatley's time each summer. So the Salem, Oregon cook makes sure getting good wholesome meals on it doesn't.

"I'm supervisor of our county fair's table-setting competition," she explains. "Plus I home-school our four children—Carissima, Joshua, David and Mary Katherine.

"I volunteer at church, too…and serve meals around my husband Brian's unpredictable work schedule as a carpenter."

The 30-minute menu here is one that Nanci calls on as often as every week.

"It's good year-round—for lunch, dinner or a late-night supper," she says. "When it's construction season, Brian may work until sundown. This meal's one that I can serve early to our kids and again later when he gets home.

"But I've also made it for a ladies' luncheon I hosted here…and the trifle is a mainstay on my potluck list."

Nanci suggests chicken breast and roast beef as other possible fillings for the sub sandwiches. "A kaiser or hard onion roll could replace the French bread," she shares. And a mellow Monterey Jack or Muenster could be substituted as the cheese.

"With the salad," Nanci notes, "spinach or another dark-green leaf lettuce works as well as the romaine." Meanwhile, the oil and vinegar can be replaced by an oil-based honey French dressing or a honey mustard or poppy seed dressing.

"For the trifle, if fresh berries are not available, the quick-frozen varieties will do—as will peaches or nectarines," she explains.

"It's a simple-to-make sweet perfect for summer. But we enjoy it so much, I make it all year."

ITALIAN SUBS

1 loaf (8 ounces) French bread
6 slices mozzarella cheese, *divided*
12 thin slices fully cooked ham *or* turkey
1 medium tomato, thinly sliced
1 tablespoon olive *or* vegetable oil
2 teaspoons cider *or* red wine vinegar
2-1/2 teaspoons dried basil

1/8 teaspoon pepper
1/8 teaspoon dried rosemary, crushed

Cut bread in half horizontally; set top aside. Place three slices of cheese on bottom half; layer with ham and tomato. Combine oil, vinegar, basil, pepper and rosemary; drizzle over tomato. Top with remaining cheese. Broil 4 in. from the heat for 2-3 minutes or until cheese is melted. Replace bread top. Cut into four pieces; serve immediately. **Yield:** 4 servings.

ORANGE ROMAINE SALAD

8 cups torn romaine
1 can (11 ounces) mandarin oranges, drained *or* 2 medium oranges, peeled and sliced
1 cup thinly sliced red onion
1/4 cup cider *or* red wine vinegar
3 tablespoons olive *or* vegetable oil
1 tablespoon minced fresh parsley
1 garlic clove, minced
Salt and pepper to taste

In a large bowl, combine romaine, oranges and onion. Combine vinegar, oil, parsley, garlic, salt and pepper; pour over salad and toss to coat. Serve immediately. **Yield:** 4-6 servings.

LEMON BERRY TRIFLE

5 cups cubed angel food cake
1 carton (8 ounces) lemon yogurt
1 cup whipped topping, *divided*
3 cups mixed fresh berries
Lemon peel, optional

Place cake cubes in a 2-qt. serving bowl or individual dishes. Combine yogurt and 3/4 cup whipped topping; spoon over cake. Top with berries. Garnish with remaining whipped topping and lemon peel if desired. **Yield:** 4-6 servings.

FREEZING FRESH BERRIES

Wash whole ripe berries. When dry, lay them on baking sheets liked with waxed paper and freeze until firm. Transfer to heavy-duty freezer bags and return them to the freezer. Berries may be frozen for up to 9 months.

Fast and Flavorful Food Gets Family's Vote

THERE'S no question about the kind of cooking Elizabeth Montgomery of Taylorville, Illinois, casts her vote for.

Her husband, Jim, is mayor of their town of 12,000—which includes the Montgomerys' Ellie, Maddie and Evan. "Between his meetings and our family commitments," Elizabeth comments, "we frequently have to squeeze in mealtimes. Menus that take half an hour or less are a necessity."

The one that she shares here is such a fast favorite Elizabeth serves it to her clan at least twice a month. "If Jim has an evening obligation," she notes, "we can still all eat together and discuss our day before he has to leave. Family time like that is a priority for all of us."

The biscuit squares get a head start with biscuit/baking mix and canned tuna. "Instead of the American cheese," suggests Elizabeth, "consider topping your tuna squares with slices of Swiss cheese or with shredded cheese."

The salad, she says, can be varied also by substituting your family's favorite greens for the spinach. "If you're really pressed for time, a bottled spinach dressing should work nicely besides."

As for the banana dish, "It can be prepared with walnuts, honey-roasted peanuts or another nutty topping," relays Elizabeth. "And the mayonnaise and the sugar could be replaced by a salad dressing or plain yogurt. Either way, it's an easy way to dress up bananas."

TUNA BISCUIT SQUARES

2/3 cup milk
1/3 cup mayonnaise
1/3 cup ranch salad dressing
4 cups biscuit/baking mix
2 cans (6-1/2 ounces *each*) tuna, drained and flaked
1/3 cup chopped celery
3 tablespoons finely chopped onion
2 tablespoons sweet pickle relish
1/4 teaspoon garlic powder
6 to 8 slices process American cheese
Tomato slices, optional

In a large bowl, combine milk, mayonnaise and salad dressing. Add biscuit mix; mix until blended. On a lightly floured surface, knead dough 5-8 times. Pat into a greased 13-in. x 9-in. x 2-in. baking pan. Bake at 450° for 12-15 minutes or until lightly browned. Meanwhile, combine tuna, celery, onion, relish and garlic powder. Spread over crust; top with cheese. Bake for 4 minutes or until cheese is melted. Garnish with tomato if desired. **Yield:** 6 servings.

WARM SPINACH SALAD

2 garlic cloves, minced
1/4 cup olive *or* vegetable oil
3 tablespoons cider *or* red wine vinegar
1/2 teaspoon salt
1/8 teaspoon pepper
2 packages (10 ounces *each*) fresh spinach, torn
Hard-cooked eggs and seasoned croutons, optional

In a Dutch oven, saute garlic in oil for 1-2 minutes. Remove from the heat; cool slightly. Stir in vinegar, salt and pepper. Add spinach and toss to coat. Place on plates or in bowls; top with eggs and croutons if desired. Serve immediately. **Yield:** 6 servings.

NUTTY BANANAS

3 medium ripe bananas
1/3 cup mayonnaise
1-1/2 teaspoons sugar
1/2 cup chopped pecans

Slice bananas in half lengthwise; cut each piece in half. Spread with mayonnaise; sprinkle with sugar and nuts. Serve immediately. **Yield:** 6 servings.

SALAD DRESSING SUGGESTIONS

Always dress salad greens just before serving so they won't become soggy. Don't overdress your salads. Too much dressing will weigh down the ingredients and mask their flavor. The dressing should highlight, not overpower, the salad ingredients.

Elegant Entree Makes Holiday Entertaining Easy

AS a minister's wife and home-school teacher, Hope Meece of Fowler, Indiana knows how important a family-filling fast meal can be. So she's happy to share her favorite made-in-30-minutes dinner with others.

"Frequently," she says, "4 days out of the week have church commitments for my husband, David, me and our six children—Daniel, Ashley, Timothy, Melissa, Stephen and Philip. Plus, we have chickens, a garden and fruit trees, too. I serve this meal at least monthly."

Especially around the holidays, it can be a lifesaver for her. "In addition to planning our own celebration," Hope notes, "I help out with the church Christmas party…and I sew costumes for our Nativity play besides."

Hope suggests varying her chicken with different kinds of cheeses—Monterey Jack or cheddar, for example—and replacing the ham with a favorite cold cut.

"The green beans can complement meat and fish, too," she reports. "I like to serve them at our church steak dinner." A smattering of onions can be used to pep up the mild flavor of the beans.

Spiced carrots would be a mouth-watering companion in the pan to the mushrooms, according to Hope.

Sundae options include substituting another pie filling—such as blueberry—for the cherry. Nuts, sprinkles and graham cracker crumbs could also be dusted across the top if you'd like.

Broiled Chicken Cordon Bleu

    4 boneless skinless chicken breast halves
1/4 cup butter *or* margarine, melted
    4 thin slices fully cooked ham
    4 tablespoons honey-Dijon salad dressing
    4 thin slices Swiss *or* mozzarella cheese

Place chicken on the rack of a broiler pan. Broil 4 in. from the heat for 3 minutes; turn and broil 3 minutes on the other side. Brush with butter. Continue turning and basting until juices run clear, about 4 minutes. Place a ham slice on each chicken breast; broil for 1-2 minutes. Spread 1 tablespoon dressing over each; top with cheese.

Broil for 30 seconds or until cheese is melted. **Yield:** 4 servings.

French-Style Green Beans

1/3 cup slivered almonds
    3 tablespoons butter *or* margarine
    1 package (10 ounces) frozen French-style green beans, thawed
1/4 teaspoon salt

In a skillet, saute almonds in butter for 1-2 minutes or until lightly browned. Add beans and salt; cook and stir for 1-2 minutes or until heated through. **Yield:** 4 servings.

Sauteed Mushrooms

1/4 cup butter *or* margarine
    1 pound fresh mushrooms, sliced
    1 tablespoon lemon juice
    1 tablespoon soy sauce

In a skillet, melt butter. Add mushrooms, lemon juice and soy sauce. Saute for 6-8 minutes or until mushrooms are tender. **Yield:** 4 servings.

Cherry Cheesecake Sundaes

    1 cup cherry pie filling
    2 teaspoons almond extract, *divided*
    1 package (3 ounces) cream cheese, softened
1/4 cup confectioners' sugar
    1 tablespoon milk
Vanilla ice cream

In a small bowl, combine the pie filling and 1 teaspoon extract; set aside. In a small mixing bowl, beat the cream cheese, sugar, milk and remaining extract. Spoon ice cream into four dessert dishes; top with cream cheese and cherry mixtures. **Yield:** 4 servings.

Poultry Pointer

Boneless skinless chicken breast halves should be placed 4 inches from the broiler's heat source to prevent burning the top before the inside is done.

Our Most Memorable Meals

*Individual cooks share family-favorite recipes that
we combined for unforgettable meals you'll surely savor.*

Popular Foods From the Past Still a Hit Today

FOODS that appeared on the dinner table years ago can still be real family-pleasers today.

"The recipe for Barbecued Round Steak came from a 1950s television program called *Kay's Kitchen*," shares Ray Sholes of Butler, Pennsylvania. "I gave it a try, and my family gave it rave reviews. It makes a colorful entree served with fresh green beans."

"I've been sharing the recipe for Favorite Cabbage Salad for over 45 years!" proclaims Jenison, Michigan cook Edna Culbertson. "It's easy to make and is great to take along for potlucks."

Dorothy Lama of Lindsay, California found pretty Baked Calico Rice in a salad oil ad in the *Ladies' Home Journal* back in 1948. "It's still a favorite not only for its good taste, but for its simplicity of preparation," says Dorothy.

Apples are a favorite ingredient of Leona Pecoraro of Ravenden, Arkansas. "I make 'apple everything' in fall when the new crop is in," states Leona. "I was happy to add delicious Apple Walnut Squares to my recipe file."

BARBECUED ROUND STEAK

✓ Uses less fat, sugar or salt. Includes Nutritional Analysis and Diabetic Exchanges.

        3 tablespoons all-purpose flour
    1/2 teaspoon salt, optional
    1/2 teaspoon pepper
1-1/2 pounds round steak, cut into four pieces
        4 teaspoons vegetable oil
    1/2 cup chopped celery
    1/2 cup chopped onion
        1 garlic clove, minced
        1 can (10-3/4 ounces) condensed tomato soup, undiluted
        3 tablespoons brown sugar
        2 tablespoons Worcestershire sauce
        1 tablespoon vinegar
        2 teaspoons prepared mustard

In a shallow bowl, combine flour, salt if desired and pepper; dredge the meat. In a large skillet, brown meat on both sides in oil. Remove and keep warm. In the pan drippings, saute celery, onion and garlic for 3-4 minutes. Combine soup, brown sugar, Worcestershire sauce, vinegar and mustard; stir into the vegetables. Return meat to the pan. Cover and simmer for 1-1/2 to 2 hours or until meat is tender. **Yield:** 4 servings. **Nutritional Analysis:** One serving (prepared without salt) equals 374 calories, 735 mg sodium, 95 mg cholesterol, 28 gm carbohydrate, 38 gm protein, 12 gm fat. **Diabetic Exchanges:** 4 lean meat, 1-1/2 starch, 1 vegetable.

FAVORITE CABBAGE SALAD

        1 small head cabbage, shredded
    1/2 cup chopped green pepper
    1/2 cup chopped onion
        3 tablespoons mayonnaise
        2 tablespoons vinegar
        1 tablespoon sugar
    1/4 teaspoon salt
        4 bacon strips, cooked and crumbled

In a large bowl, combine cabbage, green pepper and onion. In a small bowl, combine mayonnaise, vinegar, sugar and salt. Pour over cabbage mixture and toss to coat. Cover and refrigerate for at least 4 hours. Stir in bacon just before serving. **Yield:** 6-8 servings.

BAKED CALICO RICE

        1 can (28 ounces) diced tomatoes, undrained

1 cup chopped onion
1 cup chopped celery
3/4 cup chopped green pepper
2/3 cup uncooked long grain rice
1/3 cup vegetable oil
1 bay leaf
1 to 2 teaspoons salt
1/4 teaspoon pepper

In a 2-qt. baking dish, combine ingredients; mix well. Cover and bake at 350° for 1 to 1-1/4 hours or until rice is tender, stirring occasionally. Discard bay leaf before serving. **Yield:** 4-6 servings.

APPLE WALNUT SQUARES

1/2 cup shortening
1 cup sugar

1 egg
1-1/2 cups all-purpose flour
1-1/2 teaspoons baking soda
1/2 teaspoon salt
2-1/2 cups finely chopped peeled tart apples
1/2 cup packed brown sugar
1 cup chopped walnuts
1 teaspoon ground cinnamon
1 teaspoon vanilla extract

In a mixing bowl, cream shortening and sugar; beat in egg. Combine flour, baking soda and salt; gradually add to the creamed mixture and mix well (dough will be stiff). Stir in apples. Spread batter into a greased 13-in. x 9-in. x 2-in. baking pan. Combine brown sugar, walnuts, cinnamon and vanilla; sprinkle over batter. Bake at 350° for 30-35 minutes or until golden brown. Cool. Cut into squares. **Yield:** 12-16 servings.

Comforting Foods Fit For Company

WELCOME family and friends into your home with the aroma of this mouth-watering meal.

"Sicilian Meat Roll is always a big hit with company, and the leftovers are good either hot or cold," explains Mrs. W.G. Dougherty of Crawfordsville, Indiana. "My sister-in-law shared this recipe years ago, and it became our family's favorite meat loaf. The addition of ham and mozzarella is a colorful surprise and adds terrific flavor."

Elizabeth Ewan's mother served noodles with cottage cheese as a main dish on many a meatless Friday. "I altered the recipe a little as a side dish, but Parmesan Noodles still makes a good main dish," says this Parma, Ohio cook. "The special blend of flavors makes it companionable to any meal."

Why serve plain salad when you can whip up Three-Step Salad from Les Cunningham of San Diego, California? "If you don't try this refreshing salad, you have missed the best! The crisp greens and bright oranges make it colorful, and the sweet caramelized almonds create a unique crunch," shares Les. "This salad is a special treat for family and company."

Guests will rave over Pull-Apart Herb Bread. "The ingredients are so simple and the results so spectacular, I'm always willing to share the secret," smiles Evelyn Kenney of Hamilton, New Jersey. "The best part of having this bread is tearing it apart and eating it warm."

SICILIAN MEAT ROLL

2 eggs
1/2 cup tomato juice
3/4 teaspoon dried oregano
2 garlic cloves, minced
1/4 teaspoon salt
1/4 teaspoon pepper
2 pounds ground beef
3/4 cup soft bread crumbs
2 tablespoons minced fresh parsley
8 thin slices fully cooked ham
1-1/2 cups (6 ounces) shredded mozzarella cheese
3 thin slices mozzarella cheese

In a large bowl, combine eggs, tomato juice, oregano, garlic, salt and pepper. Add beef, bread crumbs and parsley; mix well. On a piece of heavy-duty foil, pat meat mixture into a 12-in. x 10-in. rectangle. Place the ham and shredded cheese on loaf to within 1/2 in. of edges. Roll up, jelly-roll style, beginning with the short end and peeling foil away while rolling. Place on a greased baking pan with seam side down; seal ends. Bake, uncovered, at 350° for 1 hour and 10 minutes. Top with sliced cheese; bake 5 minutes longer or until cheese is melted. **Yield:** 8 servings.

PARMESAN NOODLES

2 packages (3 ounces *each*) cream cheese, softened
1/2 cup butter *or* margarine, softened, *divided*
2 tablespoons minced fresh parsley
1 teaspoon dried basil
1/2 teaspoon lemon-pepper seasoning
2/3 cup boiling water
1 garlic clove, minced
6 cups hot cooked thin noodles
2/3 cup grated Parmesan cheese, *divided*
Additional parsley, optional

In a small bowl, combine the cream cheese, 2 tablespoons butter, parsley, basil and lemon-pepper seasoning. Stir in water; keep warm. In a saucepan, saute garlic in remaining butter until lightly browned. Place noodles in a serving bowl; top with garlic mixture. Sprinkle with half of the Parmesan cheese; toss lightly. Spoon cream sauce over noodles and sprinkle with remaining Parmesan. Garnish with parsley if desired. **Yield:** 8 servings.

THREE-STEP SALAD

1/2 cup sliced almonds
3 tablespoons sugar
6 cups torn romaine
1 can (11 ounces) mandarin oranges, drained
1 cup sliced celery
3 green onions, sliced
DRESSING:
1/2 cup vegetable oil
1/4 cup vinegar
2 to 3 tablespoons sugar
1/2 teaspoon salt
1/2 teaspoon ground mustard
1/4 teaspoon garlic powder

In a small saucepan over medium heat, cook and stir almonds and sugar until almonds are coated and lightly browned, about 4 minutes. Spread the almonds on heavy-duty foil to cool; gently break apart. In a large salad bowl, combine romaine, oranges, celery and onions. Top with almonds. In a jar with tight-fitting lid, combine the dressing ingredients; shake well. Pour over the salad and toss gently. **Yield:** 8 servings.

PULL-APART HERB BREAD

1 garlic clove, minced
1/4 cup butter *or* margarine, melted

2 tubes (10 to 12 ounces *each*)
refrigerated biscuits
1 cup (4 ounces) shredded cheddar cheese
1/4 teaspoon dried basil
1/4 teaspoon fennel seed
1/4 teaspoon dried oregano

In a skillet, saute garlic in butter; set aside. Separate biscuits; place half in an even layer in a greased 9-in. springform pan. Brush with butter mixture; sprinkle with half of the cheese and herbs. Repeat. Place the pan on a baking sheet. Bake at 375° for 20-25 minutes or until golden brown. Remove from the pan; serve warm. **Yield:** 8 servings.

Festive Fare Will Have All Eyes Smiling

FOLKS will think they have the luck of the Irish when you set this St. Patrick's meal on the table.

"The comic strip *Maggie and Jiggs* inspired me to serve Corned Beef 'n' Cabbage Casserole," laughs Jasper, Alabama cook Daisy Lewis. "Whenever Maggie asked Jiggs what he would like her to cook, he answered, 'Corned beef and cabbage'. My husband liked this meal, too."

The recipe for Irish Soda Bread came all the way from Tipperary, Ireland, where Anne Flanagan's great-grandmother lived. "I have eaten soda bread in New York, Philadelphia and Los Angeles, but none compare with what my grandmother made for St. Patrick's Day," remarks Anne from her Laguna Hills, California home.

Pauline Albert of Catasauqua, Pennsylvania found the recipe for Molded Vegetable Salad years ago in an old cookbook. "By using different colored gelatins, it blends in well with special holiday dinners," says Pauline. "Of course, I use lime for our St. Patrick's Day celebration. Whatever the holiday, this salad is a big hit."

Dolly Piper's mother always made Rhubarb Custard Pie with the first rhubarb of the season. "It's one of my earliest memories of a favorite treat, so I feel lucky to have this recipe," declares this Racine, Wisconsin cook. "Mother was famous for her gorgeous pies."

CORNED BEEF 'N' CABBAGE CASSEROLE

- 1 medium head cabbage, shredded (about 8 cups)
- 1 small onion, chopped
- 1 cup water
- 1 can (15-1/2 ounces) white hominy, rinsed and drained
- 3/4 pound thinly sliced corned beef, chopped
- 1/4 teaspoon salt
- 1/4 teaspoon pepper
- 1/4 teaspoon hot pepper sauce

In a large Dutch oven or saucepan, combine cabbage, onion and water; bring to a boil. Reduce heat; cover and simmer for 15 minutes or until the cabbage is tender. Add hominy, corned beef, salt, pepper and hot pepper sauce; simmer for 5 minutes. **Yield:** 6 servings.

IRISH SODA BREAD

- 4 cups all-purpose flour
- 1/4 cup sugar
- 2 teaspoons baking powder
- 1-1/2 teaspoons baking soda
- 1/2 teaspoon salt
- 6 tablespoons shortening
- 1/2 cup raisins
- 1 tablespoon caraway seeds
- 1-1/4 cups buttermilk
- 1 egg, lightly beaten
- 2 tablespoons butter *or* margarine, melted

Cinnamon-sugar

In a large bowl, combine flour, sugar, baking powder, baking soda and salt. Cut in shortening until mixture resembles coarse crumbs. Stir in raisins and caraway. Combine buttermilk and egg; add to the crumb mixture. Turn onto a lightly floured surface and knead gently 5-6 times. Divide dough in half; shape into two balls. Place on a lightly greased baking sheet. Pat each ball into a 6-in. round loaf. Using a sharp knife, cut a 4-in. cross about 1/4 in. deep on top of each loaf. Brush with butter and sprinkle with cinnamon-sugar. Bake at 375° for 40-45 minutes or until golden brown. **Yield:** 2 loaves.

MOLDED VEGETABLE SALAD

(Not pictured)

☑ Uses less fat, sugar or salt. Includes Nutritional Analysis and Diabetic Exchanges.

- 1 package (6 ounces) lime gelatin
- 1/4 teaspoon salt, optional
- 1-1/2 cups boiling water
- 3/4 cup cold water
- 3 tablespoons vinegar
- 1 cup chopped celery
- 1 cup chopped tomato
- 1 cup thinly shredded lettuce
- 3/4 cup thinly sliced radishes
- 1/4 cup finely chopped green pepper
- 4 teaspoons grated onion

Dash pepper

In a bowl, dissolve gelatin and salt if desired in boiling water. Add the cold water and vinegar. Chill until partially set. Fold in remaining ingre-

dients. Pour into a 4-cup mold that has been lightly coated with nonstick cooking spray. Chill until firm. Unmold onto a serving platter. **Yield:** 8 servings. **Nutritional Analysis:** One 1/2-cup serving (prepared with sugar-free gelatin and without salt) equals 38 calories, 77 mg sodium, trace cholesterol, 8 gm carbohydrate, 2 gm protein, trace fat. **Diabetic Exchanges:** 1-1/2 vegetable.

RHUBARB CUSTARD PIE

1-1/2 cups all-purpose flour
   1/4 teaspoon salt
   1/2 cup shortening
   1/4 cup cold water

3 to 4 cups diced fresh *or* frozen rhubarb,
   thawed and drained
  2 eggs
1-1/2 cups sugar
  2 tablespoons cornstarch
  3/4 teaspoon ground nutmeg

Combine flour and salt in a mixing bowl. Cut in shortening until mixture resembles coarse crumbs. Sprinkle with water, 1 tablespoon at a time, and toss lightly with a fork until the dough forms a ball. On a floured surface, roll out dough to fit a 9-in. pie plate. Place rhubarb in pie shell. In a small bowl, beat eggs. Add sugar, cornstarch and nutmeg; mix well. Pour over rhubarb. Bake at 375° for 45 minutes or until crust is golden brown and filling is bubbly. **Yield:** 6-8 servings.

Tasty Dinner Showcases Regional Recipes

THERE'S no need to travel further than your kitchen to treat your family to a taste of the country.

"I was fortunate to visit my grandmother's birthplace in Hawaii, where I met relatives who taught me how to make Tropical Pork Chops," explains Jeanette Babineau of Grand Junction, Colorado. "It's been a family favorite since I brought the recipe home. The pineapple is a sweet surprise."

In the South, a dish like Home-Style Green Beans is called "comfort food". "We serve it with corn bread, and they go great together," tells Thomasville, Georgia cook Nancy Reichert. "I make this as a side dish with any of my favorite entrees. It's so simple to prepare I can serve it up in no time."

Onion Cheese Custard Bread is wonderful for a brunch or luncheon menu. "The first time I made it, my family and friends loved it and just had to have the recipe. The custard texture makes it very different," says Joan Kinsinger from her Utica, New York home. Served with a tossed salad and dessert, it could even make a light meal.

From New Town, North Dakota, Carla Hodenfield says, "These moist Spice Cupcakes with creamy caramel frosting are a delicious treat. The recipe has been in my family for years. When I was growing up, it seemed these cupcakes were always in the freezer, just waiting to be snitched one at a time!"

TROPICAL PORK CHOPS

1/3 cup ketchup
2 tablespoons prepared mustard
2 tablespoons brown sugar
1 tablespoon cider vinegar
1-1/2 teaspoons soy sauce
1/8 teaspoon garlic salt
1/8 teaspoon onion salt
Dash cayenne pepper
4 boneless pork loin chops
Salt and pepper to taste
1/4 cup chopped onion
2 garlic cloves, minced

1 tablespoon vegetable oil
1/3 cup water
1/4 cup pineapple tidbits
Hot cooked rice

In a saucepan, combine the first eight ingredients. Cover and simmer until sugar is dissolved, about 10 minutes. Remove from the heat; set aside. Season pork chops with salt and pepper. In a skillet, cook pork, onion and garlic in oil until meat is browned. Add water and reserved sauce. Cover and cook over medium-low heat for 20-25 minutes or until the meat is no longer pink, adding more water if needed. Stir in pineapple and heat through. Serve over rice. **Yield:** 4 servings.

HOME-STYLE GREEN BEANS

3/4 pound fresh green beans, cut into
    2-inch pieces
1-1/2 cups water
6 bacon strips, cooked and crumbled
1 tablespoon seasoned salt

In a saucepan, combine beans and water; bring to a boil. Reduce heat; cover and simmer for 10 minutes. Add the bacon and seasoned salt; simmer 10-15 minutes longer. Serve with a slotted spoon. **Yield:** 4 servings.

ONION CHEESE CUSTARD BREAD

3/4 cup chopped onion
1 tablespoon vegetable oil
1-1/2 cups buttermilk
1 egg, lightly beaten
1-1/2 cups biscuit/baking mix
1 cup (4 ounces) shredded sharp cheddar
    cheese, *divided*
2 teaspoons poppy seeds
2 tablespoons butter *or* margarine, melted

In a skillet, saute onion in oil until golden brown, about 7 minutes. Set aside to cool. In a bowl, combine buttermilk and egg. Stir in biscuit mix, onion and 1/2 cup cheese. Pour into a greased 9-in. round baking pan. Sprinkle with poppy seeds and remaining cheese. Drizzle with butter. Bake at 400° for 30-35 minutes or until golden brown. Cool slightly. Cut into wedges. **Yield:** 8 servings.

SPICE CUPCAKES

2 cups water
1 cup raisins
1/2 cup shortening

1 cup sugar
1 egg
1-3/4 cups all-purpose flour
1 teaspoon baking soda
1/2 teaspoon salt
1/2 teaspoon *each* ground allspice, cloves,
    cinnamon and nutmeg
1/4 cup chopped walnuts

FROSTING:
1 cup packed brown sugar
1/3 cup half-and-half cream
1/4 teaspoon salt
3 tablespoons butter *or* margarine
1 teaspoon vanilla extract
1-1/4 cups confectioners' sugar
Coarsely chopped walnuts, optional

In a saucepan, bring water and raisins to a boil. Reduce heat; simmer for 10 minutes. Remove from heat and set aside (do not drain). In a mixing bowl, cream shortening and sugar. Add egg and raisins. Combine dry ingredients; add to creamed mixture and mix well. Stir in walnuts. Fill greased or paper-lined muffin cups with 1/3 cup batter each. Bake at 350° for 20-25 minutes or until the cupcakes test done. Cool for 10 minutes; remove from pan to a wire rack. For frosting, combine brown sugar, cream and salt in a saucepan. Bring to a boil over medium-low heat; cook and stir until smooth. Stir in butter and vanilla. Remove from heat; cool slightly. Stir in confectioners' sugar until smooth. Frost cupcakes; top with nuts if desired. **Yield:** 14 cupcakes.

Southwestern Menu Adds Sizzle To Supper

IS YOUR FAMILY tired of the same old thing for supper? Spice up meal monotony with this zesty Southwestern-style menu.

Carolyn Deming of Miami, Arizona has a large collection of recipes with a Southwest flavor. "Arizona Chicken is one of my husband's favorites," declares Carolyn. "The moist, flavorful chicken suits any occasion, plus it can be prepared for any number of guests."

When Estelle Stimel's menu features poultry, she reaches for Vegetable Rice Medley with its subtle sage flavor. "The zesty onion and crunchy celery make a superb combination, and it's easy to make," explains this Conway, Arkansas cook.

Chili Cornmeal Crescents are tender, light and delicious, with a bit of chili tang. "The zip and texture inspire requests for the recipe every time I serve them," shares Marion Lowery of Medford, Oregon.

A plentiful zucchini crop led Anne MacDonald of Alma, Quebec to make Orange Zucchini Cake. "It's a lovely cake with a tangy orange flavor—and the cream cheese frosting is a must," assures Anne.

ARIZONA CHICKEN

✓ Uses less fat, sugar or salt. Includes Nutritional Analysis and Diabetic Exchanges.

6 boneless skinless chicken breast halves (1-1/2 pounds)
1/4 cup vegetable oil, *divided*
1 medium onion, sliced
4 cups chopped fresh tomatoes
2 celery ribs, sliced
1/4 cup water
1/4 cup sliced stuffed olives
2 teaspoons garlic powder
2 teaspoons dried oregano
1 teaspoon salt, optional
1/4 teaspoon pepper
1/2 pound fresh mushrooms, sliced

In a skillet, brown chicken on both sides in 2 tablespoons of oil. Remove and set aside. In the same skillet, saute onion in remaining oil until tender. Add tomatoes, celery, water, olives, garlic powder, oregano, salt if desired and pepper; bring to a boil. Cover and simmer for 15 minutes. Return chicken to pan. Simmer, uncovered, for 15 minutes. Add mushrooms; simmer 15 minutes longer or until meat juices run clear. **Yield:** 6 servings. **Nutritional Analysis:** One serving (prepared without salt) equals 277 calories, 137 mg sodium, 73 mg cholesterol, 11 gm carbohydrate, 29 gm protein, 13 gm fat. **Diabetic Exchanges:** 3 lean meat, 2 vegetable, 1 fat.

VEGETABLE RICE MEDLEY

1 cup chopped onion
1 cup chopped celery
1 cup sliced fresh mushrooms
1/2 cup chopped green pepper
1/4 cup butter *or* margarine
2-1/2 cups cooked rice
3/4 teaspoon salt
1/2 teaspoon rubbed sage
Pinch pepper

In a large skillet, saute onion, celery, mushrooms and green pepper in butter until tender, about 8 minutes. Stir in rice, salt, sage and pepper; reduce heat to low. Cook and stir 3-4 minutes longer or until heated through. **Yield:** 6 servings.

CHILI CORNMEAL CRESCENTS

✓ Uses less fat, sugar or salt. Includes Nutritional Analysis and Diabetic Exchanges.

1 package (1/4 ounce) active dry yeast
1-3/4 cups warm water (110° to 115°)
1 egg
2 tablespoons olive *or* vegetable oil
1-1/2 cups cornmeal
1/3 cup sugar
1 tablespoon chili powder
1 teaspoon salt
4 to 4-1/2 cups all-purpose flour

In a small bowl, dissolve yeast in water. In a mixing bowl, beat egg and oil. Add cornmeal, sugar, chili powder, salt, yeast mixture and 2 cups flour; mix well. Add enough remaining flour to form a soft dough. Turn onto a floured surface; knead until smooth and elastic, about 6-8 minutes. Place in a greased bowl, turning once to grease top. Cover and let rise in a warm place until doubled, about 1 hour. Punch dough down; divide in half. Roll each portion into a 12-in. circle. Cut into 12 wedges. Roll up each wedge, starting with wide end. Place on greased baking sheets; curve into

a crescent shape. Cover and let rise until doubled, about 30 minutes. Bake at 375° for about 20 minutes or until browned. Cool on wire racks. **Yield:** 2 dozen. **Nutritional Analysis:** One roll equals 129 calories, 106 mg sodium, 9 mg cholesterol, 25 gm carbohydrate, 3 gm protein, 2 gm fat. **Diabetic Exchanges:** 1-1/2 starch, 1/2 fat.

ORANGE ZUCCHINI CAKE

1/2 cup golden raisins
1 cup boiling water
3/4 cup sugar
1/2 cup vegetable oil
2 eggs
1/2 cup All-Bran cereal
1-1/2 teaspoons grated orange peel
1 teaspoon vanilla extract
1 cup all-purpose flour
1 teaspoon baking powder
1 teaspoon ground cinnamon
1/2 teaspoon baking soda
1/2 teaspoon ground nutmeg
1/4 teaspoon salt
1 cup thinly shredded zucchini
FROSTING:
1 package (3 ounces) cream cheese, softened
1 tablespoon butter *or* margarine, softened
1 teaspoon grated orange peel
1-1/2 cups confectioners' sugar
1/2 to 1 teaspoon water

Place raisins and water in a bowl; let stand for 5 minutes. Drain; set raisins aside. In a mixing bowl, combine sugar, oil and eggs; mix well. Stir in cereal, orange peel and vanilla. Combine dry ingredients; add to sugar mixture. Mix well. Stir in zucchini and raisins. Pour into a greased 11-in. x 7-in. x 2-in. baking pan. Bake at 325° for 30-35 minutes or until a toothpick inserted near the center comes out clean. Cool. In a mixing bowl, beat cream cheese, butter and orange peel until light and fluffy. Gradually add sugar and water; beat until smooth. Frost cooled cake. Refrigerate leftovers. **Yield:** 8-10 servings.

Cooking for Two

*These perfectly portioned recipes fit the bill
when cooking for one or two.*

BACON-CHEESE ENGLISH MUFFINS

Violena Carver, Potosi, Missouri

*This wonderful recipe is just too good to keep to my-
self! My daughter shared it with me. The portions
are just right to suit my appetite, and the muffins are
so pretty when they're pulled from the oven with the
cheese all bubbly and hot. I also serve these to guests.*

    2 English muffins, split and toasted
    2 tablespoons mayonnaise
    4 tomato slices
    4 onion slices
    4 process American cheese slices
    4 bacon strips, cooked and crumbled

Spread muffin halves with mayonnaise; top with
tomato, onion and cheese. Broil 4 in. from the heat
for 3-4 minutes or until the cheese is melted. Top
with bacon. Serve immediately. **Yield:** 2 servings.

DOUBLE PEANUT BUTTER COOKIES

Jeannette Mack, Rushville, New York

*The extra taste of peanut butter in the middle of the
cookie is a delicious surprise the first time you bite into one. It's a nice, soft cookie and fun to make with
little helpers.*

1-1/2 cups all-purpose flour
    1/2 cup sugar
    1/2 teaspoon baking soda
    1/4 teaspoon salt
    1/2 cup shortening
    1/2 cup creamy peanut butter
    1/4 cup light corn syrup
    1 tablespoon milk
Additional peanut butter

In a large bowl, combine flour, sugar, baking soda
and salt. Cut in shortening and peanut butter
until mixture resembles coarse crumbs. Stir in the
corn syrup and milk; mix well. Shape into a 2-in.
roll; wrap in waxed paper or foil. Refrigerate for at
least 3 hours. Cut into 1/4-in. slices; place half of
them 2 in. apart on ungreased baking sheets. Top

each with 1/2 teaspoon of peanut butter. Cover
with remaining slices; seal edges with a fork. Bake
at 350° for 12-14 minutes or until lightly browned.
Cool for 2 minutes; remove from pans to wire
racks to cool completely. **Yield:** about 2 dozen.

PORK 'N' BEAN SALAD

LaVerne Stetler, Escalon, California

*This recipe from my aunt was an immediate hit. I had
pork and beans and mayonnaise in the pantry and all
the vegetables in my garden. It's great for a picnic because it travels well in a cooler and is so colorful.*

✓ Uses less fat, sugar or salt. Includes Nutritional
Analysis and Diabetic Exchanges.

    1 can (16 ounces) pork and beans, drained
    1/2 cup chopped tomato
    1/2 cup chopped celery
    1/4 cup chopped green pepper
    3 tablespoons mayonnaise
    2 tablespoons chopped onion

Combine ingredients in a small bowl. Cover and
refrigerate for 2 hours. Refrigerate leftovers. **Yield:**
4 servings. **Nutritional Analysis:** One 1/2-cup
serving (prepared with fat-free mayonnaise)
equals 139 calories, 564 mg sodium, 8 mg cholesterol, 27 gm carbohydrate, 6 gm protein, 2 gm fat.
Diabetic Exchanges: 1-1/2 starch, 1 vegetable.

FROTHY ORANGE SODA

Diane Widmer, Blue Island, Illinois

*We enjoy this delicious shake after dinner, when we
want something cool and refreshing. It makes a lovely treat, and it brings back memories of soda-foun-
tain drinks.*

    1 cup orange juice
    1 cup vanilla ice cream
    1 cup lemon-lime soda

Place orange juice and ice cream in a blender;
cover and process until smooth. Stir in soda. Pour
into glasses. **Yield:** 2 servings.

CHICKEN STUFFED BUNDLES

Kathryn Burris, Mariposa, California

This recipe has been in our family for about 40 years! My four kids loved this dish growing up, and it's still their number one request when they come to dinner.

- 1/2 cup chopped cooked chicken
- 1 tablespoon chopped celery
- 1/4 teaspoon dried minced onion
- 1/4 teaspoon dried parsley flakes

GRAVY:
- 1 can (14-1/2 ounces) chicken broth
- 1 can (10-3/4 ounces) condensed creamy chicken mushroom soup, undiluted
- 1/4 teaspoon dried minced onion
- 1/8 teaspoon dried sweet pepper flakes, optional

DOUGH:
- 1 cup all-purpose flour
- 1 tablespoon baking powder
- 1 teaspoon sugar
- 1/2 teaspoon salt
- 1 tablespoon shortening
- 6 tablespoons water

Combine the first four ingredients; set aside. In a large saucepan, combine gravy ingredients; mix well. Warm over low heat. In a bowl, combine the first four dough ingredients; mix well. Cut in shortening until mixture resembles coarse crumbs. Stir in water; knead gently. Roll dough to 1/8-in. thickness; cut into six squares. Place a heaping tablespoonful of chicken mixture in the center of each square. Fold dough over and press edges together firmly to seal. Drop bundles into simmering gravy. Cover and cook over medium heat for 15-20 minutes or until pastry flakes. **Yield:** 2-3 servings.

GREEN RICE

Nancy Beatty, Springfield, Illinois

My mother-in-law always served green rice with her chicken casserole. She was a great cook, and the local newspaper featured her several times as "cook of the week".

- 1/2 cup thinly sliced green onions with tops
- 2 tablespoons butter *or* margarine
- 1-1/2 cups chicken broth
- 2/3 cup uncooked long grain rice
- 1/4 cup finely chopped green pepper
- 1/4 cup minced fresh parsley *or* 4 teaspoons dried parsley flakes
- Dash pepper
- 1/4 cup shredded cheddar cheese, optional

In a skillet, saute onions in butter until tender. Stir in the broth, rice, green pepper, parsley and pepper; bring to a boil. Remove from the heat; pour into a greased 1-qt. baking dish. Cover and bake at 350° for 25 minutes or until rice is tender. Top with cheese if desired; bake 3 minutes longer or until melted. **Yield:** 2-3 servings.

CHOCOLATE WAFFLE COOKIES

Pat Oviatt, Zimmerman, Minnesota

I've had this recipe for years. It's economical to make, yet results in a delicious cookie.

- 1/4 cup butter *or* margarine, softened
- 6 tablespoons sugar
- 1 egg
- 1/2 teaspoon vanilla extract
- 1 square (1 ounce) unsweetened chocolate, melted
- 1/2 cup all-purpose flour
- Confectioners' sugar

In a mixing bowl, cream butter and sugar; beat in egg and vanilla until light and fluffy. Blend in chocolate. Add flour; mix well. Drop by rounded teaspoonfuls 1 in. apart onto a preheated waffle iron. Bake for 1 minute. Remove to a wire rack to cool. Dust with confectioners' sugar. **Yield:** about 1-1/2 dozen.

TUNA FISH SPECIAL

Gerry Tressler, St. Petersburg, Florida

(Not pictured)

The variety of flavors gives this dish a special taste everyone loves. No matter how many different tuna salad recipes I've tried, this one still tops our list!

- 1 can (6 ounces) tuna, drained and flaked
- 1 cup frozen peas, thawed
- 1/2 cup chopped celery
- 1/4 cup sliced green onions
- 1/3 cup mayonnaise
- 1 teaspoon lemon juice
- 1/2 teaspoon soy sauce
- 1/8 teaspoon curry powder
- Dash garlic powder
- 2 tablespoons slivered almonds, toasted
- 1 cup chow mein noodles
- Lettuce leaves, optional

In a bowl, combine tuna, peas, celery and onions. In another bowl, combine mayonnaise, lemon juice, soy sauce, curry and garlic powder; stir into tuna mixture. Stir in almonds; top with noodles. Serve on lettuce if desired. **Yield:** 2 servings.

BAKED SWISS STEAK

Dolores Wynne, Clearwater, Florida

This dish is one of my husband's favorites, so I make it often. It's also a handy recipe—while it's in the oven, you can do other things. The meat becomes very tender, and the vegetables add delicious flavor.

    1/2 to 3/4 pound boneless round steak
    2 tablespoons all-purpose flour, *divided*
    1/2 teaspoon salt
    2 tablespoons vegetable oil
    1 can (14-1/2 ounces) stewed tomatoes
    1/2 cup chopped carrot
    1/4 cup chopped celery
    1 tablespoon chopped onion
    1/4 teaspoon Worcestershire sauce
    2 tablespoons sharp cheddar cheese

Cut meat into two portions; pound to 1/4-in. thickness. Combine 1 tablespoon flour and salt; coat meat on both sides. In a skillet, brown meat in oil. Transfer meat to a greased shallow 2-qt. baking dish; set aside. To pan drippings, add tomatoes, carrot, celery, onion, Worcestershire sauce and remaining flour. Bring to a boil over medium heat; cook and stir for 2 minutes. Pour over meat. Cover and bake at 350° for 1-1/2 hours or until the meat is tender. Sprinkle with cheese; return to the oven until cheese is melted. **Yield:** 2 servings.

SAVORY STRING BEANS

Ina Reed, Kingman, Arizona

I love making this dish when I can pick the beans right out of the garden and put them into the pot. The fresh taste is unbeatable. I've also made it with beans purchased at the store. Either way, you'll find this recipe a winner.

    4 bacon strips
    2 cups fresh *or* frozen cut green beans
       (1-1/2-inch pieces)
    1 cup water
    1/2 cup chopped onion
    2 tablespoons minced fresh basil *or*
       2 teaspoons dried basil
    1 bay leaf
    1/4 teaspoon dill seed
    1/4 teaspoon garlic powder
    1/8 to 1/4 teaspoon salt
    1/8 teaspoon pepper

In a skillet, cook bacon until crisp. Remove bacon; crumble and set aside. Drain, reserving 1 tablespoon drippings. Add beans, water, onion and seasonings to drippings; bring to a boil. Cook, uncovered, for 15-20 minutes or until beans are

tender. Discard bay leaf. Stir in bacon. **Yield:** 2 servings.

RICH MASHED POTATOES

Bessie Hulett, Shively, Kentucky

I created this recipe to serve my husband and me, but it's so tasty I also prepare it for special occasions when we have dinner guests. The secret to the fluffy texture is making sure the potatoes are well drained, and heating the butter and cream before adding them.

    2 medium potatoes (about 3/4 pound),
       peeled and cubed
    3 tablespoons whipping cream
    1 tablespoon butter *or* margarine
    1/4 teaspoon salt
    1/8 teaspoon pepper
Minced fresh parsley

Place potatoes in a saucepan; cover with water. Cook until tender, about 10-12 minutes; drain. Add cream, butter, salt and pepper; mash until smooth. Sprinkle with parsley. **Yield:** 2 servings.

BANANA RICE PUDDING

Ruth Ann Stelfox, Raymond, Alberta

This is an old family recipe my mother used to make. With seven children in the house, she made larger quantities, but I adjusted the ingredients to be just right for the two of us.

    1 cup hot cooked rice
    1/3 cup sugar
    1/3 cup whipping cream, whipped
    1 large firm banana, sliced
Fresh mint, optional

In a bowl, combine rice and sugar; mix well. Cool completely. Fold in whipped cream and banana. Cover and refrigerate until ready to serve. Spoon into serving dishes; garnish with mint if desired. **Yield:** 2 servings.

TOP-BANANA TREAT

Cut a peeled banana in half horizontally. Place it, cut side up, on a baking sheet sprayed with nonstick cooking spray. Sprinkle with brown sugar, cinnamon and nutmeg; broil until sugar is bubbly.

BAKED HAM AND CHEESE SANDWICHES

Norma Curtis, Ithaca, Michigan

I collect cookbooks and enjoy reading them much like a novel. But when I start cooking, I create my own recipes to suit my taste. I used to cater parties and found I often had to be resourceful. This sandwich is one of my creations that is easy to cook for two and even one!

    4 slices bread
    2 slices fully cooked ham
    2 slices cheddar cheese
    2 eggs
1-1/4 cups milk
    1 tablespoon prepared mustard
    1 tablespoon minced fresh parsley *or* 1
       teaspoon dried parsley flakes
Fresh asparagus tips, cooked
Shredded cheddar cheese, optional

Place two slices of bread in a greased 11-in. x 7-in. x 2-in. baking dish or two individual baking dishes. Top each with a slice of ham and cheese; top with remaining bread. In a small bowl, beat the eggs, milk, mustard and parsley. Pour over sandwiches. Let stand for 5 minutes; carefully turn sandwiches over and let stand 5 minutes longer. Bake, uncovered, at 350° for 30-35 minutes. Top with asparagus and cheese if desired. Bake 5 minutes more or until cheese is melted and a knife inserted into the egg mixture comes out clean. Serve immediately. **Yield:** 2 servings.

CARROT RAISIN SALAD

Marlene Reilly, Nescopeck, Pennsylvania

If you like carrots, here's a great recipe. It's very easy to prepare. My mother made it every holiday, using either regular or golden raisins. This was one of the first recipes I tried on my husband when we were newlyweds. He was skeptical because he didn't like raisins, but now this is one of his favorite salads.

1/2 pound carrots, shredded
1/3 cup golden raisins
1/3 cup plain yogurt
    2 tablespoons mayonnaise
    1 teaspoon honey
Dash cinnamon, optional
Lettuce leaves

Combine the carrots, raisins, yogurt, mayonnaise, honey and cinnamon if desired in a small bowl. Chill for several hours or overnight. Serve in a lettuce-lined bowl. **Yield:** 2 servings.

THE SCOOP ON RAISINS

If raisins clump together, put them in a strainer and rinse with hot water. Or pop them in the microwave and heat at high power for 10 to 20 seconds.

COFFEE LOVER'S DESSERT

Louise Stuhr, Chatham, New Jersey

This recipe caught my mother's eye back in 1925. It appeared in the local newspaper published in Jamaica, New York. Dad bought a paper every day so he could read while commuting on the El train. It quickly became my brothers' and my favorite dessert.

  10 to 12 large marshmallows
1/2 cup brewed coffee
1/2 cup whipping cream, whipped

In a heavy saucepan, combine marshmallows and coffee; cook and stir over low heat until melted. Remove from the heat and cool to room temperature. Fold in whipped cream. Spoon into individual dessert dishes. Chill. **Yield:** 2 servings.

SAUSAGE POTATO SKILLET

Amelia Bordas, Springfield, Virginia

(Not pictured)

During my childhood, I lived in an Italian neighborhood in New Jersey. Since both my parents were working, I went home for lunch with my Italian girlfriend. Lunch was always the same—sausage, fried potatoes, green peppers and onions—but I could never get enough of my favorite meal.

    2 fresh Italian sausage links, cut into
       1/2-inch pieces
    1 tablespoon vegetable oil
    1 small onion, sliced
1/4 cup *each* sliced green and sweet red
       pepper
    2 small potatoes, sliced
    2 cups water
Salt and pepper to taste

In a skillet, brown sausage in oil. Add onion and peppers; saute until vegetables are tender. Add potatoes and water; bring to a boil. Reduce heat; cover and simmer for 15 minutes or until potatoes are tender. Drain; add salt and pepper. **Yield:** 2 servings.

SPECIAL SALMON STEAKS

Ruby Williams, Bogalusa, Louisiana

After all of our children were married and gone, I prepared this easy and elegant entree often for my husband and me, especially on our wedding anniversary. It was one of our favorite dishes. We found that one of the nicest ways to enjoy each other's company was to have a great meal together.

  2 salmon *or* halibut steaks (8 ounces each)
  2 tablespoons butter *or* margarine, melted
  2 tablespoons lemon juice
  1 green onion, sliced
  1 tablespoon minced fresh parsley
1/4 teaspoon garlic salt
1/8 teaspoon lemon-pepper seasoning

Place salmon in a lightly greased 8-in. square baking dish. Top with butter and lemon juice. Combine onion, parsley, garlic salt and lemon-pepper; sprinkle over salmon. Bake, uncovered, at 400° for 15-20 minutes or until fish flakes easily with a fork. **Yield:** 2 servings.

TESTING FISH FOR DONENESS

To test fish for doneness, prod it with a fork at its thickest point. Properly cooked fish is opaque, has milky white juices and flakes easily. Undercooked fish is translucent, and the juices are clear and watery.

HERBED POTATO WEDGES

R.V. Taibbi, Honolulu, Hawaii

I'm a widower and cook mainly for myself. This recipe is simple to make and I've used it many times over the years. Since it makes enough for two, I'll wrap half of the baked potato wedges in foil and freeze them for another time. Then I simply warm them in the toaster oven or microwave for a fast and flavorful side dish.

✓ Uses less fat, sugar or salt. Includes Nutritional Analysis and Diabetic Exchanges.

  3 tablespoons grated Parmesan cheese
  1 tablespoon dried basil
1/4 teaspoon salt, optional
1/4 teaspoon pepper
  1 large unpeeled baking potato, cut into wedges
  2 teaspoons vegetable oil

In a shallow bowl, combine Parmesan cheese, basil, salt if desired and pepper. Brush cut sides of potato wedges with oil; dip into cheese mixture. Place in a greased 8-in. square pan. Bake, uncovered, at 400° for 20-25 minutes or until tender. **Yield:** 2 servings. **Nutritional Analysis:** One serving (prepared without salt) equals 190 calories, 183 mg sodium, 7 mg cholesterol, 25 gm carbohydrate, 6 gm protein, 8 gm fat. **Diabetic Exchanges:** 1-1/2 starch, 1-1/2 fat.

WALDORF SALAD FOR TWO

Mildred Cummings, Cincinnati, Ohio

The pear and hint of orange are a nice surprise in this salad. It's a little different than traditional Waldorf salad and always brings rave reviews. The colorful combination of ingredients complements any meal.

  1 small apple, diced
  1 small pear, diced
  1 celery rib, diced
  2 tablespoons chopped walnuts
1/4 cup mayonnaise *or* salad dressing
  1 tablespoon orange juice
  2 lettuce leaves

In a small bowl, toss the apple, pear, celery and walnuts. Combine mayonnaise and orange juice; spoon over salad and toss to coat. Serve on lettuce. **Yield:** 2 servings.

CHOCOLATE SHORTBREAD

Sarah Bueckert, Austin, Manitoba

This recipe has been in my files for a long time…probably from when I first learned to bake. Any chocolate lover will like these melt-in-your-mouth cookies. I make them year-round with variations. They're even richer with a thin coat of icing or as a sandwich cookie with frosting in the middle.

1/4 cup butter (no substitutes), softened
1/4 teaspoon vanilla extract
1/2 cup all-purpose flour
1/4 cup confectioners' sugar
  1 to 2 tablespoons baking cocoa

In a mixing bowl, cream the butter. Add vanilla and mix well. Combine flour, sugar and cocoa; add to creamed mixture. Beat until dough holds together, about 3 minutes. Pat into a 9-in. x 4-in. rectangle. Cut into 2-in. x 1-1/2-in. strips. Place 1 in. apart on ungreased baking sheets. Prick with a fork. Bake at 300° for 20-25 minutes or until set. Cool for 5 minutes; remove to a wire rack to cool completely. **Yield:** 1 dozen.

SPANISH CHICKEN AND RICE

Mary Nelms, Jacksonville, Florida

I've had this recipe for over 50 years and have probably made it hundreds of times. This dish can be prepared quickly. The portions are just right for two people, and any leftovers are just as delicious the next day.

 2 tablespoons all-purpose flour
 1 teaspoon salt, *divided*
 1/4 teaspoon pepper
 2 bone-in chicken breast halves
 1 tablespoon butter *or* margarine
 1/2 cup chopped onion
 1/4 cup chopped green pepper
 1 garlic clove, minced
 1 jar (2-1/2 ounces) sliced pimientos, drained
 1/2 cup uncooked rice
 1-1/4 cups chicken broth
 1/2 teaspoon ground turmeric
 1/8 to 1/4 teaspoon chili powder

Combine flour, 1/2 teaspoon of salt and pepper in a large resealable plastic bag. Add chicken and shake until well coated. In a skillet, brown chicken in butter over medium heat. Remove chicken; set aside and keep warm. In the pan drippings, saute onion, green pepper and garlic until tender. Add pimientos and rice. Reduce heat; cook for 2 minutes, stirring occasionally. Stir in broth, turmeric, chili powder and remaining salt; bring to a boil. Pour into an ungreased 2-qt. baking dish; top with chicken. Cover and bake at 350° for 45 minutes or until chicken juices run clear and rice is tender. **Yield:** 2 servings.

ZIPPY CARROTS

Mina Dyck, Boissevain, Manitoba

This recipe originally didn't call for green pepper, but when I was making it one time, I noticed some in the refrigerator and decided to add it. It gave a little extra zip, so I've kept it a part of the recipe. This makes plain carrots special and adds nice color to a meal.

☑ Uses less fat, sugar or salt. Includes Nutritional Analysis and Diabetic Exchanges.

 1 tablespoon butter *or* margarine
 1-1/2 cups sliced carrots
 1 garlic clove, minced
 1 tablespoon water
 2 tablespoons diced green pepper
 2 teaspoons ketchup
Pinch chili powder

In a small saucepan, brown butter over medium heat. Add carrots and garlic; cook and stir for 1 minute. Add water; cover and cook until carrots are crisp-tender, about 6 minutes. Add green pepper; cook 2 minutes longer. Remove from the heat; stir in ketchup and chili powder. **Yield:** 2 servings. **Nutritional Analysis:** One 3/4-cup serving (prepared with margarine) equals 100 calories, 209 mg sodium, 0 cholesterol, 12 gm carbohydrate, 1 gm protein, 6 gm fat. **Diabetic Exchanges:** 2 vegetable, 1 fat.

CORN BREAD LOAF

Edna Bjork, Norwalk, Iowa

We like corn bread with our chili, and this makes just enough for two people. I received the recipe from a quilting friend at church and have shared it with many others. Another way that my husband and I like eating corn bread is straight out of the oven, buttered and topped with syrup.

 1/2 cup cornmeal
 1/2 cup all-purpose flour
 2 tablespoons sugar
 2 teaspoons baking powder
 1/4 teaspoon salt
 1 egg, beaten
 1/2 cup milk
 2 tablespoons shortening, melted

In a bowl, combine the cornmeal, flour, sugar, baking powder and salt. In another bowl, blend egg, milk and shortening; stir into dry ingredients. Pour into a greased 8-in. x 4-in. x 2-in. loaf pan. Bake at 425° for 15-18 minutes or until a toothpick inserted near the center comes out clean. Cool for 10 minutes; remove from the pan and serve warm. **Yield:** 1 loaf.

LIME DELIGHT

Nancy Vavrinek, Adrian, Michigan

Created by my husband's cousin, this salad appeared in her church's recipe book. Since it's quick and easy to prepare, I make it often for my husband and me now that we're "empty nesters".

 1 can (8 ounces) crushed pineapple, undrained
 1/4 cup lime gelatin powder
 1/2 cup cream-style cottage cheese
 1 cup whipped topping

In a small saucepan, bring pineapple to a boil over medium heat. Remove from the heat; stir in gelatin until dissolved. Chill until slightly thickened, about 30 minutes. Stir in the cottage cheese and whipped topping. Refrigerate. **Yield:** 2 servings.

TANGY MINI MEAT LOAVES

Paula Martin, Paxinos, Pennsylvania

It's fun to make miniature meat loaves instead of one big loaf...and they cook up quickly in a skillet rather than in the oven. The unique combination of flavors gives the ground beef zip.

- 1/2 pound ground beef
- 1/2 cup sliced onion
- 1/4 cup dark corn syrup
- 3 tablespoons steak sauce
- 2 teaspoons spicy brown mustard

Shape beef into four small loaves, 1/4 to 1/2 in. thick. Cook in a skillet over medium-high heat for 3-4 minutes on each side or until no longer pink. Remove to a serving plate and keep warm. Drain all but 1 tablespoon drippings; saute onion in drippings until tender. Add corn syrup, steak sauce and mustard; bring to a boil. Pour over meat loaves and serve immediately. **Yield:** 2 servings.

VINEGAR NOODLES

Jeanette Fuehring, Concordia, Missouri

I work in a beauty salon, and one of my clients shared this recipe with me many years ago. The name of this dish intrigued me, so I gave it a try. It's a refreshing summer favorite, and now, it goes hand in hand with barbecue at our house.

- 1 cup uncooked spiral noodles
- 1/2 cup thinly sliced cucumber
- 1/4 cup thinly sliced onion
- 6 tablespoons sugar
- 1/4 cup water
- 3 tablespoons vinegar
- 3/4 teaspoon prepared mustard
- 3/4 teaspoon dried parsley flakes
- 1/4 to 1/2 teaspoon pepper
- 1/4 teaspoon salt
- 1/8 teaspoon garlic salt

Cook noodles according to package directions. Drain and rinse in cold water. Place in a bowl; add cucumber and onion. Combine remaining ingredients in a jar with tight-fitting lid; shake well. Pour over noodle mixture and toss to coat. Cover and refrigerate for at least 1 hour. **Yield:** 2 servings.

CALICO SALAD

Pat Wasing, Houston, Texas

My husband suggested I share this salad recipe. It's one of his favorites, which I created a long time ago in a moment of panic. I'd opened the refrigerator to get out the makings for a plain green salad and discovered I had only a couple lettuce leaves. The cottage cheese was a perfect substitute. Celery, radishes, green pepper and dill pickle add a nice, refreshing crunch and a pretty color.

☑ Uses less fat, sugar or salt. Includes Nutritional Analysis and Diabetic Exchanges.

- 1/2 cup cottage cheese, drained
- 1/3 cup chopped celery
- 1/3 cup chopped radishes
- 1/4 cup chopped green pepper
- 2 tablespoons chopped dill pickle

Dash pepper
Lettuce leaves

In a small bowl, combine cottage cheese, celery, radishes, green pepper, pickle and pepper; mix well. Cover and refrigerate for at least 1 hour. Serve on a bed of lettuce. **Yield:** 2 servings. **Nutritional Analysis:** One 1/2-cup serving (prepared with fat-free cottage cheese) equals 54 calories, 429 mg sodium, 5 mg cholesterol, 6 gm carbohydrate, 8 gm protein, trace fat. **Diabetic Exchanges:** 1 very lean meat, 1 vegetable.

FRESH STRAWBERRY SAUCE

Joyce Courtney, West Chester, Ohio

This sauce was first served to me by my mother, who was a wonderful cook. During the months when strawberries are so plentiful, I like to keep this sauce on hand so I can improvise a delightful dessert for just the two of us. It's delicious over ice cream or angel food cake.

☑ Uses less fat, sugar or salt. Includes Nutritional Analysis and Diabetic Exchanges.

- 1 cup sliced fresh strawberries
- 1 tablespoon sugar
- 3/4 teaspoon cornstarch
- 1/8 teaspoon almond extract

Ice cream *or* angel food cake

Combine the strawberries and sugar in a small bowl; cover and refrigerate for 2-3 hours. Drain, reserving juice. Set strawberries aside. Add water to juice to measure 1/2 cup; pour into a saucepan. Stir in cornstarch until smooth. Bring to a boil; boil and stir for 2 minutes. Remove from the heat; stir in almond extract. Pour over strawberries; fold gently. Chill. Serve over ice cream or angel food cake. **Yield:** 3/4 cup. **Nutritional Analysis:** One 1/4-cup serving of sauce equals 35 calories, 1 mg sodium, 0 cholesterol, 9 gm carbohydrate, trace protein, trace fat. **Diabetic Exchange:** 1/2 fruit.

Stuffed Zucchini

Ruth Fluckiger, Tolland, Connecticut

I came up with this recipe after being challenged to find different ways to cook this plentiful summer vegetable.

    2 medium zucchini
    1/2 pound ground beef *or* bulk Italian
        sausage
    1/4 cup chopped onion
      1 garlic clove, minced
    2/3 cup seasoned bread crumbs
    1/3 cup milk
    1/8 teaspoon dill weed
      1 cup spaghetti sauce
    1/2 cup shredded cheddar cheese

Cut zucchini in half lengthwise. Scoop out pulp, leaving a 1/4-in. shell. Chop pulp; set pulp and shells aside. In a skillet, brown meat, onion and garlic; drain. Add pulp, bread crumbs, milk and dill. Spoon into zucchini shells. Place in a greased 2-qt. baking dish. Top with spaghetti sauce; sprinkle with cheese. Cover and bake at 325° for 30 minutes or until zucchini is tender. **Yield:** 2 servings.

Pretty Pepper Soup

Bessie Hulett, Shively, Kentucky

I like to create new dishes for my husband and me. This pretty soup is one of our favorites.

      1 bacon strip
      1 large sweet red pepper, chopped
    1/4 cup chopped onion
      2 garlic cloves, minced
      1 tablespoon tomato paste
    1/8 teaspoon paprika
      3 to 4 drops hot pepper sauce
    Dash cayenne pepper
      1 cup chicken broth, *divided*
      1 tablespoon butter *or* margarine
      1 tablespoon all-purpose flour
    1/2 cup whipping cream
    1/4 teaspoon salt
    Chives and additional chopped red pepper,
        optional

In a skillet, cook bacon until crisp. Remove to paper towel to drain. To the drippings, add red pepper, onion and garlic; saute until onion is tender, about 4 minutes. Stir in the tomato paste, paprika, hot pepper sauce and cayenne until well blended. Add 1/4 cup broth. Reduce heat; simmer, uncovered, for 5 minutes. Remove from the heat; cool for 10 minutes. Puree in a blender or food processor; set aside. In a saucepan over low heat, melt butter. Stir in flour; cook and stir for 2 minutes.

Gradually add remaining broth; bring to a boil over medium heat. Cook and stir for 2 minutes; reduce heat to low. Gradually stir in cream and salt. Add puree; heat through. Crumble bacon over top. Garnish with chives and red pepper if desired. Serve immediately. **Yield:** 2 servings.

Summer Squash Saute

Maxine Lynch, Boise City, Oklahoma

Yellow squash with colorful bell peppers makes an attractive and delicious combination.

✓ Uses less fat, sugar or salt. Includes Nutritional Analysis and Diabetic Exchanges.

      1 bacon strip, diced
      1 tablespoon finely chopped onion
      1 tablespoon *each* finely chopped green,
        sweet red and yellow pepper
      1 garlic clove, minced
      1 medium yellow summer squash, cut into
        1/2-inch cubes

In a skillet, cook bacon until crisp. Stir in onion, peppers and garlic; cook for 2 minutes or until vegetables are tender. Add squash; cover and cook over medium heat for 3-4 minutes or until tender. **Yield:** 2 servings. **Nutritional Analysis:** One 3/4-cup serving (prepared with turkey bacon) equals 77 calories, 191 mg sodium, 12 mg cholesterol, 10 gm carbohydrate, 5 gm protein, 3 gm fat. **Diabetic Exchanges:** 2 vegetable, 1/2 fat.

Dinette Cake

Margaret Sanders, Indianapolis, Indiana

(Not pictured)

Pieces of this cake can be wrapped individually and frozen. Then thaw for a quick dessert.

    1-1/2 cups all-purpose flour
        1 cup sugar
        2 teaspoons baking powder
      1/2 teaspoon salt
      2/3 cup milk
      1/3 cup vegetable oil
        1 egg
        1 teaspoon vanilla extract
    Fresh fruit *or* ice cream, optional

In a mixing bowl, combine flour, sugar, baking powder and salt. Add milk, oil, egg and vanilla; beat for 1 minute. Pour into a greased 9-in. square baking pan. Bake at 350° for 30-35 minutes or until a toothpick inserted near the center comes out clean. Cool on a wire rack. Serve with fruit or ice cream if desired. **Yield:** 8-9 servings.

QUICK-STUFF PORK CHOPS

Katie Koziolek, Hartland, Minnesota

I was creating recipes to teach pork cookery to high school classes when I discovered this pan-grill method of preparing meat. The results are tender and juicy. This 15-minute entree is just right for a busy cook— it's delicious, and the portions are perfect for two people.

```
1/4 teaspoon dried thyme
1/4 teaspoon rubbed sage
1/8 teaspoon salt
1/8 teaspoon pepper
  2 boneless pork loin chops (3/4 inch
    thick)
  1 tablespoon butter or margarine
  2 tablespoons chopped celery
  2 tablespoons chopped onion
1/4 cup thinly sliced carrot
1/2 cup chicken broth
3/4 cup herb-seasoned stuffing
```

Combine thyme, sage, salt and pepper; sprinkle on both sides of pork chops. In a skillet, cook chops in butter for about 5-6 minutes on each side or until juices run clear. Transfer to a serving platter and keep warm. In the pan drippings, saute celery, onion and carrot over medium heat until tender. Stir in broth and stuffing; heat through. Spoon over chops; serve immediately. **Yield:** 2 servings.

BACON CORN CHOWDER

Joan Baskin, Black Creek, British Columbia

I've served this chowder for so many years that I don't remember where I got the recipe. It's one of my husband's favorite meals. It serves the two of us generously. If there's some left over, I freeze it for another time.

```
  6 bacon strips, diced
3/4 cup diced celery
  1 small onion, diced
  1 cup diced uncooked potato
  1 cup water
  1 can (14-3/4 ounces) cream-style corn
  1 cup milk
1/2 teaspoon seasoned salt
1/2 teaspoon salt
1/4 teaspoon garlic powder
1/8 teaspoon pepper
```

In a saucepan, cook bacon, celery and onion over medium heat for 10-15 minutes or until bacon is cooked; drain. Add potato and water. Cover and simmer for 20 minutes or until potato is tender. Stir in remaining ingredients; heat

through (do not boil). Refrigerate or freeze leftovers. **Yield:** 4 servings.

AUTUMN DESSERT

Lanny Lightner, Denver, Colorado

This instant dessert satisfies my sweet tooth in about 10 minutes! There's no crust to prepare and no need to use the oven. It's just right for two, so there are no leftovers to tempt me later. I was inspired to create this recipe to make a very simple dish and to save time.

```
  1 large ripe pear or tart apple, peeled and
    thinly sliced
1/2 cup water, divided
  2 tablespoons sugar
  1 tablespoon raisins, optional
  1 teaspoon butter or margarine
1/8 teaspoon ground cinnamon
Dash ground nutmeg
  1 tablespoon cornstarch
  2 slices cinnamon bread, toasted
Ice cream or whipped cream, optional
```

In a saucepan, combine pear, 1/4 cup water, sugar, raisins if desired, butter, cinnamon and nutmeg. Cook over medium heat for 8-10 minutes or until fruit is tender. Combine cornstarch and remaining water until smooth; add to fruit mixture. Bring to a boil, stirring constantly. Cook and stir for 1-2 minutes or until thickened. Serve warm over cinnamon toast. Top with ice cream or whipped cream if desired. **Yield:** 2 servings.

SWEET POTATO PUFFS

Bernice Morris, Marshfield, Missouri

(Not pictured)

Even children love this treat, though sweet potatoes may not be their favorite vegetable. The marshmallow surprise inside delights them.

```
  1 cup mashed sweet potato (without
    added milk or butter)
  1 tablespoon brown sugar
1/4 teaspoon salt
1/8 teaspoon ground cinnamon
  6 large marshmallows
1/3 to 1/2 cup graham cracker crumbs
```

Combine sweet potato, brown sugar, salt and cinnamon; shape a small amount around each marshmallow. Roll in crumbs. Place on a greased baking sheet. Bake at 350° for 6 minutes or until lightly puffed (do not overbake or marshmallows will melt). **Yield:** 2 servings.

GLAZED HAM SLICES

Leona Luecking, West Burlington, Iowa

Besides being a great cook, my mom could put a meal together in no time at all. A creative cook, she didn't always measure everything, which made it look so easy. This recipe of hers is quick to put together. The sauce is simple but delicious.

     1/4 cup packed brown sugar
 1-1/2 teaspoons all-purpose flour
     1/2 teaspoon ground mustard
       2 tablespoons ginger ale
       1 tablespoon vinegar
       2 fully cooked ham slices (1/2 to 3/4
          pound and 1/2 inch thick)

In a skillet, combine brown sugar, flour, mustard, ginger ale and vinegar. Bring to a boil over low heat; cook and stir for 2 minutes or until sugar is dissolved and sauce is thickened. Add ham slices and heat through. **Yield:** 2 servings.

SKILLET STUFFING

Ruby Williams, Bogalusa, Louisiana

Corn bread is a staple in the South. Besides serving it with a meal, we use it in many other ways, creating a variety of delicious side dishes. This is simple and fast to prepare and makes the right amount for two.

     1/2 cup crushed corn bread stuffing *or*
          crumbled day-old corn bread
     1/2 cup cooked rice
       2 hard-cooked eggs, chopped
     1/2 cup chicken broth
     1/4 cup chopped celery
       2 tablespoons chopped onion
       2 tablespoons butter *or* margarine
       1 teaspoon minced fresh parsley
     1/4 teaspoon poultry seasoning, optional
Salt and pepper to taste

In a bowl, combine the first four ingredients; set aside. In a skillet, saute celery and onion in butter until tender. Add the corn bread mixture and seasonings; mix well. Cook over medium heat until lightly browned. **Yield:** 2 servings.

SWEET-SOUR RED CABBAGE

Karen Gorman, Gunnison, Colorado

The first time I bought a red cabbage, I didn't quite know what to do with it, but after some experimenting, I came up with this recipe. It has now become my fall "comfort food". This side dish is compatible with a variety of meat entrees, but I especially like it with a pork roast or chops.

       2 tablespoons cider vinegar
       1 tablespoon brown sugar
     1/4 teaspoon caraway seed
     1/4 teaspoon celery seed
       2 cups shredded red cabbage
     1/2 cup thinly sliced onion
Salt and pepper to taste

In a small bowl, combine vinegar, brown sugar, caraway and celery seeds; set aside. Place cabbage and onion in a saucepan; add a small amount of water. Cover and steam until tender, about 15 minutes. Add vinegar mixture and toss to coat. Season with salt and pepper. Serve warm. **Yield:** 2 servings.

A GOOD HEAD OF CABBAGE

Choose cabbage with fresh, crisp-looking leaves that are firmly packed; the head should be heavy for its size. Avoid any cabbage with dull, withering leaves or brown spots.

INDIVIDUAL APPLE COBBLER

Lucy Holland, Derby Line, Vermont

This recipe was given to me in an exchange with a homemakers group several years ago. Apples are a vibrant part of the color around New England in autumn. Once the harvest is in, apple treats pop up everywhere.

       2 cups sliced peeled tart apples
       3 tablespoons brown sugar
       1 teaspoon lemon juice
     1/4 teaspoon ground cinnamon
     1/3 cup all-purpose flour
       1 tablespoon sugar
       1 teaspoon baking powder
       3 tablespoons milk
       2 tablespoons butter *or* margarine, melted
Half-and-half cream, optional

Gently toss apples, brown sugar, lemon juice and cinnamon. Divide between two ungreased 10-oz. custard cups. In a bowl, combine flour, sugar and baking powder; stir in milk and butter just until moistened. Spoon over apples. Bake at 400° for 20 minutes or until top is golden. Serve warm with cream if desired. **Yield:** 2 servings.

Braised Lamb Shanks

Jeanne McNamara, Camillus, New York

A friend shared this recipe with me many years ago. My son-in-law loves these lamb shanks as part of a hearty meal with baked potatoes, a hot vegetable and fresh fruit salad. Of course, I always include mint jelly on the side.

2 lamb shanks (about 3 pounds)
1 cup beef broth
1/4 cup soy sauce
2 tablespoons brown sugar
1 garlic clove, minced
2 teaspoons prepared mustard

Place lamb in a greased 2-1/2-qt. baking dish. Combine broth, soy sauce, brown sugar, garlic and mustard; pour over meat. Cover and bake at 325° for 1-1/2 to 2 hours or until the meat is tender. **Yield:** 2 servings.

Cheddar Green Beans

Linda Poole, Rainbow, Texas

This dish was my grandmother's way of getting us young kids to eat our green vegetables. She was a wonderful cook and inspired me to get creative in my cooking. Sunday dinner was always served at noon at her house, and everything on the table was homemade and delicious.

1 package (9 ounces) frozen cut green
  beans
1 tablespoon finely chopped onion
1 garlic clove, minced
1 teaspoon butter *or* margarine
Salt and pepper to taste
2 tablespoons shredded cheddar cheese

Cook beans according to package directions. Meanwhile, in a skillet, saute onion and garlic in butter until tender. Drain beans; add to onion mixture and toss to coat. Sprinkle with salt and pepper. Top with cheese just before serving. **Yield:** 2 servings.

Bacon-Wrapped Potatoes

LaVerna Mjones, Moorhead, Minnesota

I received this recipe years ago from a dear friend. It's a deliciously different new twist to a plain baked potato. I recently served these scrumptious potatoes to visiting relatives from Norway, and they were a big hit. I love to cook and even wrote my own cookbook several years ago.

1 small onion, thinly sliced
2 medium baking potatoes, halved
  lengthwise
4 bacon strips

Layer onion slices on cut side of two potato halves; top with other potato half. Wrap each potato with two bacon strips. Secure with toothpicks. Place on a lightly greased baking pan. Bake, uncovered, at 325° for 1 hour and 20 minutes or until potato is tender and bacon is crispy. Discard toothpicks. **Yield:** 2 servings.

Second-Time Around Taters

Cut leftover baked potatoes into 1/2-inch pieces; toss with a little oil. Bake, uncovered, at 425°, turning occasionally, until crisp and golden brown, about 45 minutes. Season to taste with salt and pepper. Or try chili powder, cayenne pepper or minced fresh herbs.

Date Pudding

Opal Hamer, St. Petersburg, Florida

This pudding has been our family's favorite dessert for Thanksgiving and Christmas for over 65 years...and it's still on the menu. At Christmas, I top each serving with a touch of green-tinted whipped cream and a red maraschino cherry. Whenever I bring this pudding to a potluck supper, it gets rave reviews.

3/4 cup chopped dates
1/2 cup chopped walnuts
6 tablespoons sugar
1 egg
2 tablespoons milk
1/2 teaspoon vanilla extract
2 tablespoons all-purpose flour
1/2 teaspoon baking powder
Pinch salt
1 tablespoon butter *or* margarine
Whipped cream

In a bowl, combine dates, walnuts and sugar. In another bowl, beat egg, milk and vanilla. Add to date mixture; mix well. Combine flour, baking powder and salt; add to the date mixture. Spread into a greased 1-qt. baking dish; dot with butter. Bake at 325° for 30 minutes or until a knife inserted near the center comes out clean. Serve with whipped cream. **Yield:** 2 servings.

DEVILED CRAB CASSEROLE

Helen Bachman, Champaign, Illinois

After creating this recipe, I later pared it down to serve two. I serve this entree often, since it's so easy to assemble. Along with a green salad, dessert and coffee, this casserole makes a quick, delicious lunch or dinner.

1 can (6 ounces) crabmeat, drained,
   flaked and cartilage removed
1 cup dry bread crumbs, *divided*
3/4 cup milk
1/4 cup chopped green onions
2 hard-cooked eggs, chopped
1/2 teaspoon salt
1/4 teaspoon Worcestershire sauce
1/8 teaspoon ground mustard
1/8 teaspoon pepper
6 tablespoons butter *or* margarine, melted,
   divided
Paprika

In a bowl, combine crab, 3/4 cup of bread crumbs, milk, onions, eggs, salt, Worcestershire sauce, mustard and pepper. Add 4 tablespoons of butter; mix well. Spoon into a greased 1-qt. baking dish. Combine remaining bread crumbs and butter; sprinkle over casserole. Sprinkle with paprika. Bake, uncovered, at 425° for 16-18 minutes or until golden brown and edges are bubbly. **Yield:** 2 servings.

CHECKING CRABMEAT

Taste canned crabmeat—if it has a metallic taste, let it soak in ice water for 5 minutes. Drain and blot dry before using.

CRANBERRY PEARS

Leila Ryan, McDonough, Georgia

I had an abundant pear crop one summer, so I was on the lookout for new pear recipes. I ended up devising one of my own by substituting pears for apples in a chunky applesauce recipe. I usually serve it at lunch instead of a rich dessert and also find it makes a refreshing side dish.

3/4 cup water
1/2 cup sugar
1/2 teaspoon ground cinnamon
2 large ripe pears, peeled and quartered
1/2 cup fresh *or* frozen cranberries

In a saucepan, combine water, sugar and cinnamon. Add pears; bring to a boil over medium heat. Stir in cranberries. Reduce heat; cover and simmer for 10 minutes or until tender, stirring occasionally. Serve warm or chilled. **Yield:** 2 servings.

WHITE BEANS AND SPINACH

Lucia Johnson, Massena, New York

This recipe is a variation of one I received from my Italian mother. I've prepared spinach like this for years—especially since my children like it this way! It complements a variety of main courses, and whenever I serve it to guests, they really enjoy it.

8 cups torn fresh spinach
2 tablespoons water
2 garlic cloves, minced
1/4 teaspoon salt
Dash cayenne pepper
Dash ground nutmeg
3/4 cup canned white kidney *or* great
   northern beans

Combine spinach, water and garlic in a skillet; cover and cook over medium heat for 3 minutes or until tender, stirring occasionally. Sprinkle with salt, cayenne and nutmeg. Gently stir in beans; heat through. **Yield:** 2 servings.

CHOCOLATE PUDDING CAKE

Helene Belanger, Denver, Colorado

I have no idea where I got this recipe...the card is yellow with age! The dense chocolate taste makes it rich with flavor, and it's a satisfying dessert topped with ice cream or whipped cream. I'm pleased to share one of my favorites with you!

1/2 cup biscuit/baking mix
2 tablespoons sugar
2 teaspoons baking cocoa
3 tablespoons milk
1/2 teaspoon vanilla extract
TOPPING:
3 tablespoons brown sugar
1 tablespoon baking cocoa
1/2 cup boiling water
Ice cream *or* whipped cream, optional

In a small bowl, combine baking mix, sugar and cocoa. Stir in milk and vanilla. Spoon into two greased 8- or 10-oz. custard cups. For topping, combine the brown sugar and cocoa in a bowl. Stir in boiling water. Pour over batter. Bake at 350° for 25 minutes or until a toothpick inserted in the cake layer comes out clean. Top with ice cream or whipped cream if desired. **Yield:** 2 servings.

Index

C

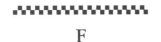

T

V

Y

Z